THE EVERYTHING® GUIDE TO THE MIDDLE EAST

Dear Reader,

My introduction to the Middle East began in the Northeast—the Northeastern part of the United States. I grew up in a neighborhood that was populated heavily with Syrian and Lebanese immigrants who added flavor to our multiethnic enclave. My exposure to their culture prompted me to learn more about their homelands and the rest of the Middle East.

Later, I visited Turkey and Morocco, where I learned more about the region. My experiences as an International Business and Management professor and writer broadened my knowledge of the Middle East through contacts with business professionals and students from various countries. Those experiences were a continuation of my vow to learn as much as I could about the diverse region we label the Middle East—and led to this opportunity to share my knowledge with you.

Hopefully, through these pages you will find the region as fascinating as I do.

Arthur G. Sharp, MA

Welcome to the EVERYTHING® Series!

These handy, accessible books give you all you need to tackle a difficult project, gain a new hobby, comprehend a fascinating topic, prepare for an exam, or even brush up on something you learned back in school but have since forgotten.

You can choose to read an Everything® book from cover to cover or just pick out the information you want from our four useful boxes: e-questions, e-facts, e-alerts, and e-ssentials.

We give you everything you need to know on the subject, but throw in a lot of fun stuff along the way, too.

We now have more than 400 Everything® books in print, spanning such wide-ranging categories as weddings, pregnancy, cooking, music instruction, foreign language, crafts, pets, New Age, and so much more. When you're done reading them all, you can finally say you know Everything®!

QUESTION

Answers to common questions

FACT

Important snippets of information

ALERT

Urgent warnings

ESSENTIAL

Quick handy tips

PUBLISHER Karen Cooper

DIRECTOR OF ACQUISITIONS AND INNOVATION Paula Munier

MANAGING EDITOR, EVERYTHING® SERIES Lisa Laing

COPY CHIEF Casey Ebert

ASSISTANT PRODUCTION EDITOR Jacob Erickson

ACQUISITIONS EDITOR Kate Powers

ASSOCIATE DEVELOPMENT EDITOR Hillary Thompson

EDITORIAL ASSISTANT Ross Weisman

EVERYTHING® SERIES COVER DESIGNER Erin Alexander

LAYOUT DESIGNERS Colleen Cunningham, Elisabeth Lariviere, Ashley Vierra, Denise Wallace

THE
EVERYTHING®
GUIDE TO
THE MIDDLE EAST

WITHDRAWN

Understand the people, the politics, and the culture of this conflicted region

Arthur G. Sharp, MA

Aadamsmedia
Avon, Massachusetts

To my childhood neighbors who sparked
my interest in the Middle East.

An Everything® Series Book.
Everything® and everything.com® are registered trademarks of F+W Media, Inc.

Published by Adams Media, a division of F+W Media, Inc.
57 Littlefield Street, Avon, MA 02322 U.S.A.
www.adamsmedia.com

Contains material adapted and abridged from *The Everything® Middle East Book* by
Jacob M. Fellure, copyright © 2004 by F+W Media, Inc., ISBN 10: 1-59337-053-9, ISBN 13:
978-1-59337-053-4.

ISBN 10: 1-4405-2901-9
ISBN 13: 978-1-4405-2901-6
eISBN 10: 1-4405-2911-6
eISBN 13: 978-1-4405-2911-5

Printed in the United States of America.

10 9 8 7 6 5 4 3 2 1

Library of Congress Cataloging-in-Publication Data
is available from the publisher.

This book is available at quantity discounts for bulk purchases.
For information, please call 1-800-289-0963.

Contents

Acknowledgments

There is an abundance of information about the history of and current events in the Middle East available today through a variety of online sources, published books and articles, etc. Many sources are available in a "one-stop" format on the Internet. Thanks are due to the people who have assembled them all in one place, facilitated the research process, and made real-time access to information easier for people who want to increase their knowledge of the region.

The Top 10 Facts about the Middle East

1. There is more trade internationally in oil than in any other good. Despite the strong recent growth in oil production in other areas, the Middle East still exports significantly more oil than any other region in the world—the region holds about two-thirds of the 1 trillion barrels of global proved oil reserves.

2. Although many people associate the Middle East with oil, its countries export numerous other products, including dates, beans, and grapes, ores and other minerals, iron, steel, chemicals, automotive products, textiles, and clothing.

3. The value of beef exports from the United States to the Middle East in 2010 grew by more than 75 percent over 2009, reaching $261 million. Egypt is the largest importer of U.S. beef in the region.

4. One of the problems contributing to unrest in the Middle East is the imbalance between education and jobs. Many countries in the region created and made available a basic education system, but there was no concomitant growth in jobs for the people who completed their university studies.

5. The majority of Egyptian physicians speak fluent English. Many have studied in the United States or Europe.

6. Turkey and Israel dominate the list of *Forbes*' Top 40 largest publicly traded companies in the Middle East. The breakdown is Turkey (15), Israel (9), Saudi Arabia (5), Egypt (4), Morocco (3), Pakistan (3), and Jordan (1).

7. The Middle East is becoming a significant primary aluminum producer. Developments in Qatar and Saudi Arabia provide two examples of aluminum's importance in the region.

8. Saudi Arabia awarded its 2009 King Faisal International Prize in Medicine, known as the "Arab Nobel Prize," to an American Jewish cancer researcher, Ronald Levy. Levy, who is married to an Israeli, is the first Jew to receive the award in the first thirty years of its existence.

9. Arabesque music (*Arabesk* in Turkish) is a term coined by Turkish musicologists to describe Arabic-style music created in Turkey.

10. Although Arabic, Turkish, and Persian are the three most common languages in the Middle East, English is a close runner-up. It is spoken by large numbers of people in Egypt, Jordan, Israel, Iran, Iraq, Qatar, Bahrain, United Arab Emirates, and Kuwait.

Introduction

THE NEBULOUSLY DEFINED MIDDLE East is one of the most mysterious regions on Earth. Its history and culture have created a mystique that many people do not understand. If they did, they would find a region that is really not much different from any other place on the planet. Middle Easterners want the same things everybody else in the world wants: peace, prosperity, and the freedom to pursue both. None of the three is easy to earn and preserve, as recent events in the region have demonstrated.

The incredibly diverse Middle East has been particularly volatile in the early years of the twenty-first century as people in its various countries strive to free themselves from overbearing governments. They have marched in the streets, sometimes at the risk of death, to convince their leaders that the time has come for democracy in their countries.

At times, their own government officials have suppressed their demonstrations brutally, and foreign entities have interceded in their domestic affairs. For some Middle Easterners, both occurrences fall under the heading of business as usual based on imperialism and their own long-term authoritarian governments. Regardless of what the outcomes of the unrest in the region may be, they cannot mask one simple fact: Middle Easterners have a lot to be proud of as they face an uncertain—but potentially bright—future.

One of the focuses of Middle Eastern political leaders in the twenty-first century is to improve living conditions for their constituents, ranging from upgrading health care systems to creating new industries that will provide the jobs so crucial to the region. Some countries, such as the Gulf States i.e., Saudi Arabia, Kuwait, Bahrain, United Arab Emirates, and Qatar—are doing both successfully. Others, such as Egypt, Libya, and Syria, lag in both respects. But one thing is certain: the fate of the entire region hinges on several factors.

There will be no peace or prosperity in the region until long-standing problems—such as finding solutions to the Palestine-Israel enmity, or the political and religious differences and struggle for influence between Saudi Arabia and Iran—are resolved. As that happens, the geopolitical climate in the Middle East will improve, and the various states can work together to create a more stable economic environment that will allow them to rely less on Western countries for goods and services and more on one another. That is their hope—and their goal.

The history of the Middle East suggests that the people can put aside their differences to create a united front and solve their problems. They have done so in the past, although the results have not always lasted. But a region that is as rich in history and cultural advances as the Middle East has been can only look forward to greater accomplishments. The integration of technology, history, and culture is the way of the future for the Middle East, and the focus of this book.

CHAPTER 1

What Do You Mean by "Middle East"?

The term "Middle East" may seem self-explanatory, but nothing could be further from the truth. The origins of this term and its contemporary boundaries are almost as misunderstood as the region itself. By identifying and correcting these inaccuracies, you will develop a clear understanding of the Middle East and create a foundation of knowledge to build upon.

Defining the Middle East

In the early 1900s, American naval officer Alfred Thayer Mahan began using the term "Middle East." By the beginning of World War II, Westerners knew the Middle East as the area bounded by the Black Sea to the north, the Arabian Sea to the south, the Indus River (in modern-day Pakistan) to the east, and the Mediterranean and Red Seas to the west.

Today, many people have a subconscious definition of the Middle East that has been formed by the media's coverage of events in the region. Journalists' streaming images, commentary, and real-time reports provide people outside the region with up-to-the-minute news and help shape their opinions of the Middle East. This media coverage does not really define the term "Middle East," which gives outsiders some latitude in describing the region.

FACT

Approximately 3.7 billion of the world's 6.9 billion people are Christian, Muslim, or Jewish. That means slightly more than half of the people on Earth find their spiritual heritage in the Middle East, where all three major religions got their start.

The problem is not with the quality or validity of the information given, but with the lack of context. Unless viewers have a good understanding of Middle Eastern history and culture, the apparent chaos and volatility of the region is frustrating. People think something like this: "Different religious groups are in conflict, and there is some type of unrest, so it must be happening in the Middle East."

Regardless of whether this is your perspective, the media has probably played a large role in shaping your understanding of the area. In fact, most Westerners have been influenced by something even more powerful than the media, known as "Orientalism."

In 1978, Professor Edward Said, a Palestinian-American born in Jerusalem, published a book called *Orientalism*, in which he questioned the validity and motivation behind many Western perceptions of the Middle East. Through Mark Twain's caricatured Middle Eastern travelogue and countless other imaginative depictions of the Orient in popular culture, Westerners have been exposed to a voluptuous and mysterious Middle East that, for the most part, does not exist.

ESSENTIAL

Middle East writers portray an accurate picture of the region. The ancient nation of Egypt is still a vibrant cultural and intellectual center, with masterful art, music, dance, and literature. Naguib Mahfouz, one of Egypt's greatest writers, received international acclaim for his many novels and screenplays, including *The Cairo Trilogy* and *Children of the Alley*. In 1988, at the age of seventy-seven, Mahfouz was awarded the Nobel Prize in Literature.

Historically, the media and popular culture together have created a certain perception—or rather, misperception—of the Middle East. While this perception may contain seeds of truth, it is not totally accurate. In the following pages, you will find the facts you need to develop an educated understanding of the diverse regions often lumped together under the generic name of Middle East.

Geographic Boundaries

One way you can define the region's location is by finding its geographic heart. Experts and news junkies alike agree: the Middle East lies somewhere on the eastern shores of the Mediterranean. As you will quickly discover, the boundaries beyond this central point are harder to determine.

Political Boundaries

Should you draw the northern border of the Middle East in southeastern Europe, at the border between Turkey and Bulgaria, or should it stop short of Turkey at the Syrian border? Should the eastern perimeter extend through Central Asia all the way to the Pakistan/India border, or go only as far as Iraq? Should the southern line be drawn to include the African nations of Sudan and Somalia, or should it stop at Jordan and Saudi Arabia? Finally, should the western boundaries stop at the edge of the Asian continent, on the Israeli/Egyptian border, or do they stretch across North Africa to the Atlantic shores of Mauritania and Morocco? To answer these questions, start by looking at the landscape.

FACT

"Sahara" is an Arabic word meaning "desert." Early Arab merchants traveling across this massive hot spot called it as they saw it—the desert. The Sahara, which covers most of Northern Africa, comprises 3.63 million square miles. It is almost as large as Europe or the United States.

Certain realities on the ground provide obvious boundaries for the region. For instance, the Black Sea, Caucasus Mountains, and Caspian Sea combine to form a point where the area naturally breaks from the West to become the East. Similarly, the Mediterranean Sea is a significant border in any definition of the Middle East. The Sahara is another important, natural dividing line between the "Arabized" lands of North Africa and the more indigenous African regions to the south. Finally, the Indus River winds its way through modern Pakistan as a definitive boundary. Historically, this river was the easternmost edge of the early Islamic empires. The Indus remains an important line of cultural and ethnic division, separating the more "Persianized" Pashtun and Baluchi peoples from the more stereotypically "Indian" Punjabi and Sindhi groups.

Isn't It All Desert?

Although most people think "desert" when they think Middle East, the region's geography and climate is as diverse as that of the United States. Much of the Arabian Peninsula is made up of hot, sandy desert lands, but Arabia cannot be characterized as uniform. Along its western borders, mountains as high as 12,000 feet tower above the temperate Red Sea coast, while in the southeastern nation of Oman, mountains of similar stature line the entrance to the Persian Gulf's crystal blue waters.

Massive evergreens pepper the snow-covered slopes of Lebanon's ski resorts, while sunbathers enjoy its sandy beaches. The lush forests of Turkey's Black Sea coast give way to mountain peaks higher than any Rocky

Mountain high, while its Mediterranean resorts rival the famed Greek Isles. The Fertile Crescent is a well-watered region that stretches from Israel's coastal plain through northern Syria and down the banks of Iraq's Tigris and Euphrates Rivers. These lands are rich with plant life, waterfalls, and wildlife. Along with the marshy banks of the Nile River in Egypt, the Fertile Crescent has been the breadbasket of the Middle East for nearly 10,000 years. With so much diversity in landscape and climate, it is a wonder that anyone would ask, "Isn't it all desert?"

Ethnic and Linguistic Groups

Ethnicities and languages also help define the region. For example, you can easily tell if one person is from an Arabic background and another is Swedish. Even if both are speaking English, characteristics such as skin tone, hair color, and facial structure indicate that each is from a different region. Similarly, it doesn't take a linguist to hear the difference between languages such as Russian and Swahili.

Ethnic and linguistic similarities and differences help determine whether someone is European or Southeast Asian. Despite the many ethnic and linguistic differences within Europe, some groups share certain connections that make them all European. As you begin to explore the Middle East, you will find three major groups:

- **Arabs**—Numbering somewhere around 300 million, they are in the majority in the area from Syria (north) to Yemen (south) and Oman (east) to Morocco (west).
- **Turks**—Also known as Turkic peoples, this group numbers over 100 million. They are in the majority in the area from Turkey and Azerbaijan to the former Soviet republics of Central Asia.
- **Persians**—Over 30 million Farsi-speaking people are in the majority in the area from Iran to parts of Afghanistan and Pakistan.

Many use the term "Arab world" interchangeably with "Middle East," but the region cannot be so easily defined. A portion of the Middle East can be called the Arab world, but with significant Turkish and Persian populations in predominantly Arabic lands and vice versa, in the end the lines cannot be so neatly drawn according to ethnic and linguistic groups. In addition, minority groups such as the Kurds, Jews, Armenians, Circassians, and Berbers complicate the issue even more.

FACT

> The phrases *Ash-sharq al-awsat* (Arabic), *Ortadoğu* (Turkish), and *khA-vareh MeeyAneh* (Farsi) all translate as "Middle East."

However, boundaries must be drawn at some point, even if they are not perfect. Should the Middle East include Pakistan, even though most of its inhabitants are of neither Arabic, Turkish, nor Persian background? If not, should the Kurdish regions of northern Iraq, eastern Turkey, and western Iran be excluded from the Middle East? To answer these questions, examine the religious aspects of these lands.

Common Religion

Religious allegiance can be a powerful adhesive or a dangerous explosive. The Middle East has seen its share of both.

Today, Islam is the predominant religion from North Africa to Southeast Asia. This region is known as the Muslim world. You have read about the overlap between the Arab world and Middle East; the Muslim world is yet another overlay in this complex part of the globe.

ESSENTIAL

> More than 90 percent of the Middle East's people are Muslims. However, not all Arabs are Muslims, not all Middle Easterners are Arabs, not all Muslims are Arabs, and not all Middle Easterners are Muslims.

The Arab and Muslim worlds are distinct from one another and from the Middle East. Although all three are related, each is a separate entity. Nevertheless, the common beliefs and practices of Muslims in this region do help differentiate it from neighboring areas, where Islam is not the popular religion.

Islam is often the common denominator for the region's diverse tribal, ethnic, and linguistic groups. As you will discover, Islam is more than a religion. It is a complete system that determines a culture's law (commonly called shari'a law), economics, military strategy, politics, and even personal hygiene. Given this information, you can see why Islam is such an important factor. Still, it is not the only issue defining the Middle East.

Culture and History

The Middle East can be defined in a cultural sense as an area of the world where Islamic traditions are the norm. Even though close to 50 million Middle Eastern people (roughly 10 percent) are not Muslims, Islam has influenced the cultural norms and history of the region. Not only that, but Arabian culture is a great influence on the nearly 40 percent of Middle Easterners who do not consider themselves Arabs.

Arabic phrases such as *as-salaam aleikum*, literally meaning "peace be upon you," are spoken by non-Arab Muslims across the globe. Pre-Islamic traditions, mannerisms, rituals, and clothing styles originating from Arabia have been influential across Africa and Asia. Even the Arabic alphabet has been adopted by non-Arab cultures, such as the Turkic- and Farsi-speaking peoples of Central Asia.

FACT

One Thousand and One Arabian Nights is early classic literature from the Middle East. Originally called *alf layla wa layla* (1,001 nights and a night), these stories were recited orally by professional storytellers and written down in Arabic. Thanks to England's Captain Sir Richard Francis Burton, these stories were translated into English and brought to the West.

From the world's first civilization in southern Mesopotamia (now modern Iraq), to the Ottoman Empire's 500-year reign over the Middle East, the peoples of this land have a shared history. The many differences between them have caused conflict among the diverse peoples of this region. Nevertheless, they share a deep sense of heritage and connection to the land that is hard for Westerners to comprehend. Five thousand years of conflicts and alliances have forged a people with a common memory of the past that is affecting their future.

An unmistakable pride permeates the peoples of the Middle East, as they are well aware of their ancient roots and great civilizations. Because of these common memories, many people find themselves shamed and frustrated by the region's current state of affairs. In an attempt to regain lost honor, many refer to the years of European colonialism as the cause of their present impotency. In addition, many look to the United States and its current influence and see the footprints of yet another exploitive empire.

Social Identity

The last piece of this puzzle is a conglomerate of all the previous pieces. Social identity is difficult to define. At the same time, it is one of the most recognizable aspects of the Middle East. Considering geographic location, ethnolinguistic background, religious affiliation, cultural norms, and regional history, is there a common identity? Despite obvious differences, is there one factor or combination of factors that connects diverse groups? Islam could be said to be this cultural glue, but many non-Muslims consider themselves Middle Eastern. The Arabic language could arguably be the common thread, but what about all the groups that don't speak Arabic? You must consider factors such as language, religion, and history to define effectively social identity in the Middle East.

Conservative and Liberal Definitions

After exploring these issues, experts have defined the Middle East in several ways. By looking at the most limited definition on one hand and the most generous on the other, you will see the wide spectrum of ideas related to this question.

Finding the middle of the Middle East—along the eastern shores of the Mediterranean Sea—is a point on which most people can agree. This central location is in fact the most conservative definition. Based largely on geographic location, at the expense of other important factors, this definition includes only the countries of Syria, Lebanon, Israel, Jordan, and the State of Palestine.

What about Saudi Arabia, the birthplace of Islam? How about Turkey, the center of regional power from the fifteenth to the twentieth century? What about Iraq, home to the imperial Islamic city of Baghdad? Among other places, what about Egypt, the largest Arab country on the planet? This definition is much too limited.

At the other extreme, the most liberal definition uses Islam as the common bond and is almost the same as the Muslim world, minus India and Southeast Asia. This perspective would add to the conservative definition the North African countries of Mauritania, Morocco, Algeria, Tunisia, Libya, Egypt, Sudan, Eritrea, Djibouti, and Somalia; the island nation of Cyprus; the West Asian countries of Turkey, Armenia, Azerbaijan, Iran, Iraq, Kuwait, Saudi Arabia, Bahrain, Qatar, United Arab Emirates, Oman, and Yemen; and the Central Asia "stans," which include Kazakhstan, Turkmenistan, Uzbekistan, Kyrgyzstan, Tajikistan, Afghanistan, and Pakistan.

FACT

When "stan" or "istan" appears at the end of a country's name, it means "the land of" whatever group is named. For example, Afghanistan means "the land of the Afghans."

The problem with these parameters is that they might as well include parts of sub-Saharan Africa, Western China and Russia, India, and Bangladesh, as Muslims are the predominant inhabitants of these regions as well. For that matter, they should also extend their borders into the Balkans to include the largely Muslim areas in this part of the world. Again, defining the Middle East is a daunting task, but Islam cannot be the lone factor.

Boundaries for This Book

Now that you have been thoroughly exposed to the issues surrounding the question "What do you mean by 'Middle East'?" it is time for a definition. For this book, the Middle East will be defined along the following lines. It will include all of North Africa (that is, above the Sahara), West Asia (minus Cyprus), and the Central Asian countries of Afghanistan and Pakistan. This will by no means silence the ongoing academic debate. But, like life in the Middle East, this definition should be fluid and adaptable.

Most likely you are a Westerner. As a result, you have in mind a tidy Western definition of the Middle East. But remember, you are exploring a region that often operates under the attitude of I.B.M.—an acronym for these Arabic phrases:

- *Inshaa Allah*—Literally translated as "God willing," but meant more like "hopefully."
- *Bukra*—Literally meaning "tomorrow," as in "We'll get to it later."
- *Ma leysh*—Don't worry about it!

Bear in mind that the Middle East can be as hazy as its legendary sandstorms. Now that you are aware of the ways you have been influenced by the media and your culture, you can begin to expand your knowledge of a land that is both rich in history and relevant to the world's future.

CHAPTER 2

The Cradle of Civilization

The modern Middle East cannot be separated from its ancient foundations. By examining its rich historical soil, you will uncover the roots of the region's many contemporary issues. Starting from the dawn of civilization, along the Tigris, Euphrates, and Nile Rivers, you will discover the origins of such things as centralized government, organized religion, and written language. You are also likely to find a part of your own history.

Components of a Civilization

Imagine that you have been stranded for years on a remote island. You rig together a small boat and set out for home. What would be your first word upon seeing the mainland? "Civilization!" That's right. No matter how much they may enjoy periods of solitude, at some level, most people desire the comforts and security of the civilized world.

So, as you explore humanity's first civilizations, look for these simple components:

- Well-planned cities
- Large, centralized governments
- Written languages
- Organized religions
- Development of new technologies and skills
- Established trade networks
- Social class structures
- Appreciation of art and entertainment
- Professional military forces

The Sumerians

In Mesopotamia (now Iraq), more than 5,000 years before Abraham was born, the Ubaidian settlers arrived. Little is known of these ancient peoples, but most experts believe they came from the mountainous regions of contemporary eastern Turkey and northern Iran. By the fifth millennium B.C., they had developed small farming communities in the large fertile plain of the Tigris and Euphrates river valley. The rivers' constant supply of water ensured that livestock and crops flourished. As word spread of the region's bountiful lands, people from surrounding areas came to share in the wealth. Before long, small Ubaidian farming communities grew into large multiethnic cities made up of people from around the Middle East.

After centuries of intermarriage, the native tongue of an immigrant group known as the Sumerians emerged as the common regional language. Soon, this prosperous part of Mesopotamia was called Sumer, after the Sumerian newcomers. By 3500 B.C., the Sumerian civilization was in place, with the world's first large, well-planned cities, massive ziggurats (stepped pyramid-temples), and complex water-diversion and irrigation systems.

FACT

Mesopotamia is a Greek word meaning "between the rivers." It refers to the lands that lie between the Euphrates and Tigris Rivers (in modern Iraq).

The city of Kish was the center of political power for the surrounding cities, with its well-organized government and impressive public works. From this metropolis, a priest-king ruled the region with power and authority given by the gods. Nearly all of Sumer's citizens were polytheistic, meaning they believed in many gods. As prudent bureaucrats, government-installed priests welcomed the various gods of the diverse peoples, admitting them into a structured national religion.

Gods and Stars

Sumerians satisfied their fascination with the skies by using tall ziggurat towers as both observatories and temples. Elements of astronomy and astrology guided worshippers to view the heavenly lights as signs from the gods. After years of intense study, priests developed maps of the skies that included many of the constellations (which today's stargazers still use). Those priests were some of the first astronomers, with such an advanced knowledge of the stars that they could predict lunar and solar eclipses.

Priests told complex stories explaining the powers of the gods and the ways they needed to be appeased. Animal sacrifices were the primary source of tribute, but gifts of fruits, vegetables, gold, and other valuables were also made. In addition, priests recited stories of the gods battling in the heavens and creating the universe. Other popular Sumerian epics remembered the details of past wars and the characteristics of heroic leaders.

One of the tales best known today is the *Epic of Gilgamesh*. Its theme—a man escaping a great flood in a boat full of animals—may sound familiar from a more recent source, the Old Testament. The *Epic of Gilgamesh* was recounted verbally until about 2500 B.C., when the Sumerians wrote it down. Today, the only remaining texts come from Assyrian scribes who copied this famous Mesopotamian tale onto clay tablets around 700 B.C.

Amazing Inventors

The Sumerians' inventiveness led them to many firsts. Sumerians invented the wheel around 3500 B.C. By the year 3200 B.C., they had created the world's first written language. This new script consisted of lines and triangular shapes organized into small crude pictures. These symbols were made by pressing the tip of a hard reed into a soft clay tablet, resulting in wedge shapes. When archeologists discovered this ancient style of writing, they called it *cuneiform*, from the Latin word meaning "wedge."

FACT

Many ancient peoples borrowed the Sumerian cuneiform script to represent their native languages. In the Middle East today, many non-Arabic speakers use Arabic script. Similarly, Americans use Latin script even though they speak English.

Sumer was also the birthplace of the school. Although its primary function was to teach new scribes the art of reading and writing cuneiform, schools also taught some arithmetic. Students who showed exceptional promise and motivation could also take classes in religion, literature, and science in order to gain the more privileged social positions, such as priests or government officials.

The Sumerians also conceived of such common ideas as the sixty-minute hour, the 360 degrees of a circle, wheeled vehicles, and the first synthetic material, known as faience. This man-made substance was meant to replicate the rare blue-colored gemstone, lapis lazuli. By mixing glass and copper ore under extreme heat, Sumerians were able to produce a blue-colored substance resembling the coveted precious stone.

Now it is time to journey south and west, to the banks of the Nile River. Another civilization was born here, one that today boasts the world's largest ancient monuments and the most well-preserved artifacts.

The Egyptians

No one knows exactly when the waters of the Nile River were first employed to support farming, but by the year 3500 B.C., the Egyptian civilization was already well established. The country was divided into northern and southern kingdoms. The northern area, defined by its low-lying marshlands, was known as Lower Egypt. The southern portion started above the marshlands, about 100 miles from the Mediterranean coast, and rose in elevation to the Nile's first waterfall (or cataract). Because of its higher elevation, this region was known as Upper Egypt.

ALERT

The Nile River flows south to north, from the Ethiopian Highlands to the Mediterranean Sea. This means that southern Egypt is higher in elevation than northern Egypt. Northern Egypt appears to be "upper" Egypt on a map, but it is really "lower" Egypt, because of its lower elevation.

In about 3100 B.C., a man known today as King Menes joined these two regions together and set up his capital city, Memphis. This united kingdom grew to become a world power that remained at the forefront of science and technology for thousands of years.

The Information Superhighway

The Egyptians used mathematics, physics, and astronomy to construct massive pyramids. Although the Great Pyramids of Giza have flat sides that form perfect triangles, the early Egyptian pyramids were almost identical to the terraced ziggurat pyramids of Sumer. This leads many to believe that the Egyptians borrowed more ancient Sumerian technology.

Not only is there an apparent technological connection between these two ancient cultures, but there is also reason to believe that there was a free exchange of astronomical and religious learning. The ancient Egyptians shared the Sumerians' fascination with the stars. In fact, the Egyptians had detailed maps of the stars that included many of the constellations identified first by Mesopotamian stargazers. From methods of water diversion and irrigation to production of faience, numerous parallels suggest a flow of information from the Euphrates and Tigris civilization to the peoples of the Nile Valley.

Egyptians were by no means just copycats. They were quite the opposite; they expanded on Sumerian technology with bigger and better creations. They also developed their own inventions and unique cultural and religious constructs.

Genius on the Nile

Egyptians used the Nile for irrigation, but it was also their maritime highway. Simple boats, fashioned from bundles of reeds, enabled citizens to travel the length of the kingdom comfortably and quickly. Eventually, large galley ships were built that allowed goods and people access to the Nile and the unknown expanses of the Mediterranean Sea.

FACT

How about a beer? Europeans weren't the first beer lovers. Artwork from both Mesopotamia and Egypt show the production and consumption of beer and wine as early as 2500 B.C.

A system of simple pictures, known today as hieroglyphics, was used by the people of the Nile to record everything from business transactions to military victories. Egyptians also developed a symbol for the number ten. This may not seem like a great achievement, but the new mark let them record 100 items with only ten symbols instead of 100 straight lines. Around 2800 B.C., Egyptians started making sheets from papyrus plants, the ancient precursor to paper. Papyrus quickly became the writing material of choice, as it was lighter than stone or clay tablets and could be rolled into a portable scroll. In fact, papyrus was adopted by many ancient peoples and was used by the Romans until about A.D. 300.

Paintings and carvings were often used to show the gods interacting with the pharaoh, reinforcing the common belief that the ruler was in fact a god-man. With the aid of the sun god, Re, the pharaoh would govern the land and ensure favor from the gods. Egyptians had a strong view of the afterlife, in which they believed their earthly bodies and possessions would be carried on into eternity. As a result, priests invented the first methods of embalming, known as mummification. To this day, modern morticians are unable to replicate the exact methods of preservation that have kept the bodies of pharaohs and farmers intact for thousands of years.

FACT

Did you know that Jacob, father of the twelve tribes of Israel, was mummified in Egypt? According to Genesis 50:1–3, "Joseph directed the physicians in his service to embalm his father Jacob. So the physicians embalmed him, taking a full forty days, for that was the time required for embalming. And the Egyptians mourned for him seventy days."

Ancient Egypt remains one of the most studied civilizations of all time. At the same time it is one of the most mysterious. From sci-fi movies to adventure thrillers, this land has provided the Western imagination with endless fuel for dreaming. Despite all of the fiction, one thing is certain: the modern inhabitants of Egypt are proud of their heritage. Even the largely Muslim city of Cairo acknowledges its polytheistic heritage, as statues of ancient gods and pharaonic trinkets are displayed in roundabouts and sold in bazaars. Whether or not today's Egyptian Arabs are direct descendants of the pharaohs, monuments of former greatness stand beside modern high-rises, blurring the millennia into one civilization—Egypt.

The Phoenicians

Around 2500 B.C., a Canaanite group, known today as the Phoenicians, established small settlements along the northeastern Mediterranean coast, in the area currently known as Lebanon. While the settlers borrowed many aspects of Sumerian culture, they enjoyed relative independence from the Mesopotamian and Egyptian power centers.

Many Phoenicians were craftsmen and farmers, yet the region's real strength was found in its relationship with the seas. From the coastal cities of Tyre, Sidon, and Byblos, the biggest and best ships of the time were built. Utilizing their own superior shipbuilding technology, Phoenician inventors used sails to propel their ships, rather than the bulky oars and rowing crews used by other seafarers.

As masters of the Mediterranean, Phoenicians were successful traders and explorers. They entered the Atlantic Ocean to trade with Britain and traveled south through the Red Sea to the tip of Africa. With their unique glassware and purple dye, Phoenicians traveled to distant lands and returned with loads of exotic merchandise. In addition to trading their goods with distant peoples, they were also responsible for spreading Middle Eastern civilization to those they met. The wealth and reputation of the Phoenician cities grew as they dominated the marine trade routes and established distant colonies, such as the North African city of Carthage (in modern-day Tunisia) and Tarshish (possibly modern-day Cadiz) in southern Spain.

ESSENTIAL

The Phoenicians developed the first phonetically based alphabet, which was the inspiration for the Latin script English speakers use today. This form of writing was designed to simplify written language by using a single character to represent each sound.

The need to record information from large business transactions while traveling the seas pushed Phoenicians to abandon the complicated Sumerian cuneiform system and develop their own set of characters. The resulting system included twenty-two simple symbols to represent specific spoken sounds, rather than the complicated shapes and pictures used by other ancient peoples. This was the world's first alphabet, from which Hebrew, Arabic, Greek, and Latin alphabets would find their inspiration.

Although these wealthy traders dominated the seas, they were not as fortunate on land. For nearly half a century, ancient Phoenicia was occupied by foreign powers. Eventually, the weakening of these powers, combined with the maritime strength of the Phoenicians, brought Phoenician independence. A few hundred years later, they were again subjugated and enveloped into the bloodlines of Greek, Roman, and Arab conquerors. Today, Phoenician pride is kept alive in Lebanon, as some citizens identify with the glory of their ancient predecessors.

The Hittites

About 1,000 years after Menes united Upper and Lower Egypt, light-skinned Indo-Europeans known as Hittites conquered much of Asia Minor (modern-day Turkey). The Hittites subdued the indigenous peoples, imposing on them their language, culture, and laws. This was the first civilization in Asia Minor; in addition, it was the first civilization composed of peoples from the ethnic stock that would later populate Europe. Before long, Hittite aggressiveness led to clashes with Mesopotamian and Egyptian armies.

The Hittites were fierce and inventive warriors. In fact, they were the first to extract iron from ore. From this new metal, they made weapons that were much stronger than the bronze and copper ones used by everyone else. Their warrior ingenuity also produced some of the world's lightest and fastest chariots. Iron weaponry and superior chariots were a huge advantage on the battlefield, but over time knowledge of iron working spread to Mesopotamia, Egypt, and beyond.

Not Just Warriors

One of the Hittites' most distinctive attributes was their strong emphasis on justice. Their extensive law codes were not unique, but the way the Hittites implemented them was unheard of elsewhere. Most ancient communities punished lawbreakers with violent retribution. The Hittites, however, approached criminals with a desire to restore both the victim and the criminal. They did this by forcing the criminal either to return the stolen property, plus an additional fee, or, if nothing could be returned, to pay a sufficient amount, as determined by a judge.

ESSENTIAL

Having studied the ancient inhabitants of places known today as Iraq, Egypt, Lebanon, and Turkey, now consider the modern citizens of these countries. They see this ancient history as their heritage. They view these technological and scientific contributions as their own; they cherish the power and majesty that once delineated their homelands, and from it draw hope for the future.

Hittite Culture

As was the case with most ancient peoples, the Hittites believed there were many gods controlling people's emotions, the weather, fertility, war, and so on. The Hittite pantheon was made up of over a thousand gods, acquired from their Indo-European homeland, as well as Mesopotamia, Egypt, and other regions. Again, as in Sumer and Egypt, the Hittite king controlled religious and political life. Among the masses, the belief was that the king's interaction with the gods assured the health, wealth, and protection of his people. Storytelling and written literature were also important parts of Hittite culture. Scribes recorded historical and religious texts from the spoken Hittite language, using Sumerian cuneiform characters.

Cuneiform and gods weren't the only things the Hittites borrowed from other civilizations—everything from art and architecture to the use of the wheel came from other peoples. Although they introduced the world to iron, this warring people borrowed much more than they invented. Ultimately, the Hittites met the fate of their violent focus, as another invading European group, known only as "the Sea Peoples," destroyed their civilization in 1200 B.C.

The Babylonians

About the same time the Hittites were conquering Anatolia (modern-day Turkey), a tribe of Canaanites known as the Amorites moved into the central Mesopotamian region of Babylonia. They made the city of Babylon their base (near modern-day Baghdad), from which they conquered the armies of Mesopotamia. The Amorites quickly adopted the rich culture of the Sumerian civilization, which then came to be known as Babylonian civilization.

From the Sumerian story of the world's creation to their wedge-shaped cuneiform characters, Amorite scribes borrowed the history and culture of Sumer and made them their own. At the hands of the mighty warrior king Hammurabi, the new Babylonian kingdom spread its influence across the Fertile Crescent, from what is now the Persian Gulf all the way to the northeastern shores of the Mediterranean.

Hammurabi was not only a skilled fighter, but a great legislator as well. His detailed law code is the most comprehensive of any ancient civilization and is the inspiration of the popular saying "An eye for an eye and a tooth for a tooth."

FACT

"If a surgeon has removed with the bronze lancet a cataract from a nobleman, and has cured his eye, he shall take ten shekels of silver. If it be a commoner, he shall take five shekels of silver." This edict, given by the Babylonian king Hammurabi in the 1700s B.C., is a snapshot of Babylon's detailed regulatory system, as well as its scientific, social, and economic conditions.

From the birth of Babylon in 2000 B.C. to its destruction in 1530 B.C., the Babylonians carried the wonders of Sumerian civilization to new heights. Massive bridges, temples, and palaces remain to this day as evidence of Babylon's greatness. As you will discover in Chapter 3, Babylon's influence did not disappear. After nearly a thousand years of dormancy, in 605 B.C. it was revived as the militant Chaldean or Neo-Babylonian Empire.

From the impact of biblical Abraham (who was originally from the Babylonian city of Ur) to Saddam Hussein's twentieth-century delusions of a revived Babylonian Empire, this civilization has not been forgotten. In fact, thanks to the detailed writings of Abraham's descendants, a vivid picture of the entire region is available to the modern world.

The Hebrews

The Hebrew civilization doesn't start with a huge ethnic group or a mighty conquest, but with a single man and his family. Genesis 11:31 reads: "Terah took his son Abram (Abraham), his grandson Lot son of Haran, and his daughter-in-law Sarai, the wife of his son Abram, and together they set out from Ur of the Chaldeans to go to Canaan. But when they came to Haran, they settled there." From Abraham and his descendants the Hebrew civilization begins.

The biblical record explains that Abraham and his family were born and raised in "Ur of the Chaldeans." Most scholars believe this took place in about 1800 B.C., which would mean that the family lived in Ur when it was the most powerful city in Mesopotamia. The exact reason they departed from the comforts of city life is not known, but some have suggested that they may have been trying to escape the strains of Ur's swelling urban population.

Promises and Land

The text of Genesis goes on to say that Abraham and his family lived in Haran until after his father Terah's death. While in the city of Haran (today found in south central Turkey), Abraham heard the voice of his singular deity declaring, "Leave your country, your people, and your father's household, and go to the land I will show you." With these words in mind, Abraham traveled south, with most of his extended family, to the region of Canaan (modern Palestine/Israel), where he again heard the voice, this time telling him, "To your offspring I will give this land."

Because of a famine in Canaan, Abraham and his relatives wandered into Egypt, where they were called Hebrews, from the Egyptian word meaning "wanderer." After living in Egypt for a short time, Abraham returned to Canaan, where he had many children, most notably Ishmael and Isaac. Both of these sons produced children, including Jacob and Esau from Isaac. Jacob had twelve sons of his own; these men would become the leaders of the twelve Hebrew tribes.

ESSENTIAL

In the Middle East today, two groups see themselves as descendants of Abraham. Jews claim to be from the line of Isaac, and Arabs from the seed of Ishmael (*Isma`il* in Arabic).

Wanderers with Holy Words

To escape another famine, Jacob and his family wandered back into Egypt, just as Abraham had done. The biblical text says that they were very successful in Egypt, but that as a group, the Hebrews eventually were forced into slavery. During 400 years of forced labor, the Egyptians continued to refer to the wanderers as Hebrews, but the descendants of Jacob (Israel) knew themselves as Israelites.

Upon their release from Egypt, there were likely over a million Israelites under the leadership of Moses. For close to forty years this wandering mass looked for Canaan; meanwhile, Moses recorded the five books known collectively as the Torah. This massive literary work was at the center of Hebrew civilization and remains to this day a significant cultural achievement.

Kingdom of Conflict

After conquering the land of Canaan in the middle of the thirteenth century B.C., the Israelites divided the land into Israelite tribal regions. Originally set up as a theocracy administered by priests, this was followed by a long period in which wise judges ruled the people. Around 1000 B.C., a traditional monarchy was set up. At this time a king ruled the nation but, as the kingdom was still religiously based, priests retained great power.

The best-known kings, David and his son Solomon, expanded Hebrew territory to run from the Euphrates River in the north to the Red Sea in the south. Solomon developed the capital, Jerusalem, into a magnificent city that included an opulent palace and a large temple dedicated to the one deity. Inside the holy city of Jerusalem, Solomon's Temple was the focal point of Hebrew consciousness, as it was the house of the only all-powerful God.

After Solomon's death in 930 B.C., the kingdom split, with Israel in the north and Judah in the south. Within 200 years, Israel was conquered and Judah remained the only Hebrew kingdom. Within another 150 years, Judah was also conquered.

Less than 900 years after conquering Canaan, the Hebrews found themselves wandering once again, this time in Mesopotamia. It would be another half-century before they would return to Canaan, only for the region to be occupied thereafter by a succession of foreign empires. In A.D. 70, the Hebrews were forced once again to wander the earth in what is called the Diaspora, meaning "the spreading out."

You can see just how much the Middle East has given to humanity. As the descendants of the pharaohs, who built the pyramids, and of the Sumerians, who invented written language, it's easy to understand the pride of modern Middle Easterners. From the first city to the first wheel, you can see just how much the world has been influenced by the Middle East. So why is it that most people today don't also follow the polytheistic example of these civilizations? The answer to this question is found, as usual, in the Middle East.

CHAPTER 3

Rise of the Empires

For thousands of years, empires fought to take over large pieces of the planet. The Middle East has been ruled by indigenous empires from the inside out and by distant foreign regimes from the outside in. Nevertheless, the Middle East has been shaped by centuries of dictators, rebel revolts, and empires reclaiming control.

Components of an Empire

Imperialism is arguably as old as civilization itself. The earliest organized governments sought to exert their power and authority over neighboring peoples and nations, causing some historians to define them as empires. For this book, empires are defined as strong, centrally organized entities that not only control close neighbors but also expand their territories by subduing and integrating distant peoples into their domains. As you seek to understand the Middle East's turbulent history, look for these components in an empire:

- One all-powerful leader
- Sophisticated military forces
- Ever-expanding borders
- Organization of extensive territories
- Efforts to integrate diverse peoples
- Cultural, religious, and ideological control
- A massive capital city
- Attitude of global superiority

The Assyrians

Just over 5,000 years ago, the region of Assur (now northern Iraq) was under the influence of the great Sumerian civilization. The inhabitants of Assur, Assurians (Assyrians), borrowed nearly every aspect of Sumerian culture, including religion, law, and the cuneiform script. Within 1,000 years, the Amorites conquered Sumer, taking control of central and southern Mesopotamia from their capital city—Babylon. At about the same time, the Assyrians expanded their territory from northern Mesopotamia by colonizing parts of central Anatolia (Turkey).

By the 1800s B.C., Assyria's king, Shamshi-Adad, expanded his domains to cover a massive area from the southern Zagros Mountains (today, southwestern Iran) to the Mediterranean Sea. The king then divided his domain into provinces, appointed regents over these areas, connected the districts with a royal mail service, and regularly counted the people of his far-flung empire.

Because of these large-scale organizational efforts, Shamshi-Adad's kingdom is considered by many to be the world's first empire. Whether or not it was, it didn't last long. After only half a century, the Babylonian king

Hammurabi conquered Assyria, putting an end to the kingdom. This began one of the Middle East's most violent and chaotic periods.

For nearly 300 years the region was ravaged, as various migrant invaders—Assyrians, Babylonians, Hittites, and Egyptians—took turns fighting one another. Although several of the invading peoples settled in the region and established kingdoms, instability and conflict characterized this bloody period. As a result of this long tumultuous time, the Assyrians were formed into a battle-hardened warrior nation. Eventually, they used their tenacity to revive the Assyrian Empire of old. This time it would be a military state, known throughout the Middle East for its ferocious armies.

Revival

At some point around 1200 B.C., Assyria acquired the skill of iron working, probably from a Hittite fleeing his conquered kingdom. Combined with other new technologies, this skill allowed Assyria to reassert itself as a regional power. By continually raiding neighboring territories, the Assyrians gained significant plunder and tribute. Because little was done to organize or annex conquered areas, Assyria expanded slowly for nearly 400 years. Then, in 745 B.C., a new king—King Tiglath-Pileser III—ascended to the throne with a view toward global domination.

The new Assyrian leader methodically planned his invasions and intentionally relocated conquered peoples from their homelands to other parts of the empire. One famous example of this policy was the conquest of the northern Hebrew kingdom of Israel, in which the Assyrians deported the Israelites to various locations in the empire. As a result, those tribes were lost to history, never to be heard from again.

By the late 700s B.C., the Assyrian king Sargon II had stretched the empire to cover the area from the Taurus Mountains (Turkey) in the west to the Persian Gulf in the east. When Sargon's son, Sennacherib, came to power, he moved the imperial capital to Nineveh (modern-day Mosul, Iraq), home of the famous goddess Ishtar. In his new capital, the king enforced Assyrian rule, crushing even the smallest rebellions with swift brutality.

From Nineveh, Sennacherib's son Ashurbanipal continued in the ruthless Assyrian military tradition by conquering Memphis, Egypt's capital, and Susa, capital of the Elamite kingdom (modern-day southwestern Iran). Ashurbanipal not only continued to expand and organize Assyria's massive empire, but he also sought to preserve Mesopotamian history, culture, and learning by collecting a huge library in Nineveh.

Changing of the Guard

The Assyrian Empire was in full swing, with territories including most of Egypt, the entire eastern Mediterranean coast, central Anatolia, Mesopotamia, and western Aryana (Iran). By all appearances it was the world's most powerful government, and there was no reason to think things would change. After the death of Ashurbanipal, everything fell apart. It's unclear exactly what caused this rapid deterioration, but within twenty years of the king's passing, the Persians, Chaldeans, and Medes had conquered Nineveh and ended the 1,000-year reign of the Assyrians.

FACT

In 650 B.C., the Assyrian king, Ashurbanipal, built one of the ancient world's largest libraries. In 1929, archeologists uncovered this collection, finding over 20,000 cuneiform tablets with information about Middle Eastern history, literature, chemistry, astronomy, and botany.

Although the Assyrian Empire vanished from the world stage, the people of Assyria remained in their northern Mesopotamian homeland. Under Medan, Persian, Greek, and Roman rule, they preserved their ancient heritage. Eventually, Christianity became a unifying force that distinguished the Assyrians from other groups. To this day, the Assyrian Christians (known as the Nestorians) of Iraq, Iran, Turkey, and Syria differentiate themselves from neighboring Arabic, Kurdish, and Turkic peoples.

The Chaldeans, a.k.a. Neo-Babylonians

With the fall of the Assyrian war machine, the Chaldeans became the powerhouse of Mesopotamia. By 605 B.C., King Nebuchadnezzar II had declared Babylon (near modern-day Baghdad, Iraq) as the capital of his new (or "neo") Babylonian Empire. After conquests in Syria, Phoenicia (modern-day Lebanon), and Egypt, Nebuchadnezzar moved into Judah, the only remaining Hebrew kingdom. By 586 B.C. he had captured its capital city, Jerusalem, and relocated Judah's inhabitants to Babylon. Using the wealth and manpower he had acquired through conquest, Nebuchadnezzar built Babylon into the largest, most impressive city of his time.

Babylon the Great

Spreading out over 2,500 acres, this magnificent city-state boasted more than 1 million citizens. The entire city was built with bricks ornamented with colorful tile pictures. Protected by 100-foot walls, the city was divided by the winding Euphrates River. The city's magnificent processional avenues were so awe-inspiring that many argued they should be named a wonder of the ancient world. Ornately crafted entrances, such as the famous Ishtar Gate, welcomed visitors to the majesty of Babylon. From extravagant palaces to soldiers' golden helmets, their wealth was the envy of the world.

As the envy of the world, Babylon was also its target. In response, Nebuchadnezzar secured the borders of his empire with large walls and towers. For instance, at Babylonia's northeastern edge, the Medes were growing in strength. Nebuchadnezzar ordered a large wall to be built. To this day, the ruins of the Median Wall can be seen in northern Iraq.

In addition to building numerous palaces and defenses, Nebuchadnezzar also fashioned a massive ziggurat tower covered with trees, plants, and flowers. Many believe this towering desert oasis (commonly known as the "Hanging Gardens of Babylon") was built to comfort his wife, who was homesick for the landscape of her homeland in Media (present-day northwest Iran). Regardless of their purpose, these gardens, rising to heights of 300 feet, were unlike anything the ancients had ever seen. The technology used to transport water from the Euphrates River to high terrace gardens was a wonder in itself, but it was the Hanging Gardens that were chosen as one of the Seven Wonders of the Ancient World.

The Chaldeans not only revived the ancient city of Babylon, but they also continued the Mesopotamian traditions of astronomy, astrology, and mapmaking. Using clay tablets, Chaldean priest-astrologers mapped the world and the universe, placing Babylon at the center of the cosmos. A clear attitude of global superiority permeated the city and was underscored by Nebuchadnezzar's declaration that Babylon was "the belly button of the world." Contrary to Chaldean propaganda, Babylon was not the center of the universe. But, thanks to Babylonian scribes, some of the Middle East's most ancient literary and historical works were preserved.

Babylon Has Fallen

Despite the neo-Babylonian Empire's opulence and pride, its power was short lived. After less than 100 years, the Persians took Babylon, bringing an abrupt end to the Chaldean dynasty. As with the Assyrians, the people of Babylonia remained in Mesopotamia. Even as subjects of foreign kings, the Chaldeans retained their identity for hundreds of years. As early as the first century, they rejected their traditional polytheism and adopted Christianity. Today, Iraqi Catholics distinguish themselves from other Iraqi Arabs and Kurds by calling themselves Chaldeans.

FACT

During the Chaldean regime, Aramaic became the common language of the Middle East. As a result, Jesus Christ spoke a dialect of Aramaic nearly 600 years later. Today, Aramaic (also known as Syriac) remains the liturgical language of many Middle Eastern Christians.

The Medes

By helping to destroy the Assyrian Empire, the Medes found themselves on top in their corner of the world. At about the same time that the Chaldeans were setting up an empire from Babylonia, the Medes began to develop their regime from the heights of the Zagros Mountains (present-day western Iran).

The Medes used their newfound freedom to conquer parts of Anatolia (Turkey), Urartu (Armenia), Assyria, and Aryana (Iran). Soon other Aryan tribes, such as the Persians and Parthians, submitted to Median power. With an empire stretching from present-day Afghanistan to Turkey, the Medes controlled more territory than the former Assyrian Empire. Not only that, but they ruled over more land than their rivals, the Chaldeans.

The Medes were relatively limited in their cultural and political development. As a result, they borrowed many things from the Assyrians and Urartians (Armenians). Median religion, however, was somewhat unique. The priestly tribe, known as the Magi, developed a complex tradition of stories to explain the natural world. What set the religion apart from other polytheistic groups was its dualism between good and evil gods. This view eventually influenced the prophet Zarathustra (also known as Zoroaster) who rejected the Magi's pantheon for a singular deity—Ahura Mazda.

ALERT

Don't be confused by the term "Aryan." In the twentieth century, Adolph Hitler idealized an ancient race of blond-haired, blue-eyed Europeans known as the "Aryans"—this was pure myth! In reality, Aryan tribes, such as the Persians, Medes, and Parthians, lived in the Middle East and were anything but European.

Borders Without Orders

From luxurious palaces to well-engineered fortifications, the Median capital was impressive in appearance, but the empire as a whole lacked the organization and oversight of previous world powers. As a result, the Persian tribe was able to grow in strength. In 550 B.C., they conquered the Median capital, claiming the empire for themselves.

FACT

After five centuries of the Persian Magi and their polytheism, the prophet Zoroaster claimed to be in contact with the one and only deity, Ahura Mazda, meaning "Wise Master." He called his listeners to reject the many gods of the old Magi religion, which that he said was inspired by Angra Mainyu, translated as "Lie Demon." Although Zoroastrianism became the official religion of more than 1 million Middle Easterners, today there are only about 140,000 followers worldwide.

After ruling only sixty years, the Medes lost their vast empire and became subjects of the Persians. Even as the Medes lost political control, Median religion continued to reign supreme long after the Persian takeover. The Magi remained the priestly tribe of the Persians until the emperor Darius rejected traditional beliefs for the teachings of Zoroaster.

It is unclear exactly what happened to the Medes after the Persian take-over. Maybe they joined forces with their Persian cousins and helped to establish the world's most powerful empire. It's possible that they intermarried with Persians and ceased to exist as a distinct Median nation. Or perhaps they remained separate from the Persians and continued living in the mountaintops of their homeland. The world may never know exactly what happened to the Medes, but one thing is certain: their conquests prepared the way for the Persians, who shaped the Middle East and nearly conquered the known world.

The Persians

As you read earlier, the Persians were an Aryan tribe that submitted to the power of their cousins the Medes. However, they eventually organized a revolt and overtook the Median Empire. With the Median territories under his belt, Cyrus, of the prominent Achaemenian family, built a Persian empire. In 539 B.C., he conquered Babylon, adding all the Chaldean territories to his growing empire. Cyrus's grandson Darius expanded the Achaemenian dynasty by conquering lands as far east as the Indus River, in present-day Pakistan, and as far west as the Danube River, the border of modern-day Romania. With an empire stretching from Eastern Europe to India, Darius was responsible for more people and land than anyone up to his time.

Empire Management

Unlike his Median predecessors, Darius devised an ingenious organizational system to bridge the wide expanses of his empire. First, the Persian leader divided the empire into twenty regions, each governed by a leader known as the satrap. To ensure that none of his satraps were thinking of starting their own kingdom, Darius developed a secret service to inspect and investigate the various regions. He also undertook the daunting task of connecting the provinces with a system of roads. In addition, a royal mail service was established, allowing communication across the empire.

Another aspect of Persian management focused on setting standards. The popular Aramaic tongue was named the official language. Instead of cumbersome cuneiform characters, the Phoenician alphabet became the official Persian script. The Achaemenians also minted the first imperial currency and developed a standard system of weights and measures. A universal law code brought uniform justice across the empire, and the Emperor Darius's conversion to Zoroastrianism established an official Persian religion. This was the best-managed empire the world had ever seen.

Compassionate Imperialism

Known as the *shah an-shah* (king of kings), the Persian ruler made his position clear. But, compared to previous world empires, the Achaemenians had relative respect for the rights of their conquered peoples. In fact, when Cyrus conquered Babylon, he released the Jews and allowed them to return to Judah, where they remained under Persian rule with a certain amount of freedom.

ESSENTIAL

In 490 B.C., the Greeks miraculously repelled a massive Persian attack on the city of Marathon. With news of victory, their fastest runner set out to inform Athens, 26.2 miles to the south. Upon reaching Athens, the runner exclaimed "*Nike!*" meaning "victory," before dropping dead of exhaustion.

The Persians continued to rule the Middle East with their compassionate brand of imperialism until a revolt erupted among their Greek subjects in Ionia (present-day western Turkey). Darius sent his armies to quiet the unrest, but the Athenians of neighboring Greece sent reinforcements as well, creating the first Greco-Persian war. The Persians came out on top in Ionia, but a clash of civilizations had begun.

The next half-century saw repeated conflicts in which the Persians burned Athens and the Greeks defeated Persian forces in both Greece and Asia Minor. Military defeats, in-fighting, revolts, and independent-minded satraps led to a serious weakening of the Persian Empire. Under the leadership of Alexander II (known as Alexander the Great), Greek forces pushed the Achaemenians out of Anatolia (modern-day Turkey) and took the eastern Mediterranean coast, Egypt, and Mesopotamia. In 331 B.C., Persia itself came under Alexander's rule. For another 1,000 years, as Greeks and Romans built their empires, Western forces reigned in the Middle East.

The Greeks

Greek civilization stretches back nearly 4,000 years, when a people known as the Hellenes began to develop a Mediterranean civilization that would become the backbone of Western civilization. (In this book, the focus is mainly on their exploits in the Middle East.)

In 334 B.C., twenty-year-old Alexander II of Macedonia led the world's first crusade of Western imperialism. From southeastern Europe, Alexander and his soldiers traveled thousands of miles, conquering the entire Persian Empire and part of India. From North Africa to Central Asia, Alexander and his men established colonial cities that eventually became centers of Greek culture. To this day, Middle Eastern cities such as Alexandria, Egypt, and al-Iskandariyah, Iraq, remain as monuments to this world leader.

ESSENTIAL

The Greco-Persian Wars were among the most pivotal points in world history. Because of Alexander the Great's victories over the Persian Empire, Western civilization was shaped by Greek thinkers, such as Plato and Aristotle, instead of the shah or his Zoroastrian priests.

Even though Alexander was a Western conqueror, he saw himself as the successor to the Persian throne. He was responsible for opening the door for Greek culture to enter the Middle East, but he also brought the Middle East to the Greeks. In fact, Alexander and 10,000 of his men married Persian wives. Not only that, he adopted Persian dress and customs and was planning to make Babylon the capital of his empire. What was originally a clash of civilizations appeared to be changing into a marriage of civilizations. Who knows what would have happened if Alexander had carried out his plans? Instead, soon after returning to Babylon from his conquests, he died suddenly of a suspicious illness, possibly poisoning.

With Alexander's unexpected demise, it was unclear who would run the empire. As a result, it splintered into at least nine different kingdoms, some ruled by local leaders and others by Macedonian generals. By 300 B.C., four of Alexander's generals had regained control of Alexander's domains. Seleucus reigned over most of the former Persian territories; Ptolemy retained Egypt, the eastern Mediterranean coast, and part of central Anatolia; Lysimachus gained western Anatolia and Thrace (modern-day Bulgaria); and Cassander ruled over Macedonia and Greece. It was not a unified empire. Nevertheless, it allowed for the influence of Greek culture on the Middle East.

East Meets West

Soon, Greeks flocked to Alexander's colonial cities, bringing their architecture, athletics, philosophies, political systems, and language. Easterners looked to the Greeks for their social and cultural cues. From Egypt to Persia and beyond, a new Hellenistic culture emerged, as non-Greeks imitated Greeks. Eventually, Greek became the common language of the entire Middle East, and Greeks or Hellenized Easterners held all positions of power. Although some resisted Hellenization, the tides had changed, and Greek culture was firmly in place.

FACT

Persians and Hebrews were not the only ancient peoples to adopt Phoenician script; Greeks also borrowed this convenient form of writing, which was later passed on to us via the Romans. Just look at the word *alphabet*, which comes from the Greek letters *alpha* and *beta*, but is also related to the Hebrew letters *aleph* and *bet* and the Arabic letters *alif* and *baa*.

You may think that Athens was the capital of the Hellenistic world, but in reality Alexandria, Egypt, was the center of Greek influence. Ancients were awed by the brilliance of the Pharos, the gigantic lighthouse counted among the Seven Wonders of the Ancient World. From exotic markets to its distinctly Greek layout and architecture, Alexandria was the intellectual and cultural hub of the known world.

Egypt was aglow with enlightenment as philosophers and thinkers displayed more than 3,000 years of learning in museums, zoos, and the ancient world's largest library. With a multiethnic population of more than

1 million, Alexandria stood as a cosmopolitan beacon of human progress and ingenuity. Among Alexandria's many astronomers, biologists, physicians, and mathematicians whose work has been passed down, Euclid's teachings remain as the foundation for modern geometry. From the romantic exploits of Cleopatra and Mark Antony to tourists in search of the Great Pyramid, Egypt was an exotic land of mysteries—just as it is today.

Hellenism spread eastward and into Europe. Specifically in the city of Rome, Greek ideas affected government, law, politics, and religion. Eventually, this Hellenized city-state expanded its control from the Italian peninsula to Spain, North Africa, Greece, and Asia Minor. By 133 B.C., even Alexandria aligned itself with the Romans, resulting in a new Western empire.

The Romans

As with the Greeks, the Roman story is one that starts well before the Roman Empire. From as early as 800 B.C., a people known as the Latins lived on the Italian peninsula. Around 250 B.C., they began more than a century of conflict with the North African powerhouse of Carthage.

Originally established by Phoenician traders, the city of Carthage (in modern-day Tunisia) grew to control most of North Africa, Spain, and the western Mediterranean islands. As Rome expanded its territory into the Mediterranean, the two powers collided, spawning the Punic Wars.

In 218 B.C., after nearly fifty years of hostilities, a Carthaginian commander named Hannibal led an army of 40,000 men (and a large herd of elephants) from Spain across the Alps to destroy Rome once and for all. It was Hannibal's lifelong ambition to see a silence of the Romans. Instead, his invasion was his demise. In the end, Rome not only protected itself, but it captured Carthage and added its territories to its emerging empire.

With most of the Mediterranean under its power, Rome occupied the rest of the Middle East (minus Iran and Arabia). While Greek language and culture permeated the region long after Alexander's death, the strength of his empire was lost until the Roman conquests. Under the *Pax Romana*, or "Roman Peace," a Western empire once again controlled the East. This time Latin was the imperial language and Roman order was preserved at all costs. Despite many changes, Rome ruled the Middle East in various forms until the seventh century A.D.

CHAPTER 4

Ancient Judaism

Out of the foggy details of ancient monotheism mentioned in Genesis chapters 1 through 11, the Hebrew Scriptures unveil a clear plan for a monotheistic nation, fathered by Abraham, Isaac, and Jacob. This chapter takes you through the birth of this nation and its resulting religious traditions. From the twelve sons of Jacob, to the Hebrew kingdoms they established, you will find a people whose faith and folly have shaped the religious fabric of the Middle East and much of the world.

The Sons of Jacob and Their God

According to the Book of Genesis, the promises God gave Abraham were passed through his son Isaac to Isaac's son Jacob (also known by the name Israel) and Jacob's twelve sons. In Genesis 35:23–26, these sons are listed as Reuben, Simeon, Levi, Judah, Issachar, Zebulun, Joseph, Benjamin, Dan, Naphtali, Gad, and Asher. Chances are you only recognize a few of these names, but each of these men fathered a Hebrew tribe, which together came to be known as the Twelve Tribes of Israel.

The Favorite Son

The Book of Genesis explains that while living as nomads in Canaan (present-day Israel/Palestine), the sons of Abraham, Isaac, and Jacob lived quiet lives herding their livestock. Jacob favored his son Joseph over the others, creating a serious sibling rivalry. Because of their jealousy, the brothers sold Joseph to a caravan of Ishmaelite merchants. The traders took him to Egypt, where he was sold to a high-ranking Egyptian official. After years of slavery and imprisonment, Joseph became the pharaoh's right-hand man.

ALERT

Joseph was more than a shepherd! As the pharaoh's assistant, Joseph would have spoken Egyptian, become comfortable with the culture, and studied the ancient secrets of the pharaohs. Not only that, but the Book of Genesis records that after his death Joseph was mummified and placed in a sarcophagus in typical Pharaonic style.

Eventually, because of a famine in Canaan, Jacob sent his sons to Egypt in search of food. To their horrific surprise, the brothers found Joseph in charge of the food distribution. Instead of killing them for their past treachery, Joseph made peace with his brothers and requested that his father, Jacob, come to Egypt. After receiving the invitation, Jacob, his sons, and all of their families left Canaan for Egypt. On the way, Jacob is said to have made a sacrifice to God, which was followed by a vision in which he was told, "Go down to Egypt, for I [God] will make you into a great nation there."

Upon arriving in Egypt, Jacob and a few of his sons met the pharaoh and were given land in the district of Rameses. Just as the Egyptians had called Abraham a "Hebrew" (wanderer), Jacob and his offspring were given this title as they wandered into North Africa.

Israel's Faith

The Hebrew Bible gives detailed accounts of Jacob's life and interaction with his God. As a strict monotheist, he is said to have called upon everyone in his family to get rid of their foreign gods and idols. He built multiple altars for animal sacrifices, including the pillar at the city he named Bethel (meaning "house of God"), and received divine visions, including that of the famous stairway to heaven (known as Jacob's Ladder). Jacob even wrestled with God, earning the name Israel (meaning "struggles with God").

From his deathbed, Jacob gathered his sons to pass the torch of the monotheistic nation. Jacob started by adopting Joseph's sons, Ephraim and Manasseh, making them equal heirs. By doing this, Joseph's inheritance was doubled, as he moved from being the head of one tribe to the father of two tribal leaders. Jacob told his sons what role they and their descendants would play in the coming nation. In his prophetic statements, Jacob made ominous predictions for some, while others were named as future leaders.

Jacob's most notable prophecy likened Judah to a lion. He said, "The scepter will not depart from Judah, nor the ruler's staff . . . until he comes to whom it belongs and the obedience of the nations is his." Eventually, Judah's sons became the dominant Hebrew tribe. To this day, the Jews are named after the tribe of Judah. In addition, the latter part of Jacob's statement established the concept of a powerful world leader, known as the "Lion of the Tribe of Judah," who would come to rescue the Israelites from oppression.

From Slavery to Wandering

The Book of Exodus begins by explaining that the Hebrews were extremely successful in Egypt, growing to such large numbers that the Egyptians saw them as a threat to national security. After the passing of Joseph and all his brothers, a new pharaoh rose to rule the country. This king allegedly devised several plans to ensure the protection of his domains. First, he placed slave masters over the entire Israelite community, hoping to suppress any possibility of revolt. But the Hebrew population continued to multiply, causing the pharaoh to order the murder of all newborn Hebrew males.

Around 1500 B.C., a baby boy was born to the tribe of Levi. The newborn's mother saved him from the pharaoh's edict by sending him down the Nile in a papyrus basket. The pharaoh's daughter found the child, adopted him, and named him Moses.

Moses was raised as the adopted son of the king. Because of his privileged position, Moses was more than likely trained in Egyptian combat, sciences, literature, and more. Because of his upbringing, it is also likely that he felt he was above the law. In a fit of rage, Moses killed an Egyptian soldier and was forced to flee to the area of Midian (present-day northwestern Saudi Arabia). As a shepherd in Midian, Moses was watching his flocks when he heard a voice speaking to him from a burning bush. Identifying itself as the God of Abraham, Isaac, and Jacob, the voice ordered Moses to go back to Egypt, liberate his Hebrew brothers and sisters, and take them to the promised land of Canaan.

Man on a Mission

After receiving a special staff from God, Moses left Midian and joined his brother Aaron in Egypt. Together they are said to have approached the Egyptian king with the message, "The God of Israel says: 'Let my people go, so they may worship me.'" Because the Pharaoh refused to let them go, ten plagues are recorded to have visited the Egyptians. The last of these included special instructions in which each Hebrew family was to make bread without yeast, kill a lamb, and place its blood on the doorframe of their house. This blood would be a sign for God's final judgment to pass over them.

When the prescribed day came, the Israelites followed instructions, and God passed over their sons. Meanwhile, the Egyptians found all of their first-born sons and animals dead. This was the last straw, and the Pharaoh told Moses and Aaron to leave his kingdom immediately. Suddenly, Moses was leading over 1 million people out of Egypt to the land of Canaan. After 430 years, the exodus had begun!

Soon after leaving the Pharaoh's clutches, the Israelites realized the Egyptian army was coming after them. According to the Biblical record, the Hebrews were pinned in by Egypt's most advanced chariots and skilled horsemen on one side and a sea on the other. The terrified Israelites prepared for death as Moses raised his staff, summoning the power of his God to divide the waters. With walls of water on either side, the Israelites passed through the sea bottom to safety, but their pursuers were crushed as the sea collapsed on them.

FACT

Every year, modern Jews remember their liberation from Egypt by celebrating Passover (*Pesach* in Hebrew). In commemoration of the original Passover, a Seder meal is served, in which specific elements are meant to symbolize captivity in Egypt, the exodus, and promises yet to come.

The Mountain of God

Moving toward Canaan, the Israelites continued to experience supernatural wonders in the desert, as stagnant water was made drinkable, mysterious food called manna (meaning "What is it?") formed on the ground, and streams of water appeared from a rock. Three months into their journey, Moses had led the Israelites back to the region of Midian, to the Horeb Mountains where God had spoken to him from the burning bush. Here, on a mountain called Sinai, Moses again experienced a raging fire from which the voice of God declared these, the Ten Commandments:

1. You shall have no other gods before me.
2. You shall not make for yourselves idols.
3. You shall not misuse the name of God.
4. Remember the Sabbath (*Shabbat* in Hebrew) by keeping it holy.
5. Honor your father and mother.
6. You shall not murder.
7. You shall not commit adultery.
8. You shall not steal.
9. You shall not give false testimony.
10. You shall not covet.

With the Ten Commandments as their new constitution, the Israelites remained in the vicinity of Midian for another year, as God continued to inspire Moses with laws for the community and festivals of remembrance to order each year. Moses recorded all of this in a document known as "The Book of the Covenant" (found today in Exodus 20:22–23:33). Eventually, Moses was again called to the mountaintop, where he received God's laws on stone tablets, as well as instructions for the building of a tent for worship and its furnishings, including a sacrificial altar, seven-branched lamp stands (known as menorahs), and the Ark of the Covenant.

ESSENTIAL

Considered by many to be the very throne of God, the Ark of the Covenant was the most prized possession of the Israelite community. Measuring just under four feet in length and a little over two feet in width and height, this wooden chest, covered in pure gold, housed the stone tablets sent down from God. Although Indiana Jones may have discovered this holy relic in the movie *Raiders of the Lost Ark*, outside of Hollywood productions its location remains a mystery.

Movin' On

Even though the Israelites were monotheists, living in Egypt for more than 400 years had shaped their culture and beliefs, causing them to dabble in polytheism. Because Moses spent six weeks on Mount Sinai, the Hebrews thought he wasn't coming back. So they made a golden calf, likely meant to be the Egyptian fertility god Apis, put on their Egyptian jewelry, and prepared a feast. As the scriptures say, the Hebrews "ate, drank, and indulged in revelry" in front of the calf.

The sons of Levi did not take part in the idolatry. As a result, Moses designated the "Levites" as the priestly tribe. God ordered the Hebrews to leave Sinai. This began a forty-year period of desert wandering, during which the Torah was drafted and the nation of Israel was prepared to enter the promised land of Canaan.

Moses and the Levitical Law Code

With anywhere from 1 to 3 million people and their livestock, it was necessary for the Hebrews to live in tents as they moved between pasturelands and oases. In fact, the Book of Numbers (33:16–49) records that the Hebrews moved more than thirty times from Sinai until their arrival at the border of Canaan. As they wandered, Moses began to record a history of ancient monotheism, the Hebrew people, and the laws he was receiving from his God.

First, in about 1445 B.C., Moses is believed to have been inspired to write the Book of Genesis (*Bereishith* in Hebrew), followed by the Book of Exodus (*Shemoth*) and, about five years later, the Book of Leviticus (*Vayiqra*). Named after the Levite priests who were to enforce its laws, the Book of Leviticus influenced Judaism more than any of the Mosaic writings. In the Jews' monotheistic community, God's laws were indisputable and the priests were his administrators.

The first seven chapters of Leviticus established the role of animal sacrifice in ancient Judaism. Unlike previous references to sacrifice, the text goes into great detail, prescribing specific animals and procedures for certain sins and situations. The Book of Leviticus also established the Day of Atonement (*Yom Kippur* in Hebrew), as a day in which nearly everyone and everything in the community was cleansed with blood. According to the Hebrew law code, blood was necessary to cleanse the worshiper of his disobedience.

FACT

The Feast of Tabernacles (*Sukkot* in Hebrew) commemorates the forty years of wandering that occurred between the receiving of the Ten Commandments and the conquest of Canaan. From mega-cities to jungle villages, many Jews remember their forefathers' wilderness time by living for one week in an outdoor structure, known as a sukkot.

While explaining God's requirements for spiritual cleansing, the Book of Leviticus also clarified God's position on day-to-day actions and attitudes. For example, Abraham was said to have given 10 percent of his wealth to God, but the tithe (meaning "10 percent") was not established until the

Book of Leviticus commanded it. As the Israelites' primary law code, it formed the community's judicial system and holy days, but the code also set standards for personal morality, hygiene, sexuality, diet, and so on. The Book of Leviticus endorsed capital punishment, but the overriding purpose of its laws was to limit retaliation by establishing a punishment equal to the crime. The text explicitly guided the new nation with divine prohibitions, commands, and promises, bringing order to the lives of more than 1 million Hebrew people.

Moses and the Hebrew nation lived as desert nomads for another thirty years before they saw the Promised Land. Looking down on the city of Jericho, Moses completed a forty-year history of the wilderness wanderings by recording the number of men from each of the twelve tribes. Today, this ancient chronicle is known as the Book of Numbers (*Bamidar* in Hebrew). Finally, with the Israelites poised to enter Canaan, Moses was inspired to draft a second edition of the divine law code. Known as the Book of Deuteronomy (*Devarim*), this scripture restated and clarified God's promises and laws, ordered the nation to take Canaan by force, and established a man named Joshua as Moses' successor. With the death of Moses, Joshua assumed power and prepared to conquer Canaan.

Conquest, Kingdom, and Captivity

By 1400 B.C., the Torah of Moses was complete, and the Hebrews believed its message was clear. Abraham, Isaac, and Jacob had worshiped one God, who promised them a great nation that would bless the planet from a specific land, the region of Canaan. After more than 400 years of slavery and migration, the promised monotheistic nation wanted the land they had been promised.

As the Book of Joshua (*Yehoshua* in Hebrew) recounts, the city of Jericho was the first to be conquered. From there, the massive Hebrew armies overwhelmed the surrounding cities, including Hebron, Bethel, and Jerusalem. Eventually, the surrounding northern and southern regions fell, putting the Israelites in control of Canaan. Joshua is then said to have divided the land into tribal regions according to each tribe's population.

After Joshua's death, the Hebrew tribes declared the kingdom of Israel a theocracy, with their God as king; the Ark of the Covenant as his throne;

the Torah of Moses as his royal law code; and judges, priests, and prophets as his officials. This style of government continued for nearly 300 years, until Saul was named king in 1050 B.C. Forty years later, David (from the tribe of Judah) was called to rule the kingdom. During his reign, Hebrew tribal divisions were mended, Israel's capital was moved to Jerusalem (along with the Ark of the Covenant), and the kingdom's territories were expanded.

David's son Solomon continued his father's expansions by stretching Israel's domains to run from the Euphrates River in the north to the Red Sea in the south. In addition, he transformed Jerusalem into a beautiful city, building the famous Temple of Solomon as a home for God and his throne, the Ark of the Covenant. The blood of animals and the prayers of the faithful flowed from Jerusalem's magnificent temple, as it became the center of monotheistic worship for the next 1,000 years.

QUESTION

What is the official Jewish symbol?
Although the Star of David (also called the Shield of David) is recognized by many to be the symbol of Judaism, the menorah, a seven-branched lamp stand, is the most ancient symbol of the Jewish faith.

Solomon moved the Hebrew nation to a new level of success, but tribal alliances were starting to crack. Solomon's death in 930 B.C. split the Hebrews into two kingdoms, Judah in the south and Israel in the north. By 722 B.C., the northern kingdom of Israel was overrun by the Assyrian Empire. Meanwhile, the southern kingdom of Judah remained strong, until Chaldean armies captured Jerusalem and destroyed Solomon's Temple in 586 B.C. The people of Judah were taken to Babylon, where they remained in captivity until the Persians conquered Babylon in 539 B.C.

Jerusalem

Under Persian rule, the Jews were allowed to go back to Jerusalem, where they rebuilt their city, their temple, and their lives. Under successive Persian, Greek, and Roman occupations, the descendants of Judah continued to worship their God in Jerusalem, until Roman forces destroyed the temple and expelled them from the region. This great Diaspora forever changed the Jewish people and their religion, as once again they found themselves wandering.

The Message of the Tanakh

From Mount Sinai's Ten Commandments to the 613 laws found in the Torah, the law of Moses provided moral and judicial foundations for the Hebrew people. After the time of Moses, monotheism continued to evolve as poets, kings, and prophets were inspired to write about the one God.

For nearly 1,000 years the warnings, promises, and predictions of Isaiah, Ezekiel, Jonah, Malachi, and others were gathered to form a division of scriptures called the *Nevi'im* (Prophets). From the praises of David's Book of Psalms to the wisdom found in Solomon's Book of Proverbs, the Hebrews embraced a body of scriptures known as the *Kethuvim* (Writings). Together, these scriptures form the Tanakh, which is an acronym for Torah, Nevi'im, and Kethuvim. If you are not from a Jewish background, you may have never heard of the Tanakh, although you may recognize its other name, the Old Testament.

ESSENTIAL

The Tanakh, or Old Testament, is the most recognized religious text in the world, as more than half of the world's population considers at least parts of it to be sacred writings, especially the Torah and the Psalms of David.

With more than twenty-five authors writing it over a 1,300-year period, the Tanakh stands as the monotheistic masterpiece. Its message sustained the Jewish people through repeated occupations and prepared the way for new monotheistic movements, such as Christianity and Islam. To this day, it continues to influence the lives of monotheists around the globe, as they look to its pages for pictures of the past, direction for the present, and hope for the future. Although various interpretations of the Tanakh have fueled conflicts in the Middle East and beyond, the text itself offers unmistakable themes of monotheism, morality, justice, and mercy.

CHAPTER 5

Early Christianity

A part of Judaism is the belief that God would send a messenger, a messiah (*moshiach* in Hebrew) to liberate the Jewish people. Around A.D. 30, an obscure group of Messianic Jews claimed the long-awaited messiah had come. Branded heretics by some and persecuted by others, this small sect continued to gather new followers. Within 300 years, this form of Judean Messianism, known today as Christianity, spread across ethnic and religious lines, transforming the Middle East and much of the world.

First-Century Judaism

In about 150 B.C., after more than 100 years of Greek occupation, a Jewish family known as the Hasmoneans (also called the Maccabees) reclaimed Judea, Jerusalem, and the Jewish temple. The Hasmoneans placed one of their own into the position of high priest, displacing the Zadokite family, which had controlled the priesthood since the time of David. Later, another Hasmonean declared himself "King of the Jews," even though he was not from the royal line of David. As a result, the Zadokites and those who followed them protested the Hasmonean dynasty and priesthood, forming a puritan sect known as the Essenes. Eventually, in 63 B.C., the Roman general Pompey the Great occupied Judea, turning the Hasmonean leadership into subservient members of the empire.

FACT

Today, the Jewish holiday of Hanukkah commemorates the Maccabean victory over the Greeks, the subsequent cleansing of the Temple of Solomon in Jerusalem, and reinstatement of the sacrificial system in 165 B.C.

The Separatists

In the first century A.D., the Essenes (writers of the famous scrolls later called the Dead Sea Scrolls) were one of four Jewish sects, along with the Sadducees, Pharisees, and Zealots. The Essenes were a tightly knit community of ascetics who separated themselves from what they considered to be a corrupted Hebrew kingdom and religious system. In their minds, they were fulfilling the words of the prophet Isaiah when he said, "In the desert prepare the way for the Lord; make straight in the wilderness a highway for our God" (Isaiah 40:3). There were several brands of Essenic Judaism, yet all Essenes strictly adhered to the words of the Tanakh, practiced elaborate water purification rites, rejected the Hasmonean priesthood and its sacrificial services, and believed that a great war was coming. With the "Sons of Darkness and the Wicked Priest" on one side and the "Sons of Light and the Teacher of Righteousness" on the other, the Essenes were eagerly awaiting their warlord messiah.

The Privileged

The Sadducees comprised both Hasmonean priests and Hellenized aristocrats. Like the Essenes, the Sadducees recognized the Tanakh as God's only message, which translated into conservative religious views. Rejecting other Jewish sects, they denied mystical beliefs such as the resurrection of the body and the existence of spirits and angels. As overseers of the Temple, its treasury, and the sacrificial services, Sadducees held considerable influence in Judea. In addition, they controlled the Jewish religious courts and the office of high priest, and were in close contact with Roman officials. Overall, members of this sect owed their privileged positions to heredity, wealth, and/or political maneuvering.

The Scholars

The Pharisees, on the other hand, were generally self-made men who had risen to prominence through their knowledge of the Hebrew Scriptures. With a strong emphasis on individual education, the Pharisees created a power base by using their interpretations of the Tanakh and exclusive knowledge of other traditions found in what they called the "oral Torah." Unlike the Sadducees, the Pharisees believed this oral Torah had been given to Moses on Mount Sinai but was never written down; instead, sages transmitted these traditions verbally through the centuries.

ESSENTIAL

The verbal traditions of the Pharisees, or oral Torah, were finally written down in the second century to form the Mishna. Over the next few hundred years, more commentaries, known as the Gemara, were written to further explain the traditions. In the fifth century A.D., these rabbinical writings were gathered together to form the Talmud.

The Pharisees were extremely critical of the Hellenized Sadducees, rejecting their political connections to the Roman occupiers. In addition, the Pharisees desired to see the complete implementation of Halakah (Judaic law). Based on their biblical interpretations and the traditions of their rabbis (teachers), this brand of Judaism focused almost entirely on morality, spirituality, and—to some degree—mysticism.

The Freedom Fighters

The Zealot movement was born from the resentment and frustration caused by continued Roman occupation. With Rome exerting more control over the Jewish people, this nationalistic resistance group was formed. Resorting to terrorism, guerrilla warfare, assassinations, and open revolt, this sect employed common religious ideals and terminology to recruit followers and incite rebellion.

Viewed as fanatics by some and freedom fighters by others, Zealots preferred death to Roman domination. The first-century Jewish historian Flavius Josephus provides evidence of this mindset, as he tells of a group of Zealots defending the mountain fortress of Masada in A.D. 73. Josephus records that after the Zealots had withstood months of besiegement, the Roman Tenth Legion finally breached the walls of the fortress. Rather than submitting to their conquerors, the Zealot men, women, and children submitted to death, committing suicide as a group.

The Concept of Moshiach

Moshiach is a Hebrew word that is literally translated "anointed one." The term was inspired by ancient Middle Eastern coronation ceremonies, in which kings were anointed with olive oil as a sign of their authority. Known to English speakers as the messiah or the Christ, moshiach has come to be one of the most controversial and influential religious concepts of all time.

QUESTION

Is there a difference among the terms "moshiach," "messiah," and "Christ"?
Around 200 B.C., Hellenized Jews translated the Tanakh from Hebrew into Greek. In this translation, the word *christos* ("anointed one" in Greek) was used for the Hebrew word *moshiach*, also meaning "anointed one." As a result, the English terms "messiah" and "Christ" were derived from these Hebrew and Greek words, and mean the same thing.

Although many scholars believe the messianic idea was introduced well after the time of Moses, Jewish and Christian traditions contend this has always been a central theme in monotheism. References to the "Lion of Judah" and the "End of Days" in the Torah, combined with the prophets' detailed descriptions of a spectacular world leader and his utopian age of justice, have produced this powerful concept. The moshiach was believed to be a warrior king from the royal line of David and a high priest after the priesthood of Zadok. Numerous scriptures have been interpreted to describe everything from the moshiach's place of birth to his characterics and puposes.

Yeshua and His Followers

As Roman occupation forces tightened their grip on Judea, zealotry and messianism were at frenzied levels. In the midst of these turbulent times, a Jewish man named Jesus son of Joseph son of David (*Yeshua ben Yosef ben David* in Hebrew) gathered large crowds who had heard of his wise teachings and ability to heal the sick, raise the dead, and exorcise demons.

Because of his understanding of the Tanakh, authoritative declarations, birth in Bethlehem, and supernatural abilities, many believed he was either the messiah or a great prophet preparing the way. According to his followers, people from all walks of life listened to Jesus' teachings and sought his miracles. Fishermen, craftsmen, tax collectors, Zealots, Sadducees, Pharisees, and even Roman officials were attracted to this mysterious rabbi from Nazareth.

ALERT

The birth of Jesus marked the end of B.C. and the beginning of A.D. to differentiate dates. From this point on, years mentioned are A.D. unless otherwise indicated.

The Chosen One

Out of the curious crowds, twelve men in particular believed Jesus was the chosen liberator and decided to drop everything and follow him. These men are said to have traveled with Jesus for three years, teaching people to love God and others in the true spirit of the Torah. In addition, they warned their listeners to prepare for the Moshiach's Kingdom, spoken of in the Prophets and Writings. Eventually, four of Jesus' followers—Matthew, Mark, Luke, and John—are said to have recorded his life story in what are now called the Gospels.

The End of Days

Messianic fervor surrounded Jesus, as is evident in the story of his entry into Jerusalem, found in the Gospel of Matthew 21:1–16. In this account, Jesus rode into the city on a donkey as a great crowd chanted, "Praise to the Son of David!" He is then said to have gone directly to the temple, where he overturned the merchants' tables and chastised the priest in charge of the temple for allowing its precincts to be corrupted.

To the twenty-first-century Westerner, the first part of the story may conjure up quaint memories of children and palm branches at a Sunday morning church service, but the second half may seem out of character for Jesus. Wasn't he a passive teacher of love and peace? For the Jewish masses living in an age of messianic expectancy, however, everything made perfect sense; this was the beginning of God's cleansing and liberation—the messiah had come!

ESSENTIAL

Most first-century Jews believed the messiah would be a spectacular warrior and leader. His appearance would signal the "End of Days" and the establishment of a perfect age of justice and righteousness. With the moshiach leading his holy armies, the oppressive Romans would be judged, and perfect law would govern the world.

According to the prophet Zechariah (Zechariah 9:9), the King Moshiach would enter Jerusalem, "righteous and having salvation, gentle and riding on a donkey." But this was just the beginning. The prophecy continues in the next verse, "He will proclaim peace to the nations, His rule will extend from sea to sea . . . to the ends of the earth." The passage goes on to describe a great battle and the ultimate victory of God and his chosen ones. To the oppressed masses of Judea, Zechariah's prophecy was coming alive; Jesus' humble entry was the quiet before the storm. Starting with the house of God, and ending with the Romans, it was time for action!

Execution and Persecution

Three days after entering Jerusalem, Jesus and his twelve closest followers sat down to eat the Passover Seder meal. While many of them believed this was their last meal before the great battle, Jesus is said to have revealed that it was in fact the last supper before his death. According to the Gospel of Matthew, he asked his followers to think of the Passover matzo bread (representing life) as his body, and the third cup of wine (representing redemption) as his blood.

Within twenty-four hours, Jesus was arrested, convicted, and executed, Roman-style, nailed to a cross. Viewed as the messiah by some, a blasphemer by others, and a troublemaker by still others, his crucifixion dealt a deathblow to his followers. How could the mighty Lion of Judah, the warrior king, be dead? The Romans were still occupying the land, corruption remained in the religious leadership, and the one they were counting on was dead.

Renewed Purpose

The Gospels record that after three days, Jesus miraculously came back to life and visited his followers over a period of forty days. The Gospel of Luke explains:

> [Jesus] said to them, "Everything must be fulfilled that is written about me in the Law of Moses (Torah), the Prophets (Navi'im) and the Psalms (Kethuvim) . . . the Messiah will suffer and rise from the dead on the third day, and repentance and forgiveness of sins will be preached in his name to all nations, beginning in Jerusalem."

With this clarification, Jesus' disciples believed his crucifixion was the initial phase of the moshiach's great purpose. He had come first to deliver the world spiritually, as a type of sacrificial lamb, and he would return later to deliver the world physically, as the conquering warrior king.

Before ascending to heaven, Jesus is said to have left his followers with these instructions: "Go and make disciples of all nations, baptizing them in the name of the Father and of the Son and of the Holy Spirit, and teaching them to obey everything I have commanded you." As requested, Jesus' disciples spread his message, first in Jerusalem and eventually around the world.

The Acts of the Apostles (written by Luke, the author of the Gospel of Luke) records that there were about 120 disciples just after Jesus' ascension. Known as "Followers of the Way" or "Nazarenes," Jesus' disciples remained in Jerusalem, worshipping at the temple as a small Jewish sect. From the descriptions found in the Book of Acts, the Nazarenes followed communal and hierarchical structures similar to those of the Essenes. In accordance with Jesus' teachings, the Nazarenes welcomed all people, calling them to repent of their sins, accept God's forgiveness, be washed physically in water, and follow the message of the Tanakh.

Miracles and Multiplication

The movement reportedly gained about 3,000 new followers after a spectacular event on the Day of Pentecost, fifty days after Jesus' resurrection, in which the Holy Spirit of God reportedly entered each of them, causing them to speak in various Middle Eastern languages. Despite imprisonment and protest from religious leaders, the group continued to spread Jesus' message of repentance and forgiveness of sins, growing to around 5,000 people. According to Acts 5:42, "Day after day, in the temple courts and from house to house, they never stopped teaching and proclaiming the good news that Jesus is the Messiah."

ALERT

Don't be confused by the term "martyr." Although the term is used loosely today to refer to everything from freedom fighters to missionaries killed in car accidents, the early Christian martyrs were nonviolent people brutally tortured and murdered for their religious convictions.

Considered heretics by some and troublemakers by others, Jesus' followers faced increased resistance from all sides. The Book of Acts records this pressure going well beyond verbal abuse when a man named Stephen was stoned to death, becoming the group's first martyr. This event is said to have sparked a widespread persecution in which many were imprisoned or killed, forcing most of the disciples to leave Jerusalem.

Growth from Jerusalem and Antioch

Taking their new faith with them, many Nazarenes fled to Jewish communities across the Middle East. Soon the Jerusalem sect gained followers in Ethiopia, Egypt, Cyprus, Antioch (Turkey), Damascus (Syria), Rome, and beyond. While traveling to Damascus to suppress this growing sect, a Pharisee named Saul (who came to be known as Paul) is said to have had a vision in which Jesus ordered him, in effect, to stop the witch-hunt. As a result, Paul devoted his life to spreading the very message he once tried to destroy. Disciples such as Peter (also called Simon), James, the brother of Jesus (also called Jacob), John, and Philip recruited many new followers from various Jewish communities, but Paul took his message to a new group, the non-Jews (called "Greeks"). Named "apostles," from the Greek word *apostolos*, meaning "a person sent forth," charismatic teachers like Paul traveled the known world spreading Jesus' teachings.

ALERT

The followers of Jesus did not see themselves pioneering a new religion, but rather as continuing and fulfilling a very old one. As disciples of the messiah, they believed they were observing the true spirit of Judaism established in the law, the Prophets, and the Writings.

By about A.D. 40 the city of Antioch (also called Syrian Antioch) became a hub for this young Messianic movement. As a sort of Eastern capital for visiting Roman emperors, Antioch was the empire's third largest city, boasting a multiethnic population of more than 250,000. Within the city's Jewish population, many decided Jesus was the long-awaited messiah. Soon the city's gentile citizens recognized a difference between those Jews who called Jesus the moshiach and those who did not. To distinguish between the two, those Jews who followed Jesus as the Christ were labeled with the Greek word *Christian*, as the Book of Acts 11:26 states: "The disciples were called Christians first at Antioch." Though predominantly Jewish, the church in Antioch also included some gentiles. This dynamic created some disputes regarding the role of Mosaic law and other cultural issues.

With strong ties to the Jerusalem church, and its leader the apostle James, the Christians of Antioch received regular visits from Judean leaders. The apostle Peter eventually made his home in Antioch and, from this city, the apostle Paul and his companions took Jesus' message into Asia Minor (Turkey), Greece, and beyond. Within twenty years, Paul's efforts brought thousands of Jews and gentiles from across the Roman Empire into the Messianic sect known today as Christianity.

The Letters

With Christian communities stretching from Rome to Mesopotamia, the apostles were responsible for the lives of thousands from various religious and ethnic backgrounds. Not only that, but Christian communities found themselves dealing with very different issues based on their location, ethnic makeup, and so on. Some groups were unclear about issues of faith and practice, while others were discouraged by the difficult and often dangerous life of a Christian.

Because of the apostle Paul's efforts, many churches were started, but most were left with only small oral accounts of Jesus' life and ministry. Among those from Jewish backgrounds, there were many questions about the relationship between their faith in Jesus and their Judaic traditions. For those from polytheistic backgrounds, it was unclear exactly how they should live in this new faith. Between Jews and gentiles, there were disagreements about observance of certain customs, and even between Jews there were arguments about how gentiles should conduct themselves. As a result, the first formal Christian document was drafted in about A.D. 50 at the Council of Jerusalem. In this letter, the Judaic leadership decided upon standards for gentile followers of Jesus, sending the manuscript to Antioch with Jerusalem's full authority.

From Paul

Soon after this, while in Antioch, the apostle Paul drafted a long letter to the churches in Galatia, a Roman province in central Asia Minor (Turkey). This letter, known today as the Book of Galatians, was circulated among the Christian communities that Paul and Barnabas had established just a few years earlier. In these writings, Paul was inspired to clarify the message of Jesus' life, denounce those who were introducing false teachings, and remind the churches of Jesus' love for them.

Over the next twenty years, Paul traveled throughout the Mediterranean, establishing new Christian communities and writing letters to those he had been with. In these letters (known as the Pauline Epistles), Paul emphasized such themes as personal salvation through Jesus' atonement, the Jewish sacrificial system and priesthood, aspects of Christian living, and requirements for leadership in the community. As he and his audiences both faced persecution and death, his words were often meant to encourage faith and hope among people at all stratas of society in the face of adversity. Paul's message of social equity can be seen in his famous statement, "There is neither Jew nor Greek, slave nor free, male nor female, for all are one in Christ Jesus" (Galatians 3:28).

From Peter, James, John, and Judah

While Paul was writing his letters, the apostle Peter wrote several times to the churches in Asia Minor. Having been arrested and beaten for his faith, Peter wrote to people who were facing similar discrimination, threats, and imprisonment. His words encouraged Christians to stay strong in their devotion to God through tough spiritual times and physical suffering. In the end, Peter reminded the faithful to live holy lives, as the messiah would return to establish "a new heaven and a new earth."

James (the brother of Jesus), John (author of the Gospel of John), and Jude (the brother of Jesus, also called Judah) also wrote letters to Christians scattered throughout the Roman world. Similar to Paul's and Peter's writings, these letters were meant to clarify the promises of God and the role of Jesus as the Anointed One, and to direct various Christian communities in matters concerning life styles and doctrine. In addition, these authors saw their share of danger, earning them the right to encourage Christians around the world to press on, overcoming evil with good and meeting persecution with prayer.

ESSENTIAL

The Gospels, the various Epistles, and the Book of Revelation form the Christian Scriptures, known as the New Testament. Many Christians believe that these writings—twenty-seven books written by at least eight authors over a period of about seventy years—are a divinely inspired addition to the Hebrew Scriptures. While considerable debate exists regarding the exact nature of these texts, most experts agree that early Christian leaders penned them in the first century.

The Church and Rome

Within thirty years after the death of Jesus, the apostles Paul, Peter, and James, along with many other Christians, had been martyred for their beliefs. In A.D. 66, Jerusalem erupted in a massive revolt against its Roman occupiers. In response, Roman forces overwhelmed the city and destroyed the sacred Jewish temple. Hundreds of thousands of Jewish men, women, and children were killed, taken to Rome as slaves, or forced to flee Judea. The Jerusalem church met the same fate, as the people were murdered, enslaved, and exiled alongside their Jewish brothers and sisters.

Displacement

After the destruction of the temple and the subsequent Diaspora, only the Pharisees survived to maintain traditional Judaism. Sadducee priests could no longer perform their temple duties, and the group's aristocrats lost their wealth and political clout in the war. The Zealots were exterminated in the streets of Jerusalem or committed suicide in sieges, as in the famous Masada story. Finally, the Essenes remain a mystery; some believe Roman forces killed them all, while others contend they joined with the Jerusalem church, following Jesus as the moshiach.

As part of the Diaspora, Christians from Judea found themselves under increasing pressure. Roman intolerance for Christianity forced them to meet in caves, catacombs, and secret places to avoid detection. Amid rumors of disloyalty to the empire and evil practices in their ceremonies, new believers from Antioch to Rome faced uncertain times. It was in this setting that the apostle John was exiled to the island of Patmos, off the west coast of Asia Minor.

In the solitude of this island, in about A.D. 95, John is said to have received a prophetic vision in which he was shown the "End of Days." Known as the Book of Revelation, or the Apocalypse (*apokalupsis* in Greek), the prophecies found in its pages were meant to comfort the oppressed with the knowledge that good would ultimately triumph over evil. With vivid pictures of cataclysmic events, culminating around the return of Jesus and his messianic kingdom, this is the only prophetic book in the Christian Scriptures.

Martyrs

From Egypt to Mesopotamia, Christians faced brutal death sentences with surprising courage, bringing new converts with every drop of blood. In fact, the phrase "The blood of the martyrs is the seed of the Church" was coined as a result of the growth experienced during intense Roman persecutions. The most famous of the early martyrs was Ignatius, leader of the Antioch church, who was fed to wild animals in about A.D. 100. Along with Ignatius, countless other known and unknown martyrs lost their lives while spreading Jesus' message of repentance, love, and forgiveness.

FACT

Fish, anyone? During Christianity's early years, the sign of the fish is said to have become a secret symbol among the faithful. From the Greek phrase "*Iesous* (Jesus) *Christos* (Christ) *Theou* (God) *Yios* (Son) *Soter* (Savior)," the acronym *ichthys* (the Greek word meaning "fish") was developed, hence the "Christian fish."

By suppressing Jewish revolts and attempting to eliminate the instability brought by the Christian movement, Rome quickly attacked what it could not control. In 135, a messianic figure known as Simon bar Kochba led the remaining Jews of Judea in a violent revolt against the Roman Empire. After reclaiming Jerusalem and the Temple Mount, many believed he was the moshiach, but Roman forces crushed his rebellion, and all Jews were banned from Jerusalem and Judea. While nationalistic Jewish revolts could be put down, Christianity's seemed only to grow stronger during Roman persecutions.

By 284, the Emperor Diocletian found himself ruling a weakened empire crumbling from the inside out. In an effort to revive his ailing domains, he divided them into an eastern and western empire and ruled over both from his new eastern capital of Nicomedia (modern-day Izmit, Turkey) in Asia Minor. In his new city, Diocletian adopted Middle Eastern customs and ceremonies, instituted major economic reforms, and, in 303, ordered an intensified persecution of all Christians.

From Jewish Messianism to the relentless travels of a Pharisee named Paul, the story of Jesus' life inspired a new era of monotheism. By the early fourth century, Christianity was more than a sect. From North Africa to southern Europe, the Roman Empire was losing its power, not to a rival empire, but to a religious movement.

CHAPTER 6

The Byzantine Empire

After one of the most brutal periods of persecution, Christianity suddenly found itself not only accepted but endorsed by the empire. The resulting "Christianized" Roman Empire, known as the Byzantine Empire, produced one of the most influential religious/political movements of all time. But, as with all world powers, this empire would not last. Internal political/doctrinal divisions and ongoing conflicts with foreign powers weakened the empire, brought it to its knees, and led to its eventual demise.

Emperor Constantine's Conversion

In 306, following the reign of the Emperor Diocletian, Flavius Valerius Constantinus (Constantine the Great) assumed the position of co-emperor, ruling the western half of the Roman domains. With the intense power struggles between Constantine and the eastern emperor, Lucinius, the empire found itself in rapid decline, battling internal and external attacks.

In one such internal conflict, Constantine was preparing to battle against a rival Italian leader when he was said to have had a supernatural encounter that changed his life. As a solar henotheist (one who worships one god without denying the existence of others), Constantine believed he was in close contact with the Roman sun god, Sol, and is even said to have had a vision of this god. But this was a different vision. On the eve of battle, Constantine was reportedly instructed by Jesus Christ to inscribe the first two letters of the Greek word *Christos*, χ (chi) and ρ (rho), on the shields of his men, thus ensuring their victory. The following day, as he was going into battle, he believed he saw a cross over the sun with the message, "In this sign conquer." Constantine was victorious over his rival, and his victory inspired him to credit the sign of the cross and the monogram of Christ (χρ) for his success.

FACT

The Greek monogram of Christ, c (chi) overlaying r (rho), is found across the Middle East and Europe in both ancient and modern churches. From the Greek word *Christos*, the letters chi and rho are usually accompanied by the first and last letters of the Greek alphabet, alpha and omega. Altogether, this revered symbol signifies the belief that Jesus is both the messiah and the eternal God.

According to the fourth-century theologian and historian Eusebius, in 312 Constantine converted to Christianity, thus becoming the first Christian emperor. The following year the emperor issued the Edict of Milan, which called for an immediate end to all persecution of Christians throughout the empire. With the support of Constantine, the Church gained new legal rights and considerable financial support from the state. With the marriage of Church and state, each influenced the other, though Christian communities experienced the biggest changes, as their leadership was suddenly empowered and employed by the empire. In addition, many Roman citizens were now willing to align themselves with Christianity, given the religion's imperial stamp of approval.

New Religious Freedom

Although doctrinal details and issues of church government had been debated for nearly 300 years, most disputes were resolved locally or were overshadowed by the constant threat of persecution. In the absence of oppression, and with the addition of political power, what were once minor disagreements became major divisions. On the teaching of subjects from the nature of Christ to questions of moral conduct and salvation, charismatic teachers gathered followers and spread their ideas throughout the Middle East and Europe. Soon, large-scale controversies arose in which heated and often violent debates pitted Christian against Christian, with each accusing the other of heresy.

In 324, Constantine became the sole ruler of both the successful eastern and fledgling western portions of the empire. As the undisputed Roman ruler, Constantine revived his lands with the unifying power of his new religion. By reorganizing his military forces, implementing governmental reforms, and minting new gold coins, Constantine prepared the way for his broad-based plans for Roman revival.

Council of Nicaea

With the purpose of establishing Christian unity, Constantine organized the Council of Nicaea (modern-day Iznik, Turkey) in 325. The major doctrinal controversy to be addressed was the question of Christ's nature. On one side was Arius of Antioch, a controversial Egyptian Christian leader, who contended that Jesus was not of the same substance as God; on the other was the bishop and theologian Athanasius of Alexandria, who argued that Jesus was of the same substance as God. After debating the issue, 318 bishops (church leaders) drafted the famous Nicene Creed, declaring Jesus as divine and of the same substance as the Father. Because Arius rejected the council's decision, he was banished to Illyria (present-day Albania) and his movement, called Arianism, was deemed heretical.

The council also determined such things as the official date for celebrating Christ's resurrection (the Sunday after the Jewish Passover) and the roles of certain church leaders. At the conclusion of these proceedings, Constantine and his mother, Helena (a recent convert to Christianity), traveled to Jerusalem and Bethlehem, ordering the construction of church buildings over the reported sites of Jesus' birth and crucifixion. According to some traditions, Helena was even said to have found parts of the original cross.

ESSENTIAL

Today, Orthodox, Catholic, and Protestant churches continue to follow some form of Athanasius's view, believing that Jesus was of the same substance as the Father. Nevertheless, small groups, such as the Jehovah's Witnesses, hold to the Arian view that Jesus was created by the Father and was not divine.

The New City

The following year, Constantine planned the construction of a new capital to be built over the small Greek city of Byzantium. After four years of massive building projects, the "new Rome" was finally complete. On May 11, 330, Constantinople (now Istanbul, Turkey) was consecrated in a sacred ceremony and established as the new capital of the Roman Empire.

Situated on a small peninsula, known as the Golden Horn, and surrounded by the crystal-blue waters of the Sea of Marmara and the Black Sea's Bosporus waterway, the city was both beautiful and well fortified. From its ornate palaces and mosaic courtyards to its terraced garden parks and magnificent Roman architecture, Constantinople is said to have dwarfed Rome in splendor. With typical Roman baths and communal public toilets, a hippodrome, theaters, a polo field, and gymnasiums, Roman heritage was alive and well in this eastern city. As a sign of the empire's distinctly Christian orientation, the Church of Hagia Eirene (meaning "Divine Peace") was built in the heart of the majestic city.

Imperial power had shifted to Byzantium (Constantinople), leaving the city of Rome to deteriorate with little in the way of influence or resources. After watching a Middle Eastern religion transform the Roman Empire, most Middle Easterners quickly adopted Christianity as well. Constantine had succeeded in reviving the empire, but now it would be protected by Christ, and its people would be called Christians.

FACT

Despite countless wars and the ongoing Israeli/Palestinian conflict, Constantine's Church of the Nativity remains standing in the West Bank city of Bethlehem, the oldest basilica in the world.

Holy Hermits

One response to the religious freedoms offered by the Byzantine Empire was the Christian monastic movement. For hundreds of years, many Christians had found spiritual strength through enduring persecution and poverty. Now, with a Christian emperor and the Edict of Milan protecting them, Christians were able to speak and move freely. For some, this "easy" life was unfulfilling and allowed for fleshly distractions. In an attempt to regain the spiritual focus of Christianity's unpopular days, some chose to seclude themselves from society, denying their bodies basic comforts.

This ascetic lifestyle was by no means unique to Christianity. Certain Hindus, Buddhists, Greek brotherhoods, and Jewish groups (such as the Essenes) separated themselves from the world, pursuing a monastic life. The Christian monastic movement originated in Egypt around 300, with Anthony of Alexandria. As the first Christian monk, Anthony taught the earliest known rules for Christian monasticism, which were recorded by Athanasius.

Soon, Christians across the Middle East were choosing the monastic life instead of the world's vices and riches. For example, Basil the Great was a member of a wealthy family from central Asia Minor. After receiving a top-notch education in Athens and Constantinople, Basil visited several well-known monks in Egypt and Syria. The devotion of these hermits inspired Basil to reject the privileged life for a path of poverty, meditation, and learning. Around 360, Basil founded the Basilian monastic order, whose rules remain the model for nearly all of today's Middle Eastern monks.

Finally, Simeon of Antioch took his spiritual quest to the extreme, living atop a sixty-foot pillar for more than thirty years. Known as Stylites (from the Greek word *stylos*, meaning "pillar"), Simeon and others like him gave up all physical pleasures, enduring cold nights, wet winters, and scorching heat atop their pillars. Viewed as a wise holy man, Simeon's eccentric ways attracted both Christians and polytheists from around the Middle East. Following Simeon's death in 459, many people followed his example, living atop pillars to escape the world's carnality. Eventually, an entire complex was built around his pillar, which became a destination for pilgrims traveling between Jerusalem and Constantinople.

Politics and Religion

In Constantinople, imperial power combined with the divine order, blurring political and religious lines. For the first time, Christians were influencing the state from the inside. At the same time, the state was able to control Christianity. Politics and religion were inseparable, as doctrinal issues became government concerns and church leaders suddenly had the ear of the emperor. Christians enjoyed individual religious liberty, but the Church became entangled in state affairs.

Following the death of Constantine, the Byzantine Empire evolved as a Christian world power. Constantine managed to unite the eastern and western Roman domains, but the longevity of this union was by no means guaranteed. With the knowledge that religion could be an adhesive or an explosive, doctrinal controversies were as much a part of the state's business as tax plans and battle strategies.

Council of Constantinople

Under the Emperor Theodosius I, religious and political conflicts threatened the union of the empire. As a result, the emperor made a concerted effort to unify his realm under the banner of Christianity. After stamping out the last bits of polytheism, Theodosius called a church-wide council (similar to Constantine's Council of Nicaea) to solidify Christian orthodoxy.

The Council of Constantinople convened in 381, attended by 150 bishops, the emperor, and his bureaucrats. In the end, the bishops upheld the decisions of the Council of Nicaea, condemned several movements as heretical, and affirmed the doctrine of the Trinity, establishing that the Holy Spirit was of the same substance as the Father and the Son. In addition, the council decided that the bishop of Constantinople was second in command to the bishop of Rome.

Although Constantinople's decisions did set standards for Christian orthodoxy, they did not end disagreements and power plays. In fact, the empire was soon divided again, with Valentinian III ruling the "Latin" west and Theodosius II overseeing the "Greek" east. With leaders dogmatically supporting various points of theology, religious issues were often manipulated according to political aspirations and alliances.

ESSENTIAL

Today, many Orthodox churches recite their liturgies in Greek, while the tradition of most Catholic churches was Latin. The use of Greek or Latin stems back to the political and cultural differences found between those aligned with Constantinople in the east and those aligned with Rome in the west.

Council of Ephesus

In this vein, Theodosius and Valentinian called yet another church-wide council. The Council of Ephesus (in present-day Selchuk, Turkey) was held in 431 to deal with the growing controversy of Nestorianism. This argument began when Nestorius, bishop of Constantinople, refused to use the title "mother of God" for Jesus' mother, Mary. Arguing that Jesus was actually a divine person and a mortal person, both acting with one purpose, Nestorius and his followers would only recognize Mary as the mother of the human Jesus.

With Cyril, the bishop of Alexandria, leading the movement against Nestorianism, the council decided that Nestorius's teachings were heresy. In their estimation, Jesus was divine; thus, Mary was the "mother of God." As a result, Nestorians were forced to leave the empire, fleeing to Mesopotamia,

Persia, India, China, and Mongolia. In these lands, Nestorians found many converts, eventually establishing a strong Nestorian church movement.

Council of Chalcedon

Within twenty years of the Council of Ephesus, the issue of Christ's nature once again made its way to the political stage, as a Byzantine monk named Eutyches began teaching the doctrine of Monophysitism. Eutyches taught that Jesus was one divine being, with no human aspects. At the request of both Rome and Constantinople, a fourth church council was called in 451 to again establish an orthodox view of Christ's nature.

Held in what is now the Istanbul suburb of Kadikoy, Turkey, the Council of Chalcedon was attended by 600 bishops, who drafted the Chalcedonian Creed. In this document, church leaders came to a type of compromise between Nestorianism and Monophysitism, called Diophysitism. In this view, Jesus possessed two natures, divine and human, but these natures were unified in one person.

Rejected by most Middle Eastern churches (most notably the Egyptian, or Coptic, and Syrian, or Syriac, Churches), the Council of Chalcedon created great political and religious divisions that have continued into the twenty-first century. Although Church councils established orthodox dogma, they did not achieve the unity desired by most Byzantine emperors. Instead, the state's orthodoxy and ecclesiastical debates became intertwined. As "heretics" were persecuted and exiled over issues of theology, many Byzantine subjects (especially Egyptians and Syrians) became disenchanted with the leadership in Constantinople.

Looking Inside and Out

Political/religious conflicts weren't the only concern of the Byzantine emperor; foreign empires and invaders were a constant threat. By the early fifth century, a Turkish-speaking people known as the Huns had appeared from Central Asia to challenge Rome and the northern Byzantine territories. By 432 the Huns had gained so much power that Rome began to pay them not to attack Italy. About the same time, the Sassanian Empire of Iran began to challenge the eastern Byzantine borders, leading to nearly 200 years of conflict.

Turkic Trouble

With Constantinople and Rome operating independently, a young warrior named Attila united the Hunnish tribes and made his move on the Byzantines. By 447 this Turkic commander and his skilled cavalrymen had defeated Theodosius II, taking most of Asia Minor, minus the city of Constantinople. If not for a lack of siege technology, Attila would likely have taken the city as well, gaining the throne of Byzantium and changing the course of history. As it turned out, Constantinople survived, but it was forced to give the Huns part of the Balkans and a considerable payment of tribute.

From his new Balkan domains, Attila, known to Christians as "the scourge of God," moved toward Italy with his eyes fixed on Rome. Aided by his new Germanic subjects, the Ostrogoths (eastern Goths), Attila and the Huns went after the Romans, who were aided by another Germanic group, the Visigoths (western Goths). The Romans succeeded in defending themselves, but soon the Huns regrouped and took most of northern Italy. Because of Attila's death of natural causes in 453, the city of Rome was spared, but the western empire was all but gone. In 476, Roman power was finally destroyed. Germanic warriors overran the city, leaving Constantinople as the sole protector of Roman power and culture.

FACT

In the modern Republic of Turkey, schoolchildren begin their study of Turkish history with the famed Turkic leader Attila the Hun.

The Sassanians

Viewing themselves as the revived Persian Empire, members of the Sassanian family moved in the spirit of Achaemenian conquerors such as Cyrus and Darius the Great. Stretching from Mesopotamia to northern India, their empire quickly grew in wealth and might. Largely because of its position along the central corridor of the famed Silk Road, Persia played a lucrative role in connecting the markets of the East and West. The Sassanians managed to resurrect the splendor of the Persian kings, but they lacked the massive territory of the Achaemenians. In a type of déjà vu reality, the Persian Sassanians would have to clash with the "Greek" Byzantines if they were to revive Persia's former glory.

ESSENTIAL

Formerly known as the kingdom of Urartu, the Armenian Kingdom was the first to accept Christianity as a nation in 301.

With an evolved form of Zoroastrianism as their state religion, Sassanians saw little distinction between "church" and state. Like the Byzantines, the new Persian Empire was interested in keeping order. As a result, other religions were tolerated, but at times their followers met severe persecution. Nestorian Christians were able to thrive within Sassanian domains, but this was largely because they had been excommunicated from the Byzantine Church, which ensured they would not align with the Western enemy.

For nearly 300 years, Syria and northern Mesopotamia were proving grounds for these two world powers. In their battle for supremacy, the Sassanians and Byzantines traded blows, conquering and reconquering each other's lands. The region of Armenia, in eastern Anatolia (Turkey), also found itself between two giants. Although the kingdom of Armenia was not part of the Byzantine Empire, its common Christian faith made the Armenians natural allies. Nevertheless, the Sassanians also had considerable influence in Armenia, as their powerful military was a constant threat. Eventually, Armenian lands were partitioned between the Byzantines and Persians, then fully conquered by the Sassanians, and later given limited autonomy under Persian rule.

Justinian's Creations and Conquests

Out of the ashes of Attila's conquests in the west and draining wars with the Persians in the east, the Byzantine Emperor Justinian boldly moved to revive Roman glory. Starting in 527, Justinian's organizational efforts, massive building projects, and relentless military campaigns not only restored Roman glory but began a new golden age of Byzantine greatness.

Divine Order

Declaring himself Christ's co-ruler on Earth, Justinian combined political and religious offices to solidify his complete authority. Although a large bureaucracy administered imperial affairs, the emperor had the final word in foreign and domestic policies. In addition, Justinian's wife, Theodora, held considerable influence as empress, involving herself in both politics and diplomacy.

As Christ's co-ruler, Justinian recognized his responsibility to maintain justice and order. To fulfill these duties, he organized a new body of civil law based on ancient Roman laws, imperial decisions, and other legal texts. As Byzantium was now a Christian empire, Justinian revised or deleted many old laws according to biblical principles. The resulting law code remained the primary source for medieval Western lawmakers and has even influenced contemporary international law.

Divine Mortar

The new emperor also desired to elicit his subjects' respect by building awesome monuments, many of which pushed the technological limits of the time. Large basilicas and monuments were erected across the empire, including the massive Church of St. John, built over what was believed to be the apostle John's grave. Although this church was destroyed in the fourteenth century, its ruins can still be seen in the Turkish city of Selchuk, near the ancient city of Ephesus.

QUESTION

How is Christianity observed in the Middle East today?
Today there are about fourteen million Christians living in the Middle East. With large populations in Egypt, Iraq, Israel, Palestine, Lebanon, and Syria, various brands of Orthodox, Catholic, and Protestant Christianity are observed.

The most impressive of Justinian's creations was the Hagia Sophia (the church of divine wisdom), completed in 537. This feat of architectural genius amazed sixth-century observers as much as it does modern spectators. Its massive dome, combined with the sheer beauty of its ornate mosaics, silk curtains, and marble pillars (some of which were taken from the Ephesian Temple of Artemis), gave worshipers a taste of divine glory and Byzantine power.

Divine Borders

Justinian's judicial and aesthetic efforts aside, the emperor's highest ambition was to see the empire's borders expanded, especially in Europe. At the expense of his eastern borders and imperial treasury, Justinian waged a massive war from land and sea to reclaim the west. Eventually his armies repossessed Italy and southern Spain from the Germanic invaders, as well as Sicily, most of North Africa, parts of Arabia, and the Black Sea coast. In addition, after more than 200 years of conflict, the mighty Persian Empire was forced to sign a peace treaty in recognition of Byzantine superiority.

Justinian had succeeded in creating a colossal world empire, complete with a comprehensive law code, monumental structures, and vast domains. Although this was the high point of Byzantine power, it was to be short lived. Financial stresses, combined with ecclesiastical, domestic, and foreign conflicts, created rapid decline that would eventually bring the empire to ruin.

Division and Decline

Within 100 years of Justinian's victorious conquests, the empire was in trouble. With imperial coffers depleted, taxes were raised, causing resentment throughout the provinces. In addition, the army and navy were exhausted from repeated foreign attacks and revived fighting with Persia. As a result, both Byzantine and Persian armies were weakened and demoralized.

About this time, Arab armies appeared from Byzantium's southeastern borders, taking the Byzantine province of Syria in about 630. Within a decade, the Sassanian Empire was defeated as the Arabs conquered Persia and then the wealthy Byzantine province of Egypt. By about 670, Arab cavalrymen had advanced through Anatolia to the gates of Constantinople, where they were eventually forced to retreat. The Arabs had dealt a major blow to the empire's territories, but the most devastating defeats would come from within.

The Big Split

For the first 300 years of Christian history, the fish and the dove were symbols commonly used to represent Jesus Christ and the Holy Spirit. After the conversion of Constantine and the subsequent blending of Greco-Roman and Christian cultures, many pictures and symbols were used to depict Jesus, Mary, and other revered Christians, known as saints. Borrowed from pre-Christian depictions of gods and goddesses, these icons, or sacred images, were used by the Byzantines to convey biblical stories in a way that new converts and illiterate worshipers could understand.

The Byzantine Church continued to employ icons in their basilicas until the eighth century, when Emperor Leo III outlawed icons, deeming them idolatrous remnants of paganism. This ideology, known as iconoclasm, spread throughout the Eastern Church, but was quickly condemned by the western Bishop of Rome. Iconoclasm created a major division between the Western (Latin) and Eastern (Greek) churches that would never be fully repaired. By 1054, residue from the iconoclast debate, combined with heated disputes over Church leadership and authority, had led to a permanent separation of the Eastern (Greek) Orthodox and Western Roman (Latin) Catholic churches.

A State of Decline

The "Great Schism," as it came to be known, left the Byzantine Empire isolated and in a state of decline. As internal power struggles and the external military defeats chipped away at this former world power, Constantinople continued to rule smaller portions of its former territories. Foreign invaders, including the European Crusaders, pillaged Constantinople's legendary wealth, causing successive emperors to relinquish more and more territory, until only the walled city remained. After ruling the Mediterranean world for 700 years and trying to stay afloat for another 400, Byzantium was finally sunk. On May 29, 1453, Turkish forces captured the city, renaming it Istanbul (although it remained "Constantinople" in both formal and informal usage until its renaming at the fall of the Ottoman Empire in the 1920s), and making it the capital of their new Islamic empire.

ESSENTIAL

Contrary to popular belief, "Istanbul" does not mean "the city of Islam." After conquering Constantinople, the Turks used its common Greek name, *Stan Poli*, meaning "the city," which they pronounced "Istanbul."

From the seventh-century Arab invasions to four centuries of Turkish onslaughts, Constantinople had battled Muslim armies for nearly 800 years, but what was this new religious faith? Where did it come from, and what did its followers believe? In the next chapter, these questions and many others will be addressed as you discover the birth and spread of Islam.

CHAPTER 7

Early Islam

Viewed as a poet by some and a troublemaker by still others, Muhammad ibn Àbdullah believed he was a messenger of God. In the tradition of Abraham, Moses, and Jesus, Muhammad was to be the champion of monotheism among his polytheistic tribesmen. After facing severe persecution, Muhammad's followers (known as Muslims) gained a political foothold in Arabia, allowing Islam's message to travel beyond the sands of Arabia. Muhammad united the country, and within 100 years of his death, an Islamic empire stretched across the continent.

Ancient Arabia

Although most information about pre-Islamic Arabia was written after the seventh century A.D., a hazy picture of ancient Arabia can be distilled from Sumerian, Assyrian, and other sources. Known in Islamic records as the *Jahiliyyah*, meaning the "Age of Ignorance," the pre-Islamic period has often been mistaken as a time of cultural and intellectual darkness. To the contrary, as far back as 3000 B.C., port cities lined the coast of the Persian Gulf. Teeming with international businessmen, colorful spice markets, and busy shipping centers, these unique Arabian towns were lively and diverse.

Saba'

Of all pre-Islamic Arabian civilizations, the southern kingdom of Saba', or Sheba, was the most impressive. Through the biblical account of Solomon and the Queen of Sheba, many are aware of this kingdom's existence, but most are not familiar with its history or grandeur. Established sometime around 1000 B.C., in present-day Yemen, archeologists have uncovered the Sabaen culture's magnificent walled cities and fortresses, complete with temples, multilevel homes, dams, and irrigation systems.

FACT

The Sabaens worshipped many gods from their temples, including the sun goddess Shamsh and the star god Athar, but the most powerful deity was believed to be the god Mukah. Interestingly, these ancient Sabaen names have influenced modern Arabic words. For example, the Arabic *shams* means "sun," and *muqaddas* means "holy."

With their ability to irrigate large portions of land, most Sabaen families lived as farmers, but the kingdom's wealth and power was afforded by their control of the trade route between India and the Middle East. Indian spices, as well as gold, silver, and coveted Arabian incense, flowed from Sabaen ports to desert caravans, making Saba' an important player in the economics of the ancient Mediterranean world.

Bedouin and Rock City

While stationary civilizations were found along the coastal regions, mobile nomadic tribes ruled most of Arabia's interior. Known as Bedouin (desert nomads), these tribes were involved in the transportation of goods from Saba' to the rest of the Middle East. With their livelihood connected to the trade routes, various Arab tribes organized, raided, and protected caravans. In addition, some tribes managed oasis settlements, such as Mecca and Yathrib (later called Medina), which were formed along the main north-south trade route, in the western Arabian Hijaz region.

About 500 B.C., Arab nomads calling themselves Nabataeans settled in what is now southern Jordan, at the north end of the trade route between Arabia and the Mediterranean. By 100 B.C., the Nabataeans had established an impressive capital city, known today as Petra, in an area that was both defensively and economically strategic. In this magnificent city, large tombs, homes, temples, and other structures were fashioned within the red stone cliffs of a rocky desert canyon.

From their rock-hewn capital, the Nabataeans established settlements throughout the region, eventually controlling a kingdom that stretched from the Red Sea to Damascus. The physical location of their kingdom put the Nabataeans in direct contact with the Mediterranean world and its technologies, as well as Phoenician script, which they adapted in their own style. Other Arab tribes eventually borrowed this Nabataean script, which became the basis for all forms of Arabic writing.

ESSENTIAL

Although most Arabs claim to be descendants of Isma`il (Ishmael), it's not that simple. Isma`il's offspring are part of the crowd, but there are actually many non-Ishmaelite Semitic tribes that have produced nearly 300 million people from Africa to Asia who consider themselves Arab.

Although Petra flourished for several hundred years as a trading center, the Roman Empire's growth brought the Nabataean kingdom under foreign rule, eventually making it a part of the Roman province of Arabia in about A.D. 100. Over the next 500 years, other Arab tribes continued to establish small kingdoms and tribal confederacies, but none equaled the glory of the Sabeans or Nabataeans. By the late sixth century, Arabia found itself on the outskirts of the Byzantine and Sassanian empires. Arab tribes enjoyed independence, for the most part. They lacked unity and, for that matter, power, but within a short time they would find both.

The Seventh Century A.D.

Around 600, the city of Mecca, in modern-day Saudi Arabia, had blossomed into a prosperous oasis town. Benefiting from its position at the intersection of two major caravan routes and its status as a religious/cultural center, the city became very wealthy. As shrewd businessmen, Mecca's ruling tribe, the Quraish, used their resources to provide legendary hospitality to travelers and pilgrims alike.

The Culture of Mecca

As a religious center, Mecca was home to the famed Ka'ba, a cube-shaped building that housed 360 statues of Arabian gods. Each year, pilgrims from across Arabia traveled to Mecca, paying homage to the gods by offering animal sacrifices and making several laps around the Ka'ba. In addition, worshipers revered the Ka'ba's mysterious black stone (possibly a meteorite) by kissing it during their march around the sacred building. As the vast majority of Arabs were polytheistic, many rituals and beliefs reflected their desire to appease the gods and repel spirits known as *jinn*.

As a cultural center, Mecca was home to artisans, poets, and musicians who made their living from the city's reliable flow of traders and pilgrims. Of all the local artists, poets were the most respected. In fact, poetry was the most popular form of entertainment, making talented orators comparable to modern-day Hollywood stars. From romantic stories of brave warriors to the hilarious accounts of foolish men, spectators paid performers according to their skill. Verbal masters also received handsome sums for their freestyle flattery of wealthy individuals. With magical monologues and ingenious imagery, Meccan poets amazed the masses with rhythmic rhyming.

FACT

"I will grant you three wishes . . . " The popular Western image of the genie in the lamp was inspired by the ancient Arabian belief in beings known as jinn. These humanlike spirit beings were thought to wreak havoc on unprotected humans, even entering their bodies at times.

Religious Diversity

Although most Arabs in the early seventh century were polytheistic, several other traditions found their way into this region. Several shades of Christian thought (likely including some obscure groups deemed heretical by the Byzantine Church) had made their way into the Arabian Peninsula. Judaism was also a noticeable movement within Arabia. Not only had Jews gained prominence in the city of Yathrib, along the Yemen-to-Syria trade route, but they also controlled the northern oasis town of Khayber. In addition, the former kingdom of Saba' (in present-day Yemen) saw many polytheists convert to Judaism, including the king.

As monotheists settled in oasis towns and moved across Arabia's trade routes, some Arabs questioned the existence of one all-powerful God, as others leaned in the opposite direction. A mysterious group, known as the Hanifs, moved toward a more monotheistic view. Although the details of their exact theology are hazy, it seems the Hanifs elevated one deity, known as "The God" (*Allah* in Arabic), to the highest position above lesser Arabian gods and goddesses. Although the Hanifs didn't gather many followers, times were changing, as new ideas simmered in the desert.

It was in this divergent religious environment that Muhammad ibn Àbdullah, a forty-year-old Meccan from the Quraish tribe's Hashemite clan, began to question his family's traditions. Were there many gods, one God in charge of lesser gods, or one singular deity? If only one God existed, who was following the right path, the Jews or the Christians? To find answers, Muhammad secluded himself in the mountains near Mecca, fasting and meditating for weeks on end. Then one day everything changed!

Muhammad and His Followers

According to Islamic sources, in 610, while meditating in a cave outside Mecca, Muhammad was gripped by a being (believed to be the angel Gabriel) that ordered him in Arabic, "*Iqra'!*" meaning "recite" or "read." Muhammad and the presence are then said to have gone back and forth several times, with Muhammad saying he could not read and the being declaring "Recite!" as it choked him.

In great pain, Muhammad exclaimed, "What should I read?" The being is then said to have answered, "Recite! In the name of your Lord, who created man from a clot of blood. Recite! For your Lord is the most generous, He who has taught man by the pen things they know not" (Qur'an 96:1–5). Following this encounter, Muhammad returned to the city, confused and trembling with fear. Thinking he had gone insane or possibly been possessed by evil jinn, he consulted his wife Khadijah, who convinced him he was to be a prophet in the tradition of Abraham, Moses, and Jesus.

The Prophet

As Muhammad's first convert, Khadijah, a wealthy Meccan businesswoman, supported her husband both financially and emotionally in his new prophetic role. The next convert to Islam (which in Arabic means "submission [to the will of God]") was Muhammad's ten-year-old cousin Àli, followed by other friends and family, bringing the total number of followers, known as Muslims (in Arabic, "one who submits"), to about forty.

ALERT

Don't be confused by the Arabic words Islam and Muslim. Islam (meaning "submission [to the will of God]") refers to a religious tradition, while Muslim (which translates to "one who submits") denotes a person who is following the religion of Islam.

In Arabia's great poetic tradition, Muhammad amazed crowds with his use of the Arabic language, yet the meaning of his messages often left his listeners puzzled. While Mecca's poets were frequently thought to receive their words from jinn, Muhammad believed the God of Abraham was inspiring his prose. In fact, as he called his listeners to monotheism and morality, he claimed to be repeating the very words of Allah. In response, some began to memorize his sermons, while others recorded them on animal skins and sheets of papyrus.

Quraish Opposition

Soon, persecution from the polytheistic Meccans forced most of the Ummah (Muslim community) to flee to the Christian kingdom of Abyssinia, found in modern-day Ethiopia. With most of his followers safe in Abyssinia, Muhammad remained in Mecca, vehemently opposing idol worship at the Ka'ba. As more Arabs accepted his message, Muhammad instituted a bold break from Meccan tradition, calling all Muslims to pray in the direction of Jerusalem, the city of the only God.

FACT

From ancient times the Arab peoples have followed a lunar calendar, which makes each year a little more than 354 days long. In addition to this moon-based system, the Islamic calendar starts in "the year of the Hijra" (*anno hegirae* in Latin, or A.H.), on July 16, 622, when Muhammad and his followers escaped from Mecca to Medina. Because of these two factors, the date June 22, 2003, on the Christian calendar is the equivalent on the Islamic calendar of Rabi' al-Thani 22, 1424 A.H.

In 620, Muhammad's wife Khadijah and uncle Abu Talib both died. Although he inherited his wife's fortune, the absence of his uncle's political influence removed his assurance of protection. In this tribal society, family connections and alliances guided all aspects of life, and with the passing of Khadijah and Abu Talib, Muhammad was no longer protected from those who saw him as a threat. As a result, powerful members of the ruling Quraish tribe began a plot to kill Muhammad and stop his message, which was threatening their business and traditions.

After hearing of the Quraish leaders' plan, Muhammad fled, accepting an earlier invitation to come to the city of Yathrib. Known as an honest man and wise leader, Muhammad was invited to mediate between tribal disputes, which were threatening the stability of the city. In 622, Muhammad and his followers escaped at night to Yathrib, which was later named Medina, or *Medinat an-Nabi* (meaning "city of the Prophet"). This secret night journey, known as the Hijra, was so significant to the survival of Islam that it marks the beginning of the Islamic calendar.

Growth from Medina

Muhammad was extremely successful in his new home, bringing peace to the city's warring tribes and attracting many followers. In Yathrib, Jews, Christians, and Muslims lived in peace under the wisdom of their new leader. By mending relationships between warring tribes, Muhammad created a loyal and unified city. Although Meccan armies continued to hunt Muhammad, their advances were always turned back.

Separating Sheep from Goats

After several years, Muhammad had gained many new converts in Yathrib and the surrounding areas, though the Jewish tribes never accepted him as a prophet of God. Eventually, Muhammad's teachings clearly separated Islam from the traditions of Judaism. One example of this shift was Muhammad's revelation stating that the direction of prayer should be changed. Originally, Muslims were instructed to pray toward Jerusalem, but now they were to face Mecca. In addition, Muslims were called to continue with the pre-Islamic tradition of annual pilgrimages to the Ka'ba, but as Muslims they would pray to the only deity, Allah.

Muhammad's teachings also addressed basic Christian theology. "They do blaspheme who say: God is one of three in a Trinity: For there is no god except one God" (Qur'an 5:76). There is also the passage, "That they said (in boast), 'We killed Christ Jesus the son of Mary, the Apostle of God'; but they killed him not, nor crucified him, but so it was made to appear to them . . . for of a surety they killed him not" (Qur'an 4:157). This declaration, in direct opposition to the foundational Christian belief of Jesus' sacrificial death, combined with other teachings, caused many Arab Christians to question the validity of Muhammad's prophetic claims.

Muhammad's Many Roles

As a religious leader, Muhammad taught his followers to preach the message of Islam, but he also established laws and social norms for individuals and the community, known collectively today as shari'a. In addition, Muhammad trained his followers to fight for the will of God and the survival of Islam. Muhammad ordered his followers to raid caravans. Over time, the communities whose caravans had been raided banded together to stop Muslim banditry. Many battles ensued, but the Muslims were nearly always victorious, convincing many tribes to join Muhammad as the victorious Arab commander.

ESSENTIAL

Even though Islam started in Arabia, and the first Muslims were Arabs, today Arabs make up less than 10 percent of the world's 1.3 billion Muslims.

Muhammad was a clever military leader, choosing his battles wisely. In 630, after winning many campaigns and repelling repeated Meccan attacks, 10,000 Muslim warriors moved on Mecca and took the city without a fight. The victorious Muslims cleansed the Ka'ba of its idols.

With Yathrib (Medina) as Muhammad's political hub and Mecca as his religious center, many tribal leaders saw the tides changing, causing them to join the new Islamic movement. As clan solidarity and tribal honor were foundational aspects of Arab culture, thousands accepted Islam, along with their leaders. Only two years after the taking of Mecca, nearly all of the Arabian Peninsula was united under the leadership of Muhammad, but this would all be threatened very soon.

Death, Division, and Domination

In 632, after returning to Medina from a pilgrimage to Mecca, Muhammad developed a sickness that eventually took his life. On his deathbed

Muhammad is said to have challenged his followers to continue spreading Islam all the way to Constantinople. At the age of sixty-three, the founder of Islam passed on, marking the end of his revelations and the beginning of turmoil and division in the House of Islam (*Dar al-Islam* in Arabic).

Splinters and Successors

Before his death, Muhammad had named no successor and had no biological son. This presented a huge problem for his followers, as no clear leader could be agreed upon. A major dispute arose regarding who should be the new leader, known as *Khalifah* (or caliph), Arabic for "successor." Two camps arose, one proclaiming Muhammad's son-in-law and cousin, Ali ibn Abi Talib, as the rightful successor, and the other insisting upon Muhammad's closest friend, Abu Bakr as-Siddiq. This division has continued through the centuries, with one group calling themselves *Shià* (from the Arabic phrase *Shiàt Àli*, meaning "partisans of Ali"), and the other calling themselves *Sunni* (from the Arabic root meaning "custom" or "practice").

FACT

Of the more than 1 billion Muslims living around the globe, Sunnis make up about 85 percent, while Shi'ites comprise about 15 percent.

In addition to the conflict regarding leadership, issues of tribal unity put the very future of Islam in question. As you read earlier, many clan leaders had followed Muhammad because of his military success and leadership capabilities. Now, with no clear leader, many tribes went their own way, refusing to pay the required *zakat* (religious tax) to Medina.

In one of Islam's most crucial moments, Abu Bakr saved the deteriorating confederacy by challenging tribal leaders to follow the living God despite the death of Muhammad. As a result of his boldness, many tribes gained respect for Abu Bakr, resulting in his election as the first successor to Muhammad. After being named caliph, Abu Bakr organized war parties to subdue those tribes that had abandoned their commitments to Islam. In what became known as the Wars of the Apostasy, Muslim forces succeeded in stamping out all rebel groups, making them sign peace treaties recognizing Islamic rule.

Conquests of the Caliphs

Through internal disagreements and bloody Arab-on-Arab wars, the Islamic armies moved forward in conquest into the Byzantine and Persian Empires. After leading the faithful for only two years, Abu Bakr died, but not before pointing to Ùmar ibn al Khattab as the next caliph. As Muhammad's second successor, Ùmar found himself responsible for defending and expanding the borders of the new Islamic empire.

On the western front, in Syria and Palestine, Muslim armies moved forward, defeating Byzantine forces left weakened by years of war with the Persians. With a similar situation in the east, depleted Persian forces lost battle after battle to Muslim war parties. By 640, Ùmar's men had subdued Persia, Egypt, and most of the eastern Mediterranean, including the ancient cities of Damascus and Jerusalem.

ESSENTIAL

The Arabic word *jihad* is possibly one of the most controversial words of the twenty-first century. On one hand, groups using the name jihad violently struggle against "infidels," fueling the belief that jihad means "holy war." On the other hand, hundreds of thousands of Muslims around the globe interpret jihad to be a nonviolent struggle against personal impurity. With various shades and interpretations of this word, it is literally translated as "a struggle," yet this particular struggle is an act of worship, with expected rewards.

Dealing with Diversity

The Muslim world had become more than an Arab confederation, as Ùmar's domains included non-Arab Egyptians, Syrians, Mesopotamians, Persians, and others, as well as substantial Christian, Zoroastrian, and Jewish populations. In order to manage these diverse lands, the caliph divided his realm into provinces, appointed governors for these areas, and implemented new systems for taxation. This system included the *jizyah* tax levied on non-Muslim subjects, who were not allowed to serve in the Muslim army.

In some cases, Christians and Jews converted to Islam to avoid the non-Muslim taxes and the social stigma related to being a *dhimmi*, or "protected" non-Muslim. Many others converted to be on the winning side, or because of frustration with the Byzantine Church, while others truly believed Muhammad to be the final messenger of God. In the same way, many Zoroastrians wanted to avoid the challenges created by dhimmi status—as a result, most rejected the Sassanian state religion with the fall of the empire.

In 644, after ten years of managing the Ummah (Muslim community) and working to expand Muslim domains beyond Arabia, Caliph Ùmar was assassinated, making Ùthman ibn Àffan the third caliph. From the Umayyad clan, Ùthman was said to be a soft-spoken leader, lacking the persona of his predecessors. Nevertheless, Ùthman managed to develop the first Muslim navy and establish a standard version of Muhammad's revelations, known as the Qur'an.

FACT

The Qur'an, Islam's most sacred text, derives its name from the Arabic verb *qara'a* (meaning "to recite"), which is also the root of the command *iqra'*, meaning "Recite!"—believed to be God's first utterance to Muhammad.

Civil Blood Makes Civil Hands Unclean

Despite his mild manner, Ùthman's decisions created many enemies. In creating an official version of the Qur'an, he had also ordered the burning of all other collections, causing some to resent his actions and leadership style. Ùthman had also relieved several officials of their duties, which translated into additional resentment throughout the Muslim community. In this climate, a disgruntled group from the Egyptian garrison camp of al-Fustat (near modern-day Cairo) traveled to Medina and murdered Ùthman as he was praying.

With Ùthman's assassination, Àli ibn Abi Talib became the fourth caliph, but not without great consequence. In fact, several of Muhammad's close friends and one of his wives, À'isha, moved to the Mesopotamian city of Basra to establish an opposition movement. In what turned out to be the first Muslim civil war, Àli's forces crushed the rebellion in the conflict we know now as the Battle of the Camel.

Àli then moved the capital of the Muslim state from the Arabian city of Medina to Kufa, in modern-day Iraq. Soon another civil war began as a rebellious governor from Syria, from the prominent Umayyad family, moved against Àli's government. Although this rebellion was put down quickly, events were set in motion that would ultimately end Àli's life and begin a new Arab dynasty.

In 661, Àli was assassinated, ending a string of rulers known as the "rightly guided caliphs." For the next chapter in Islamic history, internal divisions, corruption, and family power plays would be signatures of the caliphate. With Àli's death, his son Hasan was named caliph, but only a year later Hasan submitted to the Umayyad family and their claim to the caliphate. With the Umayyads taking control, the capital was moved from Kufa to the ancient Syrian city of Damascus, where it would remain for nearly 100 years.

The Qur'an and Hadith

According to Islamic beliefs, Muhammad's first angelic experience was only the beginning. From this visitation in 610 until his death in 632, a series of revelations was given to Muhammad in the cities of Mecca and Medina. These encounters came to him in various forms but were said to be none other than the exact words of God, as witnessed by their unparallel poetic beauty and intricacy.

Collecting the Codex

Although Muhammad's teachings were memorized and written down by many of his followers, no official compilation of these teachings was formed until sometime between 644 and 656. Known as the Qur'an, these revelations are divided into 114 chapters (*surahs* in Arabic) and more than 6,000 verses, or *ayas*. The Qur'an's major themes include God's oneness, rules for moral living, the unquestionable authority of Muhammad, and the coming Judgment Day. Reading the Qur'an is considered a sacred event, in which the worshipper is believed to be enunciating the very words of God in the same rhythmic fashion as they were first revealed. As it is believed to contain the exact expressions of God, the true Qur'an can only exist in Arabic, and any translation is considered a mere shadow of the Qur'an.

Following Muhammad's Example

According to one Qur'anic injunction, "Your companion (Muhammad) is neither astray nor being misled, nor does he say (ought) of (his own) desire. It is no less than inspiration sent down to him . . ." (Qur'an 53:2–4). This was interpreted to mean that God inspired everything Muhammad did. For example, the way he ate, walked, talked, prayed, and so on was exactly the way God wanted all humans to operate. Every aspect of Muhammad's life was to be mimicked, no matter how small or seemingly insignificant.

In addition, another Qur'anic mandate declared, "He who obeys the Messenger (Muhammad), obeys God" (Qur'an 4:80).

With this understanding that Muhammad's opinions and actions were inspired, the emerging Muslim community recognized the importance of emulating and obeying Muhammad. As a result, they began to record the things he said and did apart from his Qur'anic revelations. The "practices" or "customs" of Muhammad (*Sunnah* in Arabic) were narrated from Muslim to Muslim, until the history was eventually codified into an enormous body of writings known as the Hadith. In these records, Muhammad's decisions and actions (both public and private), along with many other details of his life, are listed for the Ummah to reference. As Muslim mothers began to teach their children in the ways their mothers had taught them, the examples found in the Hadith came to indirectly influence the majority of day-to-day Muslim life—even more so than the Qur'an!

ESSENTIAL

While the Qur'an is revered as Islam's most sacred book, the sayings and actions of Muhammad, found in the Hadith, guide the majority of an observant Muslim's daily life.

Basic Components

From the Qur'an and Hadith, Muslims have derived basic components to define their religion. The following are the common beliefs and practices, known as "Iman":

- **One God (Allah)**—All-powerful, all-knowing, merciful creator of all things
- **Heaven and hell**—The places to which every human will be resurrected, judged, and given eternal paradise or pain, according to their deeds
- **Angels and jinn**—Two distinct races of created beings, each of which can be good or evil (*Shaitan*, or Satan, is considered to be an evil jinn)
- **The prophets**—Holy men sent throughout history as messengers of God, including Adam, Noah, Moses, Jesus, Muhammad, and many others (Muhammad is considered the greatest and final prophet)
- **The sacred Scriptures**—Four divinely inspired books, including the Torah of Moses, Psalms of David, Gospels of Jesus, and Qur'an (the Qur'an is believed to be the greatest book and the only unchanged scripture)

There are also "din," the religious practices and beliefs that define the Muslim religion:

- **Profession of faith (***Shahada***)**—Saying with intent, "There is no god, except God and Muhammad is the messenger of God"
- **Daily prayers (***Salaah***)**—Five prayers completed each day, at prescribed times, with set words, and predetermined movements, while facing Mecca
- **Alms-giving (***Zakat***)**—Offering at least 2½ percent of an individual's wealth to the poor
- **Fasting (***Sawm***)**—Abstaining from all pleasures (including food, drink, sex, smoking, and so on) during the daylight hours of the month of Ramadan
- **Pilgrimage (***Hajj***)**—Traveling to the city of Mecca, Saudi Arabia (at least once in one's lifetime), to perform various rites at the Ka'ba and other significant locations

From the deserts of Arabia, Islam emerged not only as a religion but as an all-encompassing system. The words of the Qur'an and the examples in the Hadith produced an Islamic way to do just about everything. From the rules of war to proper hygiene, there were divine guidelines for all aspects of life. Shari'a (sometimes translated "Islamic law") was to influence every part of the Muslim state and the people within its borders, both Muslim and dhimmi (non-Muslim).

By the end of the seventh century, Islam had gathered the momentum needed to conquer the entire Middle East, North Africa, parts of Europe, and Central Asia. In the centuries to come, tolerant (almost secular) kingdoms and rigid dictatorial regimes would emerge, with Muslim rulers as diverse as the peoples they led.

In the next chapter, you will experience the ebb and flow of nearly 700 years of Islamic civilization. From the Arab Umayyad Empire to later Turkic Sultanates, Muslims continued to evolve in their understanding of Islam and its practical application. While Europe was mired in the Dark Ages, the Middle East was actively pursuing knowledge, leading the way in areas of science, technology, philosophy, and the arts. Muslims had defined themselves as a civilization, ensuring that Islam would be a lasting force for ages to come.

CHAPTER 8

Islamic Empires
and European Colonies

As Muslim empires rapidly expanded their territories, the Byzantine Empire continued to lose ground. Despite great divisions and continued civil wars, a series of Islamic regimes ruled the Middle East and parts of Europe with great success. From the advances of Islamic scholars, scientists, and architects to the bloody wars of occupation waged by European Crusaders, the Middle East was forever changed by an unparalleled period of conflict and transformation. This chapter offers background information you will need to understand the modern Middle East.

Umayyads in Damascus

As you read in the previous chapter, the Caliph Àli was assassinated, making his son Hasan leader of the faithful. Within a year, Hasan abdicated the caliphate to the Syrian governor, Muàwiyya, of the Umayyad family. This transition of power began a new age, in which the Muslim community would no longer be managed by pious elected leaders but by a series of predetermined wealthy kings.

For almost ninety years, the Umayyad dynasty guided the house of Islam from their opulent Syrian capital, Damascus. The Umayyads appointed Arab Muslim governors to oversee their territories, but many non-Arab or non-Muslim officials were allowed to continue leading their communities. Beyond that, educated Jews, Christians, and Zoroastrians were utilized to teach Muslims. In the great schools of Alexandria, Damascus, Antioch, and Edessa (modern-day Sanli Urfa, Turkey), Christian monks educated their Muslim conquerors in subjects such as history, philosophy, and the sciences. In addition, Byzantine and Sassanian government structures were often left in place, Greek and Persian languages were commonly used, and *masjids* (Muslim houses of worship) were built using Roman architectural styles.

FACT

How about a cup of joe? While the exact origins of the coffee bean are debated, most historians agree it was first brewed in Arabia around 675.

With the Muslim conquests of predominantly Christian lands, Islam and Christianity were coexisting as never before. When Muslim men married Christian women, their offspring were often Muslim in name, with the beliefs of their Christian mothers. According to one Muslim historian, important members of the Umayyad armies were "Arab like strangers . . . Muslims with the characteristics of Christians." As a result of these influences, a mystical undercurrent appeared within Islam by the mid-seventh century.

Blood of the Martyrs

After the death of Muàwiyya in 680, Umayyad rule was challenged as Àli's second son Husayn traveled to Mesopotamia, gathering supporters from those loyal to his father. Umayyad armies quickly engaged Husayn and his Shi'ite followers, killing them at a place called Karbala (in present-day Iraq). Instead of ending the Shi'ite movement, the death of Husayn actually gave new life to the partisans of Àli. Also, many dissatisfied Muslims rallied behind the image of Husayn's martyrdom in their opposition to the Umayyads of Damascus.

ESSENTIAL

To this day the city of Karbala, Iraq, remains one of the holiest cities in Islam, especially for Shi'ites. An annual pilgrimage to the city commemorates Husayn's martyrdom, with reenactments of his death and loud displays of mourning, including self-inflicted beatings. The death of Husayn plays such an important role in the Shi'ite movement that it is often compared to the crucifixion of Jesus in the Christian tradition.

A New Master

Of all the Umayyad caliphs, Àbd al-Malik left the greatest legacy. During his reign from 685 to 705, Àbd al-Malik used his power to do the following:

- Reorganize the imperial system of taxation.
- Make Arabic the official language (instead of Greek or Persian).
- Mint the first Islamic currency (replacing Byzantine and Sassanian coinage).
- Establish an imperial postal service.
- Re-edit the Qur'an (adding vowel signs).

Àbd al-Malik also placed new restrictions on non-Muslims and non-Arab Muslims, causing great resentment and sporadic revolts. In one such conflict, an uprising in the city of Mecca was suppressed by Umayyad troops and catapults, leaving the Ka'ba in ruins. While Àbd al-Malik instituted positive reforms, he ultimately desired complete control of his domains. Any threat of opposition, Arab, Muslim, or otherwise, would be met with swift and severe punishment. Not even the holy city of Mecca and its sacred Ka'ba were safe from Àbd al-Malik.

While trying to maintain order on the home front, Àbd al-Malik expanded Islam's territories to include new far-flung lands. In North Africa, Umayyad armies conquered the indigenous Berber tribes, moving to the shores of the Atlantic Ocean. Later, an Umayyad military leader named Tariq crossed from North Africa to Spain through an area later known as Jabal Tariq. This Arabic name was then corrupted in European languages to become "Gibraltar" (as in the Rock of Gibraltar). Eventually, Muslim forces continued through the Iberian Peninsula into southern France, only to be turned back outside of Tours (about 100 miles outside of modern-day Paris).

In the east, Muslim forces proceeded through the mountains and high plateaus of Persia to Central Asia, where they encountered warriors from nomadic Turkic tribes. After subduing the Turks, Umayyad forces moved east, to the borders of China's T'ang dynasty. While the Turkish-speaking tribes originally followed Buddhism or an ancient form of shamanism (similar to Native American religions), in time they converted to Islam. As Muslims, they then moved into Persian and Arab lands, eventually establishing their own Islamic empires.

Despite many reforms and the expansion of Umayyad territory, trouble continued to brew within the house of Islam. Tensions were high among non-Arab Muslims and others who desired a pure Islamic state but experienced Arab Umayyad domination and greed. Through civil war, revolts, and tribal rivalries, the Umayyads faced violent opposition, especially in Kufa, Iraq, the heart of the Shi'ite movement.

Sufis and Separatists

In Kufa and the surrounding areas, an overall disgust for the increasing corruption and materialism of the Umayyad royal family inspired some to protest the caliphate through nonviolent means. Drawing from the ascetic and mystical examples of Muhammad, both Shi'ites and Sunnis developed an early form of what has come to be known as Sufism. Many of these Islamic mystics adopted both monastic ideology and costume, living a life of contemplation and self-denial, shrouded in white wool garments. The Arabic word for wool, *suf*, was then used to describe this new brand of mystics, known as Sufis.

In Iraq, anti-Umayyad Sunnis rallied behind the Hashemite family of Muhammad, along with Shi'ites who revered the descendants of Ali and his wife Fatima (who was also Muhammad's daughter). In Kufa, a man named

Abu Hashim gained many followers and was called "al-Suf," leading some scholars to believe he was the father of Sufi Islam. Though many dissident groups formed, the Abbasids (followers of Muhammad's uncle, Abu al-Abbas) offered a platform to unite the opposition.

QUESTION

Who are the Sufis?
The term "Sufi" can be used to describe Muslims from both Sunni and Shi'ite backgrounds who follow a mystical path and practice an esoteric form of Islam. Many Sufis interpret the Qur'an unconventionally, distilling its words to a message of love and inner peace. In addition, most Sufis perform chants and repetitive movements meant to evoke supernatural experiences in their quest for oneness with God.

Abbasids in Baghdad

Originally based in the Shi'ite stronghold of Kufa, Iraq, the Abbasids began their offensive with propaganda rather than force. By stationing propagandists at strategic locations throughout the Middle East, Abbasids were able to encourage widespread popular dissent, which eventually led to all-out revolt. In what turned out to be Islam's third civil war, Muslims and non-Muslims banded together in revolutionary fervor, bringing the Umayyads to their knees.

In 750, the Umayyads of Damascus were defeated. Except for one prince who escaped to Spain, the entire royal family was executed, making the sons of Abbas the new leaders. Under the Abbasid dynasty, Arab and non-Arab Muslims were given equal rights. Imperial power and wealth reached new levels, and Islamic civilization enjoyed a golden age.

A City from God

During the reign of the Abbasid caliph, Abu Ja`far al-Mansur (754–775), the dynasty established itself by building a new capital city and separating from radical groups that had helped in the revolution. On the site of a small town near the ancient Mesopotamian city of Babylon, al-Mansur erected his new capital, the "City of Peace," Baghdad.

Built strategically between the Euphrates and Tigris Rivers, this unique circular city was surrounded by two walls, with four gates opening to the four corners of the empire. With nearly every major trade route crossing Abbasid lands, Baghdad's round walls formed a kind of axis for the spokes of global economics. African gold, Chinese silk, and Russian slaves were some of the exotic commodities brought to the Middle East through Baghdad's ports and markets. As Baghdad's business was booming, banking systems were established, immigrants flocked from far-off lands, and the world recognized the Abbasids as a new global power.

FACT

Thank the Middle East for your algebra homework! From basic equations offered by ancient Egyptians and Mesopotamians, the Arab mathematician Muhammad al-Khwarizmi took mathematics to another level in the ninth century. Based on the Arabic word *al-jabr* (meaning "restoration"), algebra was known as the science of restoration and balancing.

With unheard-of riches pouring into the empire, Baghdad quickly grew in size and splendor, arguably becoming the most impressive city of its time. With nearly a million inhabitants, Baghdad's gardens, fountains, palaces, and mosques filled the city with divine beauty. From the sounds of merchants selling their goods to the voice of the *mu'izzin* calling the faithful to prayer, Mesopotamia was revived with imperial power. Baghdad was the envy of the world, and Constantinople would settle for second.

Tolerance and Transformation

The Abbasids claimed legitimacy through their membership in Muhammad's Arab Hashemite clan, but with many of Iraq's inhabitants coming from Persian stock, they were greatly influenced by Iranian culture. In fact, over the centuries, Abbasid caliphs married Persian wives, making the royal family ethnically more Persian. Although non-Arab and non-Muslim peoples influenced the empire, the Abbasids ultimately identified themselves as Arab Muslims. Consequently, the Middle East was "Arabized," with non-Arabs adopting Arab customs and language. Also, the region was "Islamicized," as non-Muslims adapted to Islamic laws or converted to Islam.

One example of these changes comes from Alexandria, Egypt, in the early ninth century. Here, some of the non-Arab Coptic (Egyptian) Christian population accepted Islam, while the majority simply learned the Arabic language and adapted to Arab culture. About the same time, the famous Muslim philosopher Yaqub al-Kindi recorded the emergence of a small group of Alexandrian mystics, called Sufis. Although these men considered themselves Muslims, they were said to have had uniquely Christian beliefs and practices.

The commingling of Islamic, Christian, Persian, and Greco-Roman philosophies created new ideas, and the mixing of Arabs and non-Arabs produced new peoples. In this case, Arab Muslims were the dominant force. Thus, new beliefs were interpreted as Islamic views and new bloodlines were considered Arab.

Distinctly Shi'ite

Shi'ites, who had been a part of the Abbasid revolution but were now shunned, opposed the emerging Abbasid Sunni dynasty, believing a descendant of Ali should rule the empire. The alienation of Shi'ite groups solidified distinct doctrines regarding leadership and theology. The most visible of these was their agreement on a definitive line of imams, or infallible leaders, descending from Ali to Hasan, Husayn, and so on. Although there have since been disagreements regarding the authority of certain later imams, to this day the vast majority of Shi'ite Muslims look to a succession of divinely inspired leaders. With various types of messianic expectancy, some Shi'ites even believe an imam (or one of his descendants) will return to Earth as the Mahdi, establishing God's justice and peace around the world.

QUESTION

Is the Mahdi the same as the Messiah?
Among both Sunni and Shi'ite Muslims, the Mahdi is seen as a powerful figure who will come to Earth just before the Judgment Day. The Mahdi will rule the planet in much the same way Jews foresee the reign of the moshiach. The Mahdi's appearance is also similar to the Christian belief in Jesus Christ's second coming. (Many Muslims believe Jesus will be present in Mecca when the Mahdi is revealed.)

Umayyads in Spain

While the Abbasids were busy running their empire, the sole survivor of the Umayyad dynasty made his way to al-Andalus (Spain). Here, with the aid of Syrian troops (still present from the Umayyad conquests), prince Abd al-Rahman organized a new kingdom outside of Abbasid influence. Initially, in this revived Umayyad emirate (kingdom), Arabs ruled over the non-Arab and non-Muslim masses. In time, Spain was both Arabized and Islamicized, as many of its inhabitants learned to embrace Arabic and Islam. At the same time, many Christian and Jewish citizens chose to simply adapt to the language and culture of their new leaders.

In the Spanish capital of Cordoba, nearly half a million people enjoyed an age of scientific, philosophical, and artistic exploration. With hundreds of schools, mosques, libraries, and palaces, this Mediterranean city dwarfed all other European cities in size and splendor. By the early tenth century, the Umayyad dynasty and its subjects had developed a distinctly Andalusian culture that was known throughout the world. In an effort to establish al-Andalus and the Umayyad monarchy, Abd al-Rahman III declared himself caliph.

Although the kingdom would be dissolved in less than 100 years, various Islamic emirates continued to rule parts of Spain until 1492. Today, remnants of Arab and Muslim influence remain in Spain. This is especially true in the south, where visitors can see beautiful Islamic architecture, hear Arabic linguistic and musical influences, and taste the lingering flavors of North African cuisine.

Fractured Fraternities

In the Abbasid Empire and Umayyad Spain, religious and political factions threatened the power of Arab monarchs. From its inception, the Abbasid regime dealt with separatist groups across North Africa, including the Umayyads in Spain. In addition, Shi'ite movements in northern Iraq, Persia, and Arabia, combined with civil war at home, challenged the unity of the Islamic state.

The Mamluks

Fighting rebellion after rebellion, the Abbasids rarely enjoyed a significant period without conflict in some part of their domains. With the constant demand for skilled soldiers, the empire began training a warrior class of slave boys from Central Asian Turkish tribes, sub-Saharan African groups, and other ethnicities. Known as mamluks (meaning "those who are owned"), these boys from Christian, Buddhist, and other religious backgrounds were converted to Islam through intentional educational efforts. Soon these young men grew to be powerful military leaders and strategists. While continuing to recruit new slave boys, mamluk generals established loyal, family-like units of fierce non-Arab fighters.

In Egypt, a Turkish mamluk and Abbasid governor by the name of Ahmad ibn Tulun separated himself from Baghdad's authority, establishing his own kingdom from al-Fustat (modern-day Cairo). Although the Abbasids temporarily regained control of Egypt in 905, Egypt was again taken by Turkish and African mamluks just thirty years later. Eventually, in 969, a Shi'ite group known as the Fatimids added Egypt to its growing North African domains. Moving their capital from Tunisia to al-Fustat, the Fatimids renamed the city Al Qahirah (better known to Westerners as Cairo).

The Shi'ite Empire

This Fatimid dynasty was named after its founder, Ubayd Allah al-Mahdi Billah, who claimed to be a descendant of Fatima, the wife of Ali and daughter of Muhammad. In addition, Ubayd Allah also declared himself caliph of the Muslim world, above the Abbasid leader in Baghdad. Later he even took on the messianic title of Mahdi, bringing his followers to believe he would inspire an age of worldwide Islamic peace and justice.

The Fatimid state quickly established itself from its growing capital, Cairo. As an enthusiastic Shi'ite movement, in 972 the Fatimids completed building the famous al-Azhar mosque and university as a training center for their brand of Islam. To this day, al-Azhar is respected throughout the Muslim world as the premier Islamic university, though it is now a Sunni institution.

For the next century, the Shi'ite Fatimids surpassed the weakened Abbasid caliphate, even occupying the city of Baghdad for a short time around 1055. Eventually, the Fatimids lost power because of mamluk revolts and other opposition movements. The biggest threat came from the newly Islamicized Turkish tribes of Central Asia, who were moving southwest in the name of Sunni Islam. Over the next 200 years, Arab, Persian, and Byzantine territories were divided and conquered, changing the face of the Middle East forever.

Turkic Expansion

From their ancestral homeland around the Altai Mountains (along the modern border of Kazakhstan and Mongolia), Turkish-speaking nomads moved south and west, finding new lands and religions. The Ghaznavids established the first Turkic kingdom in what is now part of Afghanistan. After conquering most of Central Asia, the Ghaznavids moved into modern-day Pakistan and northern India in 1001. In addition to taking massive amounts of gold and jewels from Hindu temples, they left their Islamic beliefs in what would become one of the most populous Muslim areas on the planet.

By 1040, the Turkish-speaking Seljuks rolled through Central Asia and Persia into Mesopotamia and Syria. Inspired by their new religion, Sunni Islam, the Seljuks established religious schools, hoping to "purify" their domains of Shi'ite thought. Although the Seljuk sultan (king) eventually captured Baghdad, the Abbasid caliph was allowed to remain as a symbol of Sunni supremacy.

FACT

Hashish, anyone? As the Seljuks rigidly enforced their brand of Sunni Islam, a minority of fanatical Shi'ites began killing prominent Sunni political and religious leaders. According to tradition, these men carried out their suicide missions aided by the drug hashish. Whether or not they actually used drugs, these terrorists came to be known as Hashishins, meaning "takers of hashish" (which later evolved into the word "assassins").

Seljuk Turks then turned their attention to the Byzantine Empire. For nearly thirty years, Turkic and Byzantine forces repeatedly met in bloody clashes. The most important of these was waged in 1071 at Manzikert (in eastern Turkey). Here, the Seljuks defeated the Byzantines, capturing the emperor. From this victory, the Turks moved west into central Anatolia, to within 100 miles of Constantinople.

At this point, the Great Seljuk Sultanate was a vast empire, spanning east to west from Central Asia to central Anatolia and north to south from the Caucasus Mountains of Russia to the city of Mecca in Arabia. Although the

Sunni Seljuks viewed the heretical Shi'ite Fatimid sultanate as their biggest enemy, Christian Europe would soon attack. To the Holy Roman Empire, the Turkish Muslims were a major threat. Not only had the Seljuks made short work of the Byzantines, but they also controlled the Holy Land. In the eyes of many European Christians (including the pope), the holy city of Jerusalem was calling for liberation.

Europe to the Rescue—Everyone Loses

Fresh from the Great Schism of 1054 (in which the pope's Western, Latin Catholic Church and the emperor's Eastern, Greek Orthodox Church severed all ties), the Byzantines found themselves on the brink of extinction. In a desperate attempt to save itself, Constantinople called for Western European assistance. Seizing the opportunity to expand Latin influence in the Middle East, Pope Urban II rallied Catholic Christians to wage a holy war, or Crusade, to reclaim the sacred city of Jerusalem.

ALERT

Although varying accounts of Crusader conduct exist, many sources tell of bloody massacres in which Jews, Muslims, and native Christians were slaughtered at the hands of Western warriors. Today, the savagery of the "Christian" Crusades lives on in the consciousness of the region, as many Middle Eastern peoples view modern military campaigns as further Crusades for Christ.

By 1097, crusading knights from across Europe arrived in Constantinople, ready to reclaim the Holy Land. Moving quickly through the newly established Seljuk Sultanate of *Rum*, or Rome (the Arabic/Turkish term for Anatolia), Christian forces continued through Syria with victory after victory, taking the important city of Antioch by June 3, 1098. Almost a year after the capture of Antioch, the city of Jerusalem was taken as well. The liberation of Jerusalem was the stated objective of the Crusade, but after more than two years of fighting, and hundreds of thousands of lives, the Europeans occupied the entire eastern Mediterranean coast.

Colonial Kingdoms

In order to manage their newly acquired lands, knights established four colonial states, ruled from four major cities. The "Latin Kingdom of Jerusalem"—stretching from the Red Sea through Palestine to the present-day city of Beirut, Lebanon—was the largest and most powerful of the colonies. The other three states included the county of Tripoli (roughly contiguous with the modern-day country of Lebanon), the principality of Antioch (including contemporary northwestern Syria and the Hatay Province of Turkey), and the Anatolian county of Edessa (centered on the modern Turkish city of Sanli Urfa).

ESSENTIAL

During the turmoil of the Crusades, Sufism and orthodox Islam moved in opposite directions. At about this time, the Persian philosopher and theologian Abu Hamid al-Ghazali drafted a series of revolutionary works that married aspects of the two. Although his insightful writings legitimized mysticism, they also inspired many Muslims to reject rationalism.

New Alliances

Over the next two centuries, Europe launched a series of offensive and defensive Crusades, with Kurdish, Turkish, and Arab Muslims attempting to end European occupation. As the saying goes, politics makes strange bedfellows. Between Sunni and Shi'ite conflicts, Crusader and Muslim tensions, Orthodox and Catholic rivalries, and various tribal feuds, the bedfellows were strange indeed.

The most extraordinary of these alliances came as a result of a botched deal between a Kurdish general from Syria and the Fatimid caliph of Egypt. The resulting rift brought about an alliance in which Catholic Crusaders and Shi'ite Fatimids fought together against Sunni Syrians and their Kurdish commander. This unlikely relationship eventually ended in 1169, as Syrian forces returned to Egypt with overwhelming force. Thanks to the Syrians, Egypt was free of Crusaders, the Fatimids were finished, and a new Sunni regime came to power.

eventually destroying Baghdad and the Abbasid dynasty in 1258. The Mamluks of Cairo remained as the only Muslim force able to repel the might of the Mongols, but only as far as Syria.

By the late 1200s, Muslim forces decided once and for all to end the European occupation. Soon the cities of Jaffa (modern Tel Aviv, Israel), Antioch, and Tripoli all fell to Muslim forces, leaving the coastal city of Acre (north of present-day Haifa, Israel) as the last Crusader outpost in the Middle East. Despite a last-ditch Crusade, in 1291, after nearly two centuries, the last bastion of European colonialism was removed from the Middle East. Although Muslim armies had finally succeeded in expelling the Europeans from Palestine, the Mongols remained in Iraq and Iran.

Eventually, just as monotheism transformed Judea's pagan Roman occupiers (via Christianity), it again changed the region's pagan Mongol conquerors, via Islam. Known as the Il-Khans, these new Muslim converts continued to rule most of Iran and Central Asia for another 100 years.

The fall of Constantinople and the rise of the Turks, the revival of Islamic civilization and the decline of great empires—these are just a few of the monumental events that have shaped today's Middle East.

Expulsion of the Infidels

The end of Shi'ite Fatimid rule in Egypt marked the beginning of a new era of Sunni resurgence in the Middle East. Under the leadership of Salah al-Din Yusuf ibn-Ayyub (also known as "Saladin"), the Ayyubid family would wage a two-pronged jihad against European occupation and Shi'ite heresy.

As sultan, Salah al-Din was just as much a diplomat as a warrior. Not only was he able to unite Damascus and Cairo under the banner of Sunni Islam, but he also contributed to growing divisions between the "Latin" Crusaders and "Greek" Byzantines.

The unification of Syria and Egypt meant Salah al-Din could squeeze Crusader forces from all directions. By 1187, the Europeans were expelled from Jerusalem and forced to retreat to a small area along the Mediterranean coast. For the next sixty years, Salah al-Din's Ayyubid sultanate extended its influence from Cairo across North Africa to a swath of land stretching from southeastern Anatolia in the north to Yemen in the south.

FACT

Jalal al-Din Muhammad Rumi, or "Mevlana" (*Mawlana* in Arabic) as he was later known, was a masterful poet whose works are renowned throughout the world for their lyrical luster and meaningful mysticism. After Rumi's death, his followers preserved his teachings, forming the Mevlevi Sufi order. Today, pilgrims from all corners of the globe visit Konya, Turkey, in hopes of gaining wisdom and blessings at Mevlana's grave.

Between the Ayyubids in Cairo, the Abbasids in Baghdad, and the Seljuks in Konya (south-central Anatolia), the remaining coastal Crusader colony had little or no power. Nevertheless, many desired to see the European cancer completely removed. This wish was delayed, however, as both the Abbasids and Seljuks were plagued by a new group of infidels, the Mongol khans (rulers), and the Ayyubid dynasty was usurped by its own Turkish mamluks.

Under the leadership of Genghis Khan, the Mongols ravaged most of the world from Japan to Eastern Europe. Throughout the 1200s, the Mongols turned their attention to the Middle East, conquering the Seljuks in 1242 ar

CHAPTER 9

A New Empire Is Born

Crusader occupation, Mongol invasions, and internal conflicts left the Seljuk and Abbasid empires in ruins. In this power vacuum, nomadic Turkish tribesmen stepped up to try their hand at empire management. Within 200 years, three Turkish-speaking Muslim dynasties ruled an empire that stretched from Eastern Europe through the Middle East to India. Despite imperial power struggles and dynastic disputes, the Middle East led the world into a modern era of science, technology, and style.

The Aftermath of Defeat

Although European knights killed many Jews and Muslims during the Crusades, little lasting political or monetary damage was done to any of the Islamic empires. Despite random massacres of Eastern Christians, the Crusades were largely directed at non-Christians, until the sacking of Constantinople in 1204. During this series of raids, crusading knights pillaged Byzantium's ancient Roman wealth, taking massive amounts of gold, jewels, and priceless relics back to Europe as booty. With imperial treasuries emptied, the Byzantines would never fully recover, and Western Europe would never look back.

Powder Power

By the end of the 1200s, the great city of Baghdad lay in ruins, the caliph was dead, and Mongol khans ruled much of the Middle East. The mighty Arab dynasties were distant memories and, except for the Mamluks of Egypt, classical Islam's magnificent empires were extinct. From what could have been a deathblow to Islamic civilization, the Mongol hordes inadvertently provided an element that was more powerful than the pen or the sword—gunpowder.

ESSENTIAL

Just as Chinese gunpowder revolutionized Middle Eastern warfare, European armies later found new strength as they borrowed powder power from the Middle East.

The newly Islamicized Il-Khan (Mongol) dynasty remained connected to its Asian roots, creating a type of cultural and technological exchange between Far Eastern and Middle Eastern peoples. Of the many shared ideas and practices, the introduction of Chinese gunpowder made the biggest impact. As certain Middle Eastern armies transitioned from the sword to the gun, an enormous technological gap was created, similar to that between an M-16 and a musket. In time, "gunpowder empires" emerged with the ability to exert overwhelming force on the powder-deficient masses.

Cairo's Conversion

In Egypt and Syria, the Shi'ite Fatimids were a distant memory as Mamluks ruled a distinctly Sunni empire. During the Fatimid period, most of Cairo's Muslim citizens remained Sunni despite their proselytizing Shi'ite leaders, including scholars at the city's venerable al-Azhar University, which had its beginnings in 972. Even though it functioned as a Shi'ite missionary training center, the university provided the people of Cairo with access to a quality education in Arabic grammar, literature, and history, regardless of the faculty's Shi'ite leanings.

Salah al-Din had made large strides in ridding the city of what he considered Shi'ite heresy, but in the case of al-Azhar University, he and his successors ignored its potential as a Sunni institution. With the rise of the Mamluks, al-Azhar was restored to its former greatness. From that point forward it taught Sunni doctrines. In al-Azhar and other schools, some forms of scholarship were encouraged, but original ideas and philosophies were discouraged as students were taught to trust in the accomplishments of the past. From the vitality of classical Islamic intellectualism, the Mamluks inspired a long period of scholastic stagnation.

Slaves as Masters

Although the Mamluks were ethnically Turkish, Mongolian, and Circassian (a people from the Caucasus Mountains), they were not interested in their origins. Instead of ethnic pride, Islam guided the Mamluks as they ruled largely Arab lands. As a result, Arabic culture and language thrived, and Cairo emerged as the heart of the Arab world. In a political maneuver that pleased the Arab masses and satisfied Mamluk religious convictions, a series of Arab men from the fallen Abbasid dynasty were named "caliph." Although these men continued the centuries-old Arab caliphate, these caliphs were actually puppets of the Mamluks, nominally presiding over Sunni Islamic orthodoxy.

From the masterfully constructed Qait Bey Citadel in Alexandria, Egypt, (possibly built in part from the rubble of the legendary lighthouse of Alexandria), to mosques, schools, hospitals, and fountains built in Cairo, Jerusalem, Damascus, and Mecca, Mamluk monuments peppered the Middle East. In addition to architectural achievements, the Mamluk era also produced beautiful textiles, ceramics, and poetry. Conservative views may have stifled new religious and philosophical exploration, but Arab scientific and mathematical innovations continued to lead the world. Eventually, the Mamluks' piety and fatalism would lead to their end, as plague and famine were met with little response.

ESSENTIAL

In most of the Islamic world, the late thirteenth century saw conflict and upheaval. But from Cairo, the Mamluks protected their lands from foreign invaders. As a result, Cairo's greatness rallied Arab pride within the Mamluk territories, as well as Mongol- and Turkish-controlled areas. Eventually, the city was even given the title "Mother of the World."

Osman's Empire

Turkish-speaking tribes moved southwest from their Asian homeland to establish Islamic empires as early as 1001. Because of volatile situations in Asia, new Turkic tribes moved into the Indian subcontinent, Persia, Mesopotamia, and Anatolia. By the 1100s, the Seljuks were the ruling Turkic power, with most other tribes recognizing Seljuk supremacy. As the Mongols decimated the Seljuks, Turkic tribes proceeded even farther west into Byzantine lands.

Fewer than 100 miles from Constantinople, a man named Osman led his *ghazis*, or "warriors of the faith," into Byzantine territories. Called Osmanli, meaning "followers of Osman" (or Ottomans), this Turkish-speaking tribe established its own kingdom under the banner of Sunni Islam. As it turned out, the Ottomans were in the right place at the right time, with the Byzantine Empire barely alive and the Mongols unconcerned with affairs in western Anatolia.

By the mid-1300s, the Ottoman Turks expanded their rule from Anatolia into Eastern Europe. After conquering most of the Balkans, the sultan (meaning "ruler") moved his capital from the Anatolian city of Bursa to the eastern European city of Edirne (Adrianople). With the Byzantine Empire whittled down to the walls of Constantinople, and most of Anatolia under the sultan's control, the Ottomans were well on their way to building an empire. From their simple Turkish and Muslim origins, conquest had transformed the Ottomans into a powerful multiethnic and multireligious empire.

FACT

Claiming descent from the dreaded Genghis Khan, Timur the Lame (Tamerlane) spent most of his adult life conquering distant lands. From his Central Asian base, Timur eventually controlled an empire stretching from southern Russia and Anatolia to parts of China and India. Timur is even reported to have been planning to invade China, but his death in 1405 ended what could have become the world's largest empire.

With the Ottoman war machine winning victory after victory in Europe and Anatolia, a Turkic warlord from Samarqand (in present-day Uzbekistan) established his own kingdom in Central Asia. Despite several physical disabilities, Timur the Lame led a massive army through Iran and Iraq into Anatolia, conquering most of the Ottoman territories and capturing the Sultan. With the Ottomans subdued, Timur, and his descendants after him, controlled the eastern half of the Middle East for another fifty years.

Constantinople and Cairo Fall

Based largely in the Balkans, the defeated Ottomans regrouped from Timur's conquests to defend against ongoing European attacks. After many defeats, the Ottomans finally won a decisive victory at Kossova (Kosovo) in 1448. Under the leadership of the new sultan Murad II, the Ottomans expanded their territories in Eastern Europe and Anatolia, with their eyes fixed on Constantinople.

The next Ottoman leader, Sultan Mehmed II, increased the empire as he completed Muhammad's belated 800-year-old mission and captured Constantinople. In 330, Constantine had established Constantinople as the new Rome, the eternal city of Christ and the protector of Christendom. Through centuries of domination, decline, and revival, the Byzantine Empire lived on—at the very least inside Constantinople's thick walls—with the notion that God was on their side.

On May 29, 1453, God's perceived favor turned to judgment as Ottoman forces used new technology to blast cannonballs through Byzantium's previously impregnable walls. With the emperor dead, Sultan Mehmed (known in Turkish as *Fatih*, meaning "the Conqueror") established the city as his new capital, renaming it Istanbul. The fall of Constantinople and the rise of the Ottomans marked the end of one era and the beginning of another, as ancient swords were replaced by modern firepower and the world moved into modernity.

As emperor of Islamic Byzantium, Mehmed the Conqueror quickly shifted his focus from conquest to construction and control. Although the Byzantine emperor and most of his Latin soldiers were killed in the battle for Constantinople, most of the city's Greek population survived the occupation/liberation. Under Ottoman rule, Greek and Armenian Christians, as well as Jews, remained the predominant business class in Istanbul and were even given limited autonomy within their own religious communities. However, as in other Islamic empires, non-Muslims were subject to special taxes, and many churches (including the central Hagia Sophia) were converted into mosques.

Earthly Expansion and Ethnic Evolution

With news of Mehmed's victory, both European and Mamluk leaders recognized the threat of Ottoman growth. Soon, their fears were realized as Mehmed's troops spread out in all directions. In Europe, Ottomans attacked from land and sea, conquering most of Greece and the remainder of the Balkan Peninsula (including at least some parts of modern-day Croatia, Serbia, Hungary, and Romania). Eventually, Ottoman naval forces even moved across the Adriatic, taking the heel of the "boot" in Italy.

Having subjugated most of the Balkans, the Ottomans took Eastern European children from their Christian families. Similar to the Mamluk slave-warriors of other Muslim empires, non-Turkic boys were instructed in the art of war and the ways of Islam, while the girls were utilized as slaves or concubines. From these non-Turkic boys, the most skilled soldiers were chosen to join the elite Janissary Corps. The most gifted of the janissaries were allowed to take positions of power within the empire, though the Ottomans never experienced a Mamluk-style slave takeover.

Although the sultanate was never usurped by one of the janissaries, the Ottoman administration did become less Turkic as other ethnic groups joined their ranks. In addition, Ottoman officials (including the sultan) often married the most beautiful Eastern European slave girls. These and other mixed marriages produced an empire in which many of its subjects and sultans were not Turkic but Ottoman.

FACT

The English word "maraud" is defined as "the act of raiding or invading in order to gain booty." The exact origins of this term are uncertain, though some believe it was coined by Eastern Europeans who experienced the plundering Ottoman war parties led by sultans and commanders named Murad.

From Eastern Europe, the Ottomans continued around the north shores of the Black Sea, taking the region of Crimea and parts of what are now Ukraine and Russia. In time, the navy Mehmed had established controlled not only the Black Sea but most of its coastal regions as well. As they moved deeper into Anatolia, the Ottomans subdued unruly Turkic tribes, eventually clashing with soldiers from the Mamluk Empire.

Mastering the Mamluks

From the late 1300s to the early 1500s, Egypt was basically in a state of emergency as major economic problems, food shortages, and the Black Plague magnified existing dissatisfaction with the Mamluk sultans. Because of fatalistic religious ideas, little was done to contain the plague, resulting in the decimation of Cairo's population—with as many as 7,000 deaths per day during its worst period.

With Cairo in disarray, Ottoman armies moved as far south as Mamluk-controlled Syria. Hoping to repel the Ottomans, cavalrymen raced from Egypt to Syria, but Ottoman cannons overpowered the prideful Mamluks, who rejected gunpowder as a "weak man's weapon." Continuing south into Egypt, Ottoman firepower dealt the final deathblow, as the Mamluks were overrun outside Cairo in 1517.

After this great defeat, Mamluk commanders continued to hold great influence in Ottoman-controlled Egypt, eventually creating serious tensions with Istanbul. With the Ottomans on top, the Arab caliph was stripped of his honorary title, leaving the caliphate to gather dust until the 1800s, when Ottoman sultans again revived its symbolic power.

FACT

In the Middle East, the year 1517 brought an end to the Mamluk Empire, moving the Ottomans toward becoming the world's most powerful Islamic empire. In Europe in 1517, the German theologian Martin Luther announced his ninety-five disagreements with the Catholic Church, beginning a Christian movement known as the Protestant Reformation.

With the acquisition of Mamluk lands, the Ottoman Empire stretched from the borders of Austria and Russia to the deserts of Egypt and Arabia. With these lands under their influence, the Ottomans were well on their way to becoming the most powerful regime in the history of Islam. With momentum on their side, a strong leader was all that was needed to increase the empire's influence.

Sultan Süleyman and Ottoman Expansion

In 1520, a new sultan named Süleyman (Solomon) rose to the Ottoman throne. Just like his namesake, the ancient Hebrew King Solomon, Süleyman used his wisdom to expand the kingdom's territory, wealth, and global influence. Because of his foreign policy and conquests, Europeans came to know him as Süleyman "the Magnificent," while his domestic improvements inspired his subjects to call him "the Lawgiver."

In 1529, Süleyman advanced Ottoman muscle deep into Europe, sending troops as far as Germany while simultaneously besieging the Austrian city of Vienna. Although Vienna was not conquered, people across Western Europe developed a fear of the "Turks." Over the next thirty years, Ottoman territories expanded to include Mesopotamia, parts of Persia and present-day Sudan, and most of North Africa. The reign of Sultan Süleyman marked the Ottoman Empire's golden age, as it was the largest and most powerful force in the Middle East and Europe.

ALERT

According to tradition, European coffee and the crescent roll both made their début after the Ottoman siege of Vienna. As Muslim forces returned to Istanbul, the citizens of Vienna emerged from their city to discover coffee beans in abandoned Ottoman camps. Thus, coffee was introduced to Europe.

The size of the Ottoman territories alone was enough to make the empire one of the most impressive of all time, but Süleyman's diplomatic, administrative, and architectural achievements were also extraordinary. From his alliances with France and other European powers, to the building of uniquely Ottoman style mosques throughout the Middle East and Balkans, Sultan Süleyman's majesty was so well known that even Shakespeare makes reference to him in the comedy *The Merchant of Venice*. As Süleyman the Lawgiver, this sultan ran a tight ship, implementing many reforms and holding tightly to shari'a (Islamic law), which was based on the Qur'an and Hadith. The grand vizier and members of the imperial council listened to the opinions of respected clerics as they determined Ottoman law. Ultimately, Süleyman was the final authority, although officials were given considerable power, and Islamic law was held in the highest regard.

Turkic Rivalries

In Iran, the Turkish-speaking Safavids emerged in the tradition of ancient Persian kings and their Sassanian successors. After starting as a religious movement, rather than a tribal unit, the Safavids manipulated Iranian tribal politics to become an influential force. By the early 1500s, a Safavid leader named Isma'il assumed the Persian title *shah an-shah*, or "king of kings," leading many of his followers to believe he was the messiah-like Muslim figure known as the Mahdi. With a fiercely loyal Shi'ite army behind him, the shah declared Iran and Iraq as his realm. Thus the Safavid dynasty was born.

Neighbors

To the east, Turkish and Mongol warriors, claiming descent from Genghis Khan and Timur the Lame, established themselves as the Islamic Mughal (*Mongol* in Persian) Empire. With distinctly Sunni beliefs, the Mughals ruled most of present-day India, Pakistan, and Bangladesh, as well as parts of modern-day Afghanistan, from the mid-1500s to 1857. Of the Mughals' many lasting influences in India, the tomb of Mumtaz Mahal (known as the Taj Mahal) is the most impressive and well-known. For the most part, the Mughals were not involved in the Turkic rivalries. Instead, they focused on domestic issues—especially conflicts with Hindus, Sikhs, and other religious groups.

FACT

The English word *mogul*, meaning a wealthy or powerful person, was inspired by the mighty Muslim sultans of India's Mughal (Mongol) Empire.

To the north and east, another Turkish-speaking dynasty established the Uzbek kingdom in what is now northern Turkmenistan, Uzbekistan, and southern Kazakhstan. As strong Sunni Muslims, the Uzbeks were a constant threat to the Shi'ite Safavids, but they never made significant advances into Safavid territories. To the west, fellow Turkish-speaking Ottomans practiced Sunni Islam among themselves, while the Safavids unabashedly promoted Shi'ite views. In fact, the Safavids imposed their particular brand of Islam on the Persian population, transforming this historically Sunni area into the world's first large-scale popular Shi'ite state. Nevertheless, the Ottoman Empire was the biggest rival of the Safavids, who desired to expand westward into the Islamic holy lands of Iraq, Palestine, and Arabia.

A House Divided

For the next 200 years, the Ottoman and Safavid Empires remained bitter enemies, with jihad after jihad being waged on the "infidel" shah or sultan. Initially, the Ottomans held a major advantage with their black-powder-propelled cannons, allowing the Ottoman Sultan Süleyman to conquer Mesopotamia and other Persian territories in 1534. After continued conflict, the Safavids were forced to recognize Ottoman superiority by signing a peace treaty in 1555.

Following the death of Sultan Süleyman the Magnificent in 1566, attributed to natural causes, Shi'ite Ottoman subjects joined forces with their Safavid coreligionists to fight the Sunni sultan of Istanbul. Despite their desire to fight honorably and without gunpowder, the Safavids begrudgingly accepted this new explosive technology under the leadership of Shah Abbas "the Great." With both empires possessing the powder, a relative balance of power was achieved, leading to the Safavid Empire's greatest age.

Military power allowed Persia to develop institutionally and economically, despite their Ottoman neighbors. From 1588 until his death in 1629, Shah Abbas created a mighty empire by moving his capital to the economically strategic city of Isfahan (located on the Silk Road), reorganizing the government, revamping taxation systems, and utilizing the skills of both Muslim and non-Muslim subjects. Most notably, Armenian Christians were moved to his new capital because of their expertise in the silk trade. Ultimately, the city and the empire prospered until Shah Abbas' death signaled a downturn in the dynasty's power. Most of the eighteenth century was marred by instability, but in 1795, a new Turkic dynasty, the Qajars, came to rule Iran. Moving their capital to the northern city of Tehran, the Qajar dynasty controlled Persia into the twentieth century.

Euro Power

From 1400 to 1800, various Turkic dynasties battled to control the ancestral homelands of Arabs, Persians, Kurds, Armenians, and so on. Meanwhile, the offspring of the once archaic European Crusaders experienced a Renaissance, a Reformation, and several revolutions. As Middle Eastern peoples continued to make important contributions to world civilization, the glory of their governments consistently faded. Eventually, European powers used their new technologies and power to profit from the wealth of natural resources found in Africa, the Middle East, Southeast Asia, and the Americas. Thus, an age of European conquest and colonialism was born.

Throughout the 1400s, European kingdoms developed economic ties with Muslim governments in order to procure coveted spices, silks, and textiles. By the end of that century, Middle Eastern trade networks had become a vital part of the European business with Southeast Asia. As a result, European explorers such as Christopher Columbus risked their lives in order to find new ways to bypass the Middle Eastern middlemen and their high taxes.

Although Columbus never reached India by going west, in 1498 the Portuguese explorer Vasco da Gama successfully reached India by sailing south around the southern tip of Africa. This successful voyage opened the way for the Portuguese and other European powers to trade directly with India, leaving the Middle East out of the equation.

ALERT

Checkmate! This term comes from the Persian phrase *shah-mât*, "The king is dead!" Although chess is believed to have started in India, the game was introduced to Europe via the Middle East.

Although the 1500s saw continued trade between Southeast Asia and Europe, the Americas provided the biggest boost to European economies, with massive loads of gold and silver being taken back across the Atlantic. After a century of distant exploitation, the 1600s began a new era of colonialism, in which Spanish, Dutch, English, and French colonialists established long-term settlements in the Americas, Africa, and Southeast Asia.

By the 1700s, European navies controlled the world's oceans and with them the global economy. Ancient land-based Middle Eastern trade routes quickly became obsolete, causing huge economic problems for the Muslim empires. By the end of that century, the British had emerged as the world's most powerful military force, with the industrial revolution giving them an even greater advantage over other world markets. Despite troubles in the North American colonies, the British managed to effectively control the largest empire the world had yet seen.

Throughout the 1800s, the French, British, Spanish, and Italians extended their power into North Africa, while at the same time Russian and British governments vied for control of Persia and Central Asia. With the loss of its North African territories and a strong European presence in Persia and India, the Ottoman Empire was surrounded. Perceiving a squeeze play, the sultan moved quickly to protect his crumbling empire.

Division and Decay

By the early 1900s, the Ottoman Empire was a mere shadow of its former greatness; nevertheless, it remained the world's only independent Islamic empire. Despite nearly 200 years of internal revolts and external attacks, Istanbul managed to retain all of Anatolia, Syria, and Palestine, most of Arabia and Mesopotamia, and a small piece of Eastern Europe. At the same time, Greek and Slavic independence movements whittled away at the former Ottoman Balkans (a region that would eventually spark the world's first world war), while British troops occupied the nominally Ottoman province of Egypt.

QUESTION

Which came first, the ottoman footstool or the Ottoman Empire?
While the French were the first to call their footstools "ottomans," this doesn't necessarily mean they were referring to their Middle Eastern rivals. Correctly pronounced *Osmanli* (followers of Osman), "Ottoman" may have been French wordplay used to insult this Muslim empire. Either way, it appears the French desired to bring their enemies underfoot.

Following the example of European nationalistic revolutions, Arab and Armenian areas organized resistance movements, hoping to attain independence from the ailing Ottomans. With the aid of eastern Anatolia's Kurdish militiamen, the Ottomans managed to put down Armenian rebellions with overwhelming brutality. Between 1915 and 1923, an estimated 1.5 million Armenian men, women, and children were either killed or displaced from their ancient Anatolian homeland, in what some call the Armenian Genocide.

Like cornered wolves, the Ottomans unleashed their wrath on any that would threaten their failing empire. The rapid growth of European empires, and the rivalries that developed between them, created a combative climate that somehow ended up involving most of the world. From Europe's exploitation of Indian, Persian, and African lands to alliances formed between European powers and others, such as the Ottomans, or the distant and relatively young United States of America, a global powder keg was ready for a spark.

CHAPTER 10

World War and Change

As political tensions in Europe grew, the world's most powerful governments divided into two camps and went to war. As history shows, the Ottomans chose the losing side, resulting in the dismantling of their empire. From the ashes of war, the Middle East was reshaped into Western-style nation-states. Today, as modern political boundaries divide the map, empires are a distant memory. With most Middle Eastern governments less than eighty years old, national lines are fresh and, in some cases, unsettled.

Choosing Sides

Throughout the 1800s, a series of independence movements dramatically altered the face of Europe and eventually the Middle East. Based on ideals from the French Revolution of the late 1700s, Europeans of similar ethnic, linguistic, and cultural backgrounds sought to determine their own affairs. In the midst of this nationalist fervor, France, Britain, Russia, Austria-Hungary, Germany, and Italy vied for supremacy. As a result, economic rivalries and political alliances set the stage for a colossal war.

Zionism on the Horizon

Of the many European nationalist groups that emerged in the late 1800s, Jewish nationalism (the movement known as Zionism) was the only movement that desired a non-European homeland. In 1896, Theodor Herzl, a Jewish journalist from Vienna, published a book entitled *Der Judenstaat* ("The Jewish State"). Just as Serbian, German, and other nationalist leaders desired to carve out independent states, Herzl's writings articulated the need for an ethnically Jewish nation.

ALERT

The term "Zionism" is derived from Zion, the hill on which Israel's King Solomon built the first Jewish temple. Although this name has religious connotations, modern Zionism was not established as a religious movement. Quite the opposite; it began in the late 1800s as a secular political movement focused on celebrating Jewish culture and history and providing a national refuge from anti-Jewish forces.

Although Zionism did not attract large numbers during Herzl's lifetime, over the following decades persecutions inspired many to take up the cause while fleeing from Europe. In search of a homeland, some considered establishing a Jewish colony in East Africa, while others looked to Palestine as a long-lost motherland. Ultimately, they decided to colonize Palestine, but because Herzl and many other Zionists were atheists, the new "Land of Israel" would not be focused on the God of Abraham, but on secularism and Jewish heritage.

Trouble Brewing

During the first ten years of the twentieth century, alliances were formed along political and ethnic lines, which polarized Europe. With Germany and France clashing over issues in Morocco, Austria-Hungary and Russia trading insults over tensions in the Balkans, and Italy rousing German disdain by attacking Ottoman territories in North Africa, large-scale war was narrowly averted several times. Nevertheless, war was unavoidable, and the powder keg exploded in the Balkans.

On June 28, 1914, Serbian nationalists assassinated the Austrian Archduke Francis Ferdinand in Bosnia. Their goal was to force the Austro-Hungarian government to divest itself of its south-Slav provinces so they could be folded into a Greater Serbia or a Yugoslavia. Their attempt failed. Instead, Austria-Hungary declared war on Serbia, which in turn brought Russia to the aid of their fellow Slavs, the Serbians. With Russia threatening Austria, Germany declared war on Russia. Eventually, Germany also declared war on France, prompting Britain to do the same to Germany. Finally, Italy announced its hostilities toward Austria-Hungary, and Europe was embroiled in battle.

Because of Europe's global influence, what would have been a major continental war turned into the first world war. With Britain, France, Italy, and Russia as the original Allied Powers and Austria-Hungary and Germany as the initial Central Powers, Japan, China, Brazil, Liberia, the United States, and many others joined the Allies' cause, while the Ottomans and Bulgarians sided with the Austrians and Germans. With the Ottomans in the mix, the Middle East was drawn into Europe's ever-growing conflict.

FACT

World War I (1914 to 1918) saw the combined use of revolutionary technologies and firepower. Chemical weapons, machine guns, land mines, tanks, armored gunships, submarines, and bomber and fighter planes were used in concert to create more than 37 million casualties. By comparison, the entire Vietnam War saw a total of about 3.5 million casualties.

In Anatolia, the Allies attempted to take the Dardanelles (a narrow waterway connecting the Mediterranean to the Black Sea) in 1915. With control of these important straits, the Allies could use the Black Sea to squeeze the Central Powers from all sides. Because of British planning blunders, lightly armed ANZAC (Australia New Zealand Army Corps) forces, along with limited British and French troops, were sent into a hopeless battle. Unexpectedly meeting powerful Ottoman machine guns and well-fortified positions, thousands of ANZACs were gunned down day after day on the beaches of Gallipoli.

In what was supposed to be the first of many victories in Anatolia, the Allies were soundly defeated. From this overwhelming victory, an Ottoman military leader named Mustafa Kemal rose to prominence, eventually becoming the founding father of the modern Republic of Turkey. While Turkish leaders in Istanbul breathed easier at home, their control of Arab lands remained uncertain.

In Mesopotamia, British troops from India used Persian outposts to attack Ottoman positions. Hoping to take the great city of Baghdad, the British were turned back repeatedly by Ottoman resistance. In Egypt, the British officially made the region a protectorate, having occupied the area since 1882. From Cairo, the British set up their chief command center for all campaigns against the Ottoman Empire.

Lawrence of Arabia?

The most famous British support missions included the eccentric Thomas Edward Lawrence (Lawrence of Arabia), who was sent to western Arabia to aid Arab separatists. While most British soldiers viewed Arabs as uncivilized "wogs" (a derogatory term for nonwhites), T. E. Lawrence respected Arab culture, even adopting Arab clothing and mannerisms. While Lawrence of Arabia fascinated curious European crowds, most Arabs were not as impressed.

Although Lawrence is said to have unified the Arab tribes, this seems to be a bit of an exaggeration. Lawrence did develop a special relationship with a charismatic Hashemite named Faysal, but he never directly led any of the Arab tribes. Instead of T. E. Lawrence, the protectors of Mecca and Medina, Sharif Husayn (governor of western Arabia) and his sons Ali, Abdullah, and Faysal, were the most influential leaders in Arabia. Because of their Hashemite family's reported descent from Muhammad and their relationship with Istanbul, Husayn's family held great sway in the Hijaz region of western Arabia. In addition, the Saùdi family of eastern Arabia used their power to fight the pro-Ottoman Rashidi dynasty of northern Arabia. Nevertheless, the Hashemites led the fight for Arab independence.

Everyone Wants a Piece

In a type of symbiotic relationship, Arab nationalists viewed British firepower as their meal ticket to independence, while the British in turn used Arab nationalism to undermine Ottoman calls for global Islamic revolt. With Arab and British leaders united in their disdain for Istanbul, an alliance was struck in which Arab leaders were guaranteed certain territories in return for their cooperation in the war effort.

With the combination of Arab tactical superiority and British technological advantages, Arabia, Palestine, Syria, and southern Mesopotamia had fallen from Ottoman hands by October 1918.

With the Ottomans defeated in most of their Arab lands, Anatolia was their only remaining territory. In hopes of salvaging some part of their once-great empire, Istanbul chose to withdraw from the ailing Central Powers. Less than two weeks later, the Central Powers surrendered in Eurasia, ending the first global war.

ESSENTIAL

"A land without a people for a people without a land." This Zionist motto was used to convince the world that Palestine should become the Jewish homeland. In reality, by 1914, the land was occupied by more than 500,000 Arabs, whose families had lived there for more than 1,000 years. In contrast, fewer than 100,000 Jews lived in Palestine in 1914, the majority of whom had emigrated from Europe since the late 1800s.

Throughout the war, the British and French offered various portions of the Ottoman territories to other governments as incentives for their alliance. For instance, the Greeks and Italians were offered parts of western Anatolia for their partnership with the Allies. In the early years of the war, other secret arrangements were made with Russia, including the partitioning of Persian lands and the 1916 Sykes-Picot Agreement—named after its authors, Englishman Sir Mark Sykes and Frenchman François Georges-Picot. The

Sykes-Picot plan agreed on the distribution of Ottoman territories, giving the Russians much of Ottoman Anatolia while the British and French claimed Syria, Palestine, and Mesopotamia.

In addition, European Jews were promised territory in Palestine, despite previous promises to Palestine's Arab inhabitants. In a letter known as the Balfour Declaration, the British foreign secretary, Arthur James Balfour, assured the prominent Jewish tycoon Lord Rothschild that London would support the establishment of a Jewish homeland in Palestine. As a result, European Zionists (Jewish nationalists) continued to purchase plots of land in the hope that their scattered Palestinian settlements would one day be united in a viable Jewish state.

True Intentions?

As Arab leaders caught wind of the Sykes-Picot and Balfour plans, many began to question the true intentions of the West. In particular, King Husayn recognized serious contradictions between these new documents and his previous correspondence with Sir Henry McMahon, the British high commissioner in Egypt. In response, French and British delegates traveled to the Hijaz (western Arabia) to assure the Hashemite king of their postwar plans for the region.

By promising the same pieces of land to multiple peoples and governments, the Allies had managed to secure war partners for the short term. However, in the long term, Western double-talk created bitter enemies. After fighting alongside British soldiers, Arab warriors found their allegiance unappreciated. In their eyes, the West had defamed Arab honor, creating feelings of betrayal and resentment that remain to this day.

Settling Dust and Changing Maps

U.S. President Woodrow Wilson was a strong advocate of self-determination and democracy, believing all peoples should have the right to decide their own future. With the end of hostilities, Wilson sent a team to the Middle East to see what type of government the people of the region desired. The information from this fact-finding mission was presented at the 1919 Paris Peace Conference, but it was largely ignored in favor of predetermined British and French plans. Nevertheless, Wilson remained a vocal proponent of self-determination for all peoples—including non-Westerners.

FACT

U.S. President Woodrow Wilson received the 1919 Nobel Peace Prize for his attempts to broker peace during World War I and his effort to establish stable democratic nations in all parts of the world. As an advocate of the "little guy," Wilson took a personal interest in the future of Arabs, Armenians, and Kurds after the fall of the Ottoman Empire.

Getting a Piece, or Making the Peace?

The Paris Peace Conference led to anything but peace for the Middle East, especially the Arab world. In closed-door meetings, promises were betrayed as the British and French turned the Middle East into their chessboard. Without considering ethnic, religious, political, or historical realities, the European powers partitioned the region according to their own interests. In addition, aspirations for Arab independence were crushed as Faysal was forced to relinquish his position only four months after having been elected king of greater Syria. Throughout the 1920s, British and French actions seriously wounded Arab nationalism, but in time the movement would rise again.

In what was at best a well-meaning support effort, and at worst a deceptive imperialist plot, the Allies created the "mandate system." In this arrangement, Western governments would provide direct administration of areas deemed unfit for immediate self-rule. After the Paris Conference and several other meetings, the Allies determined that the "peace" of the Middle East would be assured by establishing "spheres of influence," in which varying degrees of Western oversight would be implemented.

For the first time since the establishment of Ottoman provincial boundaries hundreds of years earlier, the region was defined by new political boundaries, many of which would become today's national borders. However, for the first years of their existence, these artificial lines were more for the benefit of Western governments than Middle Eastern people.

The French sphere of influence included these territories:

- **Syria and Lebanon**—Under direct administration, a form of governance known as a "mandate"
- **Eastern Anatolia**—Loosely monitored
- **Independent Armenian region**—In northeastern Anatolia
- **Autonomous Kurdish region**—In southeastern Anatolia

The British sphere of influence included these territories:

- **Palestine, Transjordan (Jordan), and Iraq**—Under mandate (direct administration)
- **Egypt, Kuwait, southeast Arabia, and Persia**—"Protectorates" under partial administration
- **Northwest Arabia, Sudan, and the Horn of Africa**—Loosely monitored

The Italian sphere of influence included these territories:

- **Western Anatolia**—Including the Greek-administered region of Smyrna
- **Dodecanese Islands**—About fifty islands in the Aegean Sea (including Rhodes, Kos, etc.)
- **Thrace**—At the extreme southeastern tip of the Balkan Peninsula (annexed by Greece)

With the West controlling most of the Middle East politically, and with limited military action continuing throughout the region, Arab, Turkish, and Persian nationalists rallied their peoples against the "occupiers." Broken promises, gun-toting foreign soldiers, and memories of Crusaders and colonialists created resentment and suspicion among most Middle Eastern peoples. As Ottoman imperialism had come to a close, no one wanted British or French leaders to replace the sultan. At the same time, Ottoman Anatolia was not ready for Italian or Greek rule. As a result, a period of nationalistic fervor swept through the region, producing wars, revolts, and, in the end, fully independent Middle Eastern nations.

Winds of Nationalism

After the Paris Conference and several other key meetings, it became clear to people across the Middle East that the West had betrayed their trust. The Arab world was determined to see its promised independence realized at any cost. In Anatolia, Turkish nationalism would allow Ottomans to avoid territorial extinction. Finally, Persia would resist British and Russian occupation by ejecting the weak Qajar dynasty for the nationalistic regime of Reza Khan.

Dealing with Betrayal

In Egypt, forty years of colonialism and four years of obligatory support for the British war effort created great resentment. With Egyptian and Arab pride as their war cry, the Wafd Party provided a platform through which frustrated Egyptians could vent their anger and find hope for the future. As a result of widespread civil disobedience, the British protectorate was terminated in 1922, but only on paper. In reality, British troops lingered in Egypt, and the Egyptian-born King Fu'ad (formerly the Ottoman governor of Egypt) was London's puppet.

In other parts of the Arab world, the call of nationalism was also stirring people to action. In Iraq and Transjordan tensions were rising daily, especially among Iraq's Shi'ite population, whose leaders declared a jihad on all British troops. Also, the French ejection of Faysal from Syria inspired Faysal's brother, Àbdullah, to lead Arabs from the Hijaz into Transjordan to attack the French. With Faysal and Àbdullah gathering supporters across the Fertile Crescent, the British decided to use the Hashemite brothers to regain some semblance of control.

In 1921, Faysal was named king of Iraq, and Àbdullah was given the throne in Transjordan. With Arab monarchies established, nationalist movements were temporarily appeased, but a continued British presence in these areas undermined each king's credibility. In fact, in each region, Arabs began to view their king as London's "yes-man." Nevertheless, Faysal's descendants continued to rule Iraq until 1958; in Transjordan, now Jordan, Àbdullah's great-grandson Àbdullah II remains the Hashemite king.

Father and Savior

In Anatolia, the Allies were in the process of implementing the Treaty of Sèvres. As a way to punish the defeated empire, the treaty divided most of the non-Arab Ottoman territories among Greeks, Armenians, and Kurds, while the remaining areas were placed under British, French, Italian, or international rule. With the Ottoman homeland in danger of being dissolved, war hero Mustafa Kemal used his clout from the Gallipoli victory, along with his powerful persona and political panache, to unite the Ottomans under a banner of Turkish nationalism.

After centuries of intermarriage among Central Asian Turks, Eastern Europeans, Caucasians, Arabs, Persians, and other groups, Anatolia's Ottomans were not ethnically Turkic (with characteristically Asian features). Instead, they were a mix of the empires' diverse subjects. With Turkish as its root, the unique Osmanli language borrowed many words from Arabic and Persian and was written in Arabic script. Nevertheless, Ottomans were distinct from Arabs, Persians, and other neighboring ethnic and linguistic groups.

FACT

On October 29, 1923, Mustafa Kemal established the modern Republic of Turkey. He then moved to modernize and secularize his new nation by abolishing many Islamic institutions (including the caliphate), implementing Western laws, introducing European clothing styles, adopting the Latin alphabet (in place of Arabic script), and eventually removing Islam from its position as the official state religion.

Despite Anatolia's lack of Turkic blood, a Turkish identity (similar to the multiethnic American identity) gave rise to fierce nationalism and resistance. By 1920, Kemal mobilized his people to rid Anatolia of foreign occupiers—especially Greeks—and free the region of the sultan's tyranny. After intense fighting and skilled negotiations, Kemalists managed to remove European forces, overthrow the sultan, and carve out a national homeland, declaring the independent Republic of Turkey on October 29, 1923.

Over the following fifteen years, Mustafa Kemal instituted massive reforms across his new nation, patterning most of his changes after the West. In addition, he sought to modernize the haggard Ottoman homeland at all costs, including tradition. After abolishing the office of the caliph, outlawing certain traditional clothing styles, and making other direct attacks on conservative Islamic constructs, Kemal intentionally ejected religion from the Turkish state. In the end, Kemalism emerged as a type of religion, with Turkey's masses passionately devoted to their great leader. Mustafa Kemal not only saved Ottoman Anatolia from being carved into multiple states but also became Atatürk (meaning "Father of the Turks"), the founding father of modern Turkey. (The Turkish Grand Assembly bestowed the last name "Atatürk" on Mustafa Kemal on November 24, 1934.)

Reza Rising

In Persia, an unlikely figure emerged from the military to overthrow the aging Qajar dynasty. In 1921, Reza Khan realized his revolutionary dreams by taking the city of Tehran and seizing control of the nation. As king, Reza Shah Pahlavi associated himself with the ancient Aryan kings of Persia, even renaming his country "Iran," meaning "Land of the Aryans."

FACT

Since Iran's 1979 Islamic Revolution, Shi'ite clerics have ruled the nation according to their interpretation of Islamic Law. At the same time, the deposed Pahlavi family has moved to establish a freer and more democratic Iran. Today, the former shah's thirty-two-year-old son Reza Pahlavi II lives in Maryland working as an advocate for his country.

In addition, Reza built his new dynasty on the pillars of nationalism and modernization. From the example of his Turkish neighbor, Mustafa Kemal Atatürk, Reza Shah moved to implement Western-style reforms in Iran. Although many resisted his efforts, especially his moves to separate mosque and state, the Pahlavi dynasty managed to improve Iran's infrastructure, school systems, and civil laws. Despite opposition, revolt, and a short period of foreign occupation, Reza's monarchy continued for another generation, as his son Muhammad Reza Shah ruled from 1941 until the Islamic Revolution of 1979.

Memories of Imperialism

Throughout the 1920s, nationalist movements brought new hope to Middle Eastern peoples who had long been subjects of foreign and local empires. However, with British and French oversight continuing into the 1930s, many began to see the West as imperialists in disguise. Memories of Ottoman and Crusader conquerors, coupled with fresh resentment from the Allies' betrayal, inspired some Arabs to reject all Western political influences. In contrast, many of these same people embraced Western cultures, technologies, and economies.

In Palestine, local Arabs watched as European Jews continued to purchase land and build settlements. The message of the Balfour Declaration had clarified Britain's support for a Jewish homeland, and for many Palestinian Arabs this "homeland" would be nothing more than a European colony. At the same time, increasing anti-Jewish sentiments in Germany and other Eastern European countries made Palestine an attractive refuge. Increased immigration through the 1930s caused even greater tensions between Jewish newcomers and the indigenous Arab population.

ALERT

Although today's circumstances have seen Palestinians using "terrorist" measures, the situation in the 1940s saw Jewish "freedom fighters" using these same methods. Among groups such as the Stern Gang, created and led by Avragan ("Yair") Stern, and Irgun, acts of terror and sabotage took civilian and military lives from both the British and the Arabs. Their goal was to evict the British authorities from Palestine as a way to allow unrestricted Jewish immigration and create a Jewish state. Of these Jewish terrorist activities, the 1946 bombing of Jerusalem's King David Hotel killed more than 100 people.

As a result of Britain's conflicting promises, two peoples believed they would be given the same small region. For European Zionists, Palestine's Arab population would simply need to move to any of the surrounding Arab states to make way for the Jewish state. On the other hand, local Arab leaders believed they would control Palestine upon British retreat. In their view, Jewish settlers would either accept Arab rule or return to Europe.

In an attempt to rectify the situation, British officials tried to broker a compromise, but it was too little too late. Jewish settlers and Arab citizens both wanted an end to the British occupation of Palestine. In 1939, a document known as the White Paper officially ended London's support for Zionism, promising an Arab Palestinian state. One year later, Palestine remained under direct British control as a triangle of violence raged among British troops, Jewish immigrants, and the Arab inhabitants of Palestine.

Birth of the Nations

From the ashes of World War I, the Middle East was reshaped by the victorious European powers, but it was ultimately the tides of nationalism that brought the region back to life. Although Egypt was the first to officially receive its independence in 1922, British strings were still attached until 1952, when Gamal Abdel Nasser declared the Arab Republic of Egypt. That said, Turkey was actually the first truly independent Middle Eastern nation, as the shrewd nationalist Mustafa Kemal announced the independent Turkish republic in 1923.

In the mid-1920s, King Husayn of the Hijaz and his son Ali were deposed by Ibn Saùd of eastern Arabia's Saùdi kingdom. Nevertheless, the Hashemite family's honor was partially restored as Husayn's son Faysal assumed full control of an independent Iraq in 1932. Meanwhile, Àbdullah, another of Husayn's sons, held limited power over the region of Transjordan.

Two years later, in 1932, the Saùdi family announced the united kingdom of "Saùdi" Arabia. While the British directly controlled Egypt, and Iraq for a time, most of Arabia had never been under organized European authority. As a result, the formation of Saudi Arabia was not related to any British or French decisions. In fact, the Arab kingdom remained free of any Western influence until oil was discovered in 1935.

In the northern half of the Levant (present-day Syria and Lebanon), the French continued their strict control through the 1930s and until just after World War II. During their mandate, the French expanded the largely Christian area of Mount Lebanon to include surrounding lands, which were mostly inhabited by non-Christians. As a result, ancient ethnic and religious balances were disturbed, leading to a major civil war several decades later. Only after Britain and the United States pressured France to leave the region did Syria and Lebanon finally become independent nations in 1946. In that same year, the British mandate of Transjordan was terminated, and Àbdullah became monarch of the Hashemite Kingdom of Jordan.

Seeds of Conflict

With Palestine as the only remaining British-administered area, it was clear that both Jewish and Arab leaders were planning to establish their authority. In response, the United Nations proposed a plan to partition Palestine, with independent Jewish and Arab states and an international zone in Jerusalem and areas surrounding the city. Zionist leaders, desiring different borders and a much larger state, hesitantly accepted the plan as a temporary setback. However, Arab leaders rejected the plan outright, citing that it gave over half of Palestine to Jewish immigrants, who accounted for less than one-third of the region's population.

Finally, on May 13, 1948, the British gave up, and the mandate of Palestine was terminated. The next day, the independent state of Israel was established, followed hours later by an Arab declaration of war. To Palestinians and their fellow Arab neighbors, the State of Israel was simply another Western imperialist plot. Just as their ancestors had resisted Crusaders, they would repel the Zionists.

For more than fifty-five years this conflict has continued, with each side giving and receiving the sentence of death. Why do they hate each other? What are the Occupied Territories? Can there be peace between Israelis and Palestinians? The Arab-Israeli conflict has produced some of the most complex questions of this century, questions that cannot be answered with fatalistic or simplistic answers.

CHAPTER 11

Modern Middle East Mosaic

Like the ancient Middle East, today's Middle East is a crossroads of peoples and cultures. In addition to diverse clothing styles (including Western apparel), modern technologies, sprawling mega-cities, and a wide range of religious perspectives, the spectrum of facial features, skin tones, and languages is as broad in this region as any other part of the world.

Urban and Eclectic

Although most countries in the Middle East have retained parts of their traditional cultures, they have also been injected with new technologies and ideologies. The result is a unique coexistence of old and new, which can be seen in nearly all areas of daily life. In the streets of major cities such as Cairo, donkey carts drive alongside new cars, while in small villages, radios play the music of both Western pop stars and traditional Arabian singers.

In addition to technology and pop culture, economies and lifestyles have changed drastically over the past forty years. In many nations, small family-run farms are no longer able to compete with more efficient high-tech farms. As a result, farmers are forced to leave their rural homelands for the possibility of work in the cities. Because of this shift, huge urban centers have developed in once average-sized cities. In Istanbul, for example, the city's population has swelled from less than 2 million in 1960 to almost 15 million in 2011, which is one-fifth of Turkey's population.

FACT

With a population of approximately 17 million, Cairo, Egypt, is the largest city in the Middle East and is one of the planet's twenty biggest cities.

Technology and Traditions

As opposed to the lightly armed soldiers of the early twentieth century, most Middle Eastern governments are now equipped with tanks, fighter jets, radar systems, and other high-tech weaponry. Between 2004 and 2008, Saudi Arabia was the United States' biggest arms customer, paying more than $40 billion for weapons and the latest surveillance equipment.

In addition, the Saudis have received expert antiterrorist training from the United Kingdom's elite Special Air Services (SAS) unit. Even in the parts of Afghanistan ruled by the Taliban, where certain elements of modernity were banned, armored vehicles, heavy artillery, and wireless communications were used to combat coalition forces.

You will find varying levels of development in each nation. For the most part, cell phones, satellite televisions, computers, movie theaters, and automobiles are just as prevalent in the Middle East as they are in Middle America. From skyscrapers and electronic billboards to shopping malls, amusement parks, and bowling alleys, there is more than enough modern in the Middle East.

The Middle East is a land not only of external contrasts but of internal differences as well. With the rapid introduction of new technologies, most people adapted functionally to modern life while retaining traditional values, social structures, beliefs, and superstitions. Yet, technology does not produce modernity in the way many Westerners might envision. The peoples of the Middle East have their own unique ways of doing things, which are not necessarily going to be changed by highways and high-tech gadgets.

Distinctions of Diversity

The Middle East's three largest ethnic groups, which divide into Arab, Turkic, and Persian worlds, are by no means exact, as there are Turkic populations in Persian regions, Arab groups living in predominantly Turkic areas, and so on. There are other distinct minority groups throughout the Middle East whose bloodlines and/or languages are vastly different from the majority of their neighbors.

Kurds

The largest of these minority groups is the Kurds. With more than 30 million Kurdish people in the Middle East, they are hardly a minority when taken as a whole. But, because they are a people without a national homeland, they live as minorities in several nations. The most significant Kurdish populations are in the mountainous regions of eastern Turkey, northern Iraq, and western Iran, where they are actually the majority.

In Turkey, there are about 15 million Kurds (20 percent of the nation's citizens); in Iraq, there are more than 5 million (20 percent of the population); and in Iran, there are another 5 million (10 percent of the republic's people). While Kurds also live in parts of Syria, Lebanon, and the former Soviet Union, these groups account for less than 5 percent of the global Kurdish population. Of all the world's Kurds, the vast majority are Sunni Muslims, though some are Shi'ite Muslims or Christians. Others practice various forms of Zoroastrianism.

Who are the Kurds? Start by determining who they are not. Kurds are not ethnically Arabs, Turks, or Persians, nor is Arabic, Turkish, or Farsi their mother tongue. These highlanders come from the same Indo-European stock as many Iranian tribes, but their distinct Kurmanji and Sorani languages set Kurds apart. In addition, unique Kurdish clothing styles, music, and so on have developed among these mountain people.

ESSENTIAL

After being promised an independent Kurdish state in 1920, the Kurds watched Western governments divide their homeland among the newborn nations of Turkey, Syria, Iraq, and Iran.

While some believe the Kurds are descendants of the ancient Medes, their exact origins remain uncertain. As with most modern questions of ethnicity, the concept of Kurdishness has become politically charged. For some Kurds, having their traditional homeland divided among Arab, Turkish, and Iranian nations is unacceptable. In their estimation, an independent Kurdish state should be formed in the region they call Kurdistan. At the same time, many Kurds are content with life under a non-Kurdish government, as long as they are not victims of discrimination.

In response to Kurdish nationalism, the governments of Turkey and Iraq have tried to suppress any possibility of rebellion. Over the past fifteen years, thousands of Kurdish guerrillas and civilians have been shot, gassed, or tortured, while the living have been prevented from speaking their language or celebrating their heritage. Whatever their ancient roots or nationalistic aspirations, today more than 30 million people proudly consider themselves Kurds.

Armenians

North of the Kurdish region, a people known as the Armenians once inhabited a large area from Mount Urartu (Ararat) to central Anatolia (present-day Turkey). According to tradition, a man named Haik established the first Armenian kingdom around 2100 B.C. As a result, contemporary Armenians call themselves "Hay" and their nation Hayastan. Whether or not this tradition is completely accurate, most experts believe the Armenian people are a combination of ancient peoples, including the Urartians (Araratians), Hurrians, and possibly even Greek immigrants. Linguistically, Armenian is one of many languages in the Indo-European family, to which Persian, Kurdish, and Greek are also connected.

After adopting Christianity in A.D. 301, the Armenian people found themselves subject to a series of foreign rulers, including the Christian Byzantines and the Muslim Ottomans. In World War I, fearing the Christian Armenians would side with their Russian coreligionists, the Ottomans joined with Kurdish forces in a pre-emptive strike. As a result, more than a million Armenians were killed in what has come to be known as the Armenian Holocaust or Genocide.

FACT

One of the world's best-known Armenians is an American billionaire named Kirk Kerkorian. Known as the "Quiet Lion," Kerkorian was raised in a middle-class home, but became one of Las Vegas's most famous hotel and casino moguls. As of March 2011, the ninety-three-year-old Kerkorian's net worth was estimated at $3.5 billion.

With the defeat of the Ottoman Empire, the Armenians (along with the Kurds) were promised an independent Armenian state. But, as with the Kurds, the Armenians' land was divided between the newly formed Republic of Turkey and the Soviet Union. In addition, another round of violence ensued, in which most of Anatolia's Armenians were forced to evacuate or die. In what is called the Armenian Diaspora, citizens of this ancient nation were scattered from their homeland into the Soviet Union, United States, and various parts of the Middle East.

Since the newly independent Republic of Armenia was declared in 1991, nearly 4 million of the world's 6 million Armenians have been living on the eastern edge of their Middle Eastern homeland. Most of the other 2 million Armenians have made their homes in the countries of Iran, Iraq, Syria, Jordan, Israel/Palestine, Egypt, and Sudan, while about 500,000 have settled in the United States.

Proud of their ancient Christian heritage, diasporic Armenians have found a source of identity and solidarity in the church. From liturgy written and recited in the Armenian language to special cultural events and holiday celebrations, the church is a meeting point for the displaced. Because most Armenians are proud of their roots, local churches have been established around the world as a vital link to the mother church in Armenia.

Circassians

To the north of the Armenians, a people known as the Circassians (also called the Adyge or Cherkess) once inhabited a region in the Caucasus Mountains stretching from the Black Sea to the Caspian Sea. From time immemorial, these stately mountaineers have protected their ethnic identity and their homeland. By the 1200s, pressure from the Byzantine Empire moved the Circassians to reject ancient tribal beliefs for Christianity. With the rise of the Ottoman Empire, the Circassians eventually adopted Islam in the late 1600s.

By the late 1700s, the Russian Empire expanded into Circassian lands, spurring a major war between these Christian and Muslim peoples. Despite fierce resistance, the Circassians were eventually overpowered by Russia in 1864. As a result, nearly 1.5 million Circassians fled their ancient homeland for the protection of their Ottoman coreligionists. In this mass exodus, more than 90 percent of the world's Circassian population found new homes throughout the Middle East.

FACT

Circassians around the world recognize May 21 as a day of mourning for those who died or were displaced during the 1864 Circassian Diaspora.

The Circassian language, the native tongue of the indigenous people of Northwest Caucasia, is completely different from the Turkic, Semitic, or Indo-European groups. With its unusually large number of consonants and infrequent use of vowels, the Circassian language is one of the world's most unique. Although they are related to other Caucasian mountain peoples (such as the Georgians and Chechens), the Circassians are their own distinct group.

Today, more than 1.5 million Circassians live in fifty-six countries around the world. With about 500,000 living in southwestern Russia, most of the other million Circassians live as minorities in the Middle East. Turkey, with more than 200,000 Circassians, is home to the region's largest population, followed by Libya, Jordan, and Syria. There are also significant communities in Iraq, Lebanon, and Israel/Palestine. Because of recent wars in the Middle East, some Circassians have come to the United States as well.

Assyrians

In northern Iraq, northwestern Iran, and northeastern Syria (south of the mountainous Kurdish homeland and to some degree overlapping Kurdistan), nearly 3 million Assyrian Christians live as a minority in what they believe to be their ancestral homeland. Geneticists from Stanford University have determined that modern Assyrians do have a distinct genetic profile, although definitive proof of their ancient bloodlines is unavailable. Still, the Assyrians' genetics distinguish them from their Arab, Kurdish, Turkic, and Persian neighbors.

Another difference between Assyrians and other Middle Eastern populations is their language. Known as Aramaic or Syriac, the language of the Assyrians is a Semitic tongue related to Hebrew and Arabic. After centuries of Arabization, some Assyrians now speak Arabic as their first language, though their Aramaic mother tongue continues to be used in liturgical church services.

In addition to their ethnolinguistic distinctiveness, Assyrians are also proud of their ancient Christian heritage. As some of the first gentile followers of Jesus Christ, Assyrian missionaries were responsible for spreading the new faith into Persia, China, and other parts of Asia. Over the centuries, church politics and doctrinal differences have produced four main Assyrian denominations: the Apostolic Assyrian Church of the East; the Catholic Assyrian Church of the East; the Chaldean Catholic Church; and the Assyrian Orthodox Church of Antioch.

Just as their Armenian coreligionists, Assyrian Christians experienced death and dispersion during and after World War I. Known as the Assyrian Holocaust, hundreds of thousands of civilians were forced from their lands and killed by Ottoman armies. Like their Kurdish and Armenian neighbors, the Assyrians received a promise of an independent state, only to see their lands parceled out into Arab, Turkish, and Persian states.

ALERT

Don't mistake Assyrians and Syrians as the same people. Citizens of the Arab Republic of Syria are known as Syrians, while Assyrians are a distinct ethnic group. Though nearly 1 million Assyrians live in Syria, another 3 million live in other nations.

Today, there are nearly 4 million Assyrians around the globe, with more than 1 million in Iraq, just under 1 million in Syria, and more than 200,000 in Armenia. In addition, Assyrian communities can be found in Turkey, Iran, Lebanon, Jordan, other parts of the Middle East, and the United States, where nearly 500,000 Assyrians have made their homes.

Copts

The term "Copt" comes from the Greek *Aigyptos*, which comes from the ancient title *Hikaptah*, which was given to Egypt's capital, Memphis. From the late 100s to the early 300s, after millennia of polytheism, most Egyptians accepted Christianity. By the mid-600s, Arab Muslim armies had conquered Egypt, setting up military installations among the indigenous non-Arab peoples. After several hundred years of Arab occupation, Egyptian Christians began converting to Islam. As Muslims, they adopted the Arabic language and began calling themselves Arabs. Those who remained Christian continued to identify themselves as non-Arab Egyptians or Copts.

The Copts are not Arabs, nor are they of the Semitic family; they are their own subdivision within the Eastern Hamitic (Afro-Asiatic) group. Strictly speaking, Copts are a mixture of the ancient Egyptian peoples, African Nubians, Greeks, Jews, and Romans. Because Copts look much like their

Arab Muslim neighbors, a cross worn around a person's neck or tattooed on their right wrist is the most likely identifying factor.

ESSENTIAL

The Coptic language used today in most Egyptian church services is largely the same tongue spoken by the ancient pharaohs (just as modern English is largely the same tongue as Old English).

Today, there are an estimated 7 million Copts who make up about 10 percent of Egypt's total population. While the vast majority of Egyptian Christians are part of the Coptic (Egyptian Orthodox) Church, others are members of various Eastern Orthodox, Catholic, and Protestant churches. The biggest distinction between members of the Coptic Church and other Egyptian Christians is their adherence to Monophysitism, an understanding of Christ's nature that most other churches view as heresy.

As late as 1600, Arabic surpassed Coptic as Egypt's spoken language. As a result, the ancient Egyptian (Coptic) language is only used in ceremonial church services, just as Latin is recited in Roman Catholic mass. Since priests and a select few laymen are the only people who can understand the language of the pharaohs, Greek and Arabic are also used in Coptic churches.

Berbers

From the western Egyptian oasis town of Siwa to the High Atlas Mountains of Morocco and Algeria, an ancient people known as the Berbers struggle to keep their identity and language alive. "Berber" is a broad term for the indigenous tribes of North Africa who have lived in this region for thousands of years. Referenced in Egyptian texts as early as 3000 B.C., about 50 million of these diverse non-Arab peoples continue to live in the mountains and rural areas of their African homeland.

As a whole, Berbers are the ethnic majority in North Africa, but because of continued Arabization, many ethnic Berbers have adopted the Arabic language and cultural identity. In some countries, if you call someone a Berber, you are calling that person a backward country bumpkin. Because of this stigma, and the perceived superiority of Arab civilization, many ethnic Berbers now consider themselves Arabs. Nevertheless, some are strongly resisting Arabization and have launched Berber identity movements.

Nearly 80 percent of Moroccans and Algerians are ethnically Berber, while less than half of these people identify themselves as Berbers. Though more than half of Tunisians are descendants of Berber-speaking parents, only 5 percent admit they are Berbers. The same is true in Libya and Egypt, where Arabic has replaced ancient Berber dialects. Nevertheless, some Berbers remain proud of their heritage. In Algeria, many Berbers have refused to learn Arabic.

FACT

The famous Christian theologian Augustine of Hippo was a Berber. Born in A.D. 354, and raised in a part of North Africa that is now Algeria, Augustine is revered by the Roman Catholic Church as a saint. Within his many writings, this blessed Berber clarified such doctrines as original sin, free will, divine grace, and predestination.

In addition to the ongoing Arabization of Berbers, these aboriginal peoples have also come to embrace Islam. Today, most Berbers consider themselves Muslims, but the process of Islamicization was slow, starting in the late 600s and continuing into the 1500s. Because of this gradual change, most Berbers have retained pre-Islamic beliefs and ceremonies. The intermingling of Islamic and pagan traditions has produced unique "folk Islamic" practices across North Africa. With Berber language and identity on the verge of extinction, these traces of ancient religion may be the only thing Berber to survive in the twenty-first century.

Jews

The Hebrews (Egyptian for "wanderers") are an ancient people who are said to have come from the Semitic family of Abraham, Isaac, and Jacob (also known as "Israel"). Captivated by Jewish culture and faith, ethnically non-Jewish locals adopted the Jewish religion. With their conversions, people from many different ethnic backgrounds began calling themselves Jews. Thus, the distinction between ethnically Jewish people and those practicing Judaism must be made.

Nearly 2,000 years after the Diaspora, people who consider themselves Jewish are divided into two groups. European Jews, who tend to have lighter skin, are known as the Ashkenazim. In addition to their European appearance, the Ashkenazim are politically and culturally Western. In contrast, those who have lived in the Middle East, North Africa, and Spain for the past millennia usually have darker skin, making it difficult to distinguish them from other Middle Eastern peoples. Known as the Sephardim, these people have been shaped by centuries of life in the Arab and Muslim worlds.

QUESTION

Are Jews a religious group or an ethnic group?
It depends! One who is born ethnically Jewish may or may not also practice the Jewish religion. Conversely, someone who is not born a Jew can choose to formally convert and practice the Jewish religion.

Since the creation of Israel in 1948, Eastern and Western Jews have lived together in one land for more than fifty years. Although these groups share a common religion, cultural differences have been a source of ongoing tension between the Ashkenazim and Sephardim. In addition, many darker-skinned Sephardic Jews feel they are being discriminated against by European Jews. The most striking example of this is seen in the controversy over the "Jewishness" of more than 80,000 Ethiopian Jews. Despite their ancient Jewish traditions and clearly Jewish beliefs, the dark skin and African features of Ethiopia's Jewish community almost kept them from receiving Israeli citizenship. Nevertheless, it was finally decided that these Ethiopians were in fact "real" Jews.

Despite internal differences, about 5 million Jews live as a majority in the State of Israel, while another 50,000 live as minorities in Turkey, Lebanon, Morocco, and other parts of the Middle East.

Islamic Offshoots—Reformers or Heretics?

Since the death of Muhammad in A.D. 632, Muslims have been faced with the fate of all major world religions: division. For Islam, this began as Muslims tried to choose a leader after the untimely death of their prophet. With some believing their leader should be the most qualified man, and others advocating for Muhammad's closest male relative, the newly formed brotherhood was split. Over the centuries, this rift has inspired approximately 1.3 billion Muslims to call themselves Sunni, while about 257 million consider themselves Shi'ites.

ESSENTIAL

Though many non-Muslims view Islam as a monolithic religion, Islamic beliefs are as diverse and divided as any other religious movement. (Remember the Sufis, for example?)

Today, after fourteen centuries of Islamic history, many orthodox and heterodox movements have appeared. While most of these groups continue to celebrate their Islamic roots, some conservative Muslims view them as apostates and infidels. Here are a few controversial factions.

Alawites (a.k.a. Nusayri)

Found primarily in the mountains that line the northwest Mediterranean coast, today about 2 million Arabs call themselves Alawites. Inspired by the teachings of the ninth-century Shi'ite theologian Muhammad bin Nusayr, Alawites have unique beliefs and practices, which some Muslims view as blasphemy.

An almost Trinitarian concept of Ali, Muhammad, and God being one in essence is the most striking Alawite belief. This sect is also criticized for not observing Islam's five pillars, for not meeting in mosques, and for celebrating traditionally Christian and Zoroastrian holidays.

The five pillars of Islam are:

- Faith or belief in the Oneness of God and the finality of the prophethood of Muhammad

- Establishment of the daily prayers (five times a day)
- Concern for and almsgiving to the needy
- Self-purification through fasting during the month of Ramadan
- The pilgrimage to Mecca for those who are able (the *Hajj*)

Despite opposition from some Muslim leaders, Alawites believe they are Shi'ite Muslims.

FACT

Like his father before him, Syria's president Bashar al-Assad is an Alawite. Though less than 10 percent of all Syrians are Alawites, this minority has ruled the nation since 1963.

Alevi-Bektashis

As a unique synthesis of Sufism, Shi'ism, and pre-Islamic religious beliefs, Alevi-Bektashism is a flexible and complex movement. Inspired by the teachings of a twelfth-century mystic named Haji Bektash Veli, nearly 15 million Turkish and Eastern European people have combined aspects of all the major world religions with a view that holds humanity and divinity as one and the same.

Like the Arab Alawites of south-central Turkey, eastern Syria, and northeastern Lebanon, Alevi-Bektashis do not observe Islam's five pillars, though Muhammad and the Qur'an are held in high regard. If you ask an Alevi-Bektashi if he is Muslim, he most likely will reply, "I am Muslim, Jewish, Christian, Buddhist, and atheist, but most importantly I am human."

Druze (a.k.a. Mowahhidoon)

Though the exact origins of this movement are unclear, the *Mowahhidoon* (Arabic for "Monotheists") emerged in the 800s, believing they were a new interpretation of Judaism, Christianity, and Islam. In their view, the other three had lost the true meaning of religion by focusing on rituals and laws. In contrast, the Mowahhidoon sought the "pure path," which incorporated aspects of Greek philosophy and Hindu spirituality with traditional monotheism.

In the late 900s, a Mowahhidoon leader named Darazi announced that the Fatimid Caliph al-Hakim was the incarnation of God. Although many initially accepted this teaching, his followers eventually rejected Darazi. Because of Darazi's spectacular claims, outsiders used the name "Druze," a variation of Darazi's name, when referring to the Mowahhidoon.

Because members of this sect have kept the details of their religion secret, many non-Mowahhidoon have speculated about their beliefs and practices. The Mowahhidoon are by definition strict monotheists. Unlike most monotheists, the Mowahhidoon believe that each soul is reincarnated from life to life and that heaven and hell are states of mind rather than destinations. As other offshoot groups have done, the Mowahhidoon have rejected the five pillars of Islam, causing many Muslims to reject them.

Today, there are about a million Mowahhidoon living around the world, with nearly 300,000 living in Lebanon, Syria, and northern Israel. The Mowahhidoon are ethnically Arabs, yet because they do not accept converts or marry outside of the faith, they have developed a distinct, almost ethnic identity.

CHAPTER 12

Israel/Palestine— All Eyes on Jerusalem

Welcome to the contemporary Middle East! To better understand today's Middle East, you will jump right into the most complicated place in the region. Take a moment to prepare yourself for heartache produced by more than sixty years of war and injustice. Set aside your preconceived notions, and allow the stories of these two peoples to move you. Try to understand their history, their hopes, and their dreams.

Aryanism, Zionism, and Exodus

While Britain was bouncing back and forth on its plan for Palestine between 1917 and 1948, National Socialism (better known as Nazism) inspired the people of Germany as they rebuilt their devastated country after World War I. Under the banner of Nazism, Adolph Hitler began a program of nationalistic conquest. Based on a corrupted understanding of the Aryan identity, Germany seized surrounding nations seen as Aryan homelands. In addition, Nazis attempted to rid their state of all non-Aryan peoples in the years leading up to the start of World War II in 1939—and until it ended in 1945.

Although Gypsies, Slavs, and other groups were targets of Nazi racism, Jewish populations were their primary focus. After confiscating Jewish possessions, humiliating Jews with special identification symbols, and displacing Jewish families into ghettos, Aryan nationalists tried to exterminate all non-Aryans. By establishing death camps (concentration camps), Hitler's henchmen gassed, shot, raped, and starved millions.

British, American, and Soviet forces eventually defeated Germany and liberated those still living in death camps. If not for the Allied intervention, millions more would have been massacred, and most of Europe's Jewish population could have been annihilated. Nevertheless, the genocide program that became known as the Holocaust stole the lives of more than 5 million Jews and another 5 million non-Jewish civilians.

ESSENTIAL

The term "Palestinian" is translated *Filastin* in Arabic, but this does not mean they are the descendants of the ancient Philistines! About 2,000 years ago, the Romans expelled all Jews from the province of Judea, renaming it Palestine after the ancient Philistines. Over the following centuries, those living in this region were known as Palestinians, regardless of their ethnicity. Nevertheless, from about A.D. 700, most of Palestine's inhabitants were ethnically Arabs.

At the end of World War II, European and American populations felt partially responsible for the Holocaust because they did very little to prevent it as it was going on, leading many politicians to look for ways to make amends. At the same time, Jewish nationalists were calling for a refuge in

Palestine. For most Western leaders, the idea of creating a Jewish homeland was just what the doctor ordered. A Jewish state in Palestine would provide a new start for Holocaust survivors, who wished for a safe haven from any more attempts at persecution. But what about the Arab peoples who had made their start in Palestine centuries before? Was Palestine really a "land without a people," as Zionists were asking? The answers to these questions are still not clear, and the results of the solutions implemented to date have not pleased all the parties involved.

Declaration of State and War

Three years after Nazi Aryanism's greatest defeat, Jewish Zionism gained its greatest victory. European immigration had increased the Jewish population in Palestine from fewer than 175,000 in the 1931 census to more than 650,000 in 1948. With key members of the United Nations voicing their support for a Jewish state and Britain abandoning its thirty-year mandate of Palestine, Russian-born David Ben-Gurion announced the Jewish State of Israel on May 14, 1948. The next day, Arab armies made their own declaration of resistance, and the first Arab-Israeli war began.

FACT

On April 9, 1948, more than a month before the Arab-Israeli war began, future Israeli Prime Ministers Menachem Begin and Yitzhak Shamir led a group of armed Jewish radicals into the Palestinian village of Deir Yassin. When the dust settled, the bodies of 245 Palestinian men, women, and children were found, with many stuffed in wells or tied to automobiles.

Ben-Gurion united Jewish terrorist groups, lightly armed farmers, and emboldened Holocaust survivors against Jordanian, Iraqi, Egyptian, and Lebanese regular armies. With both sides focused on Jerusalem, heavy fighting plagued the holy city and its surrounding areas. After one month of intense conflict, U.N. mediator Count Folke Bernadotte organized a ceasefire. A month later, Jewish terrorists from the notorious Stern Gang assassinated the U.N. mediator, and fighting resumed.

Bolstered by new weaponry from Czechoslovakia, the Israeli army moved with fresh vigor on Arab positions, pushing them all the way to Jerusalem. After six months of renewed fighting, Arab armies were ready to throw in the towel. By July 27, 1949, the war was officially over, as Jordan and Egypt signed cease-fire agreements with the Jewish state.

As a result of the 1948 war, Israel's borders increased to include 78 percent of the land formerly known as Palestine. The remaining 22 percent was divided between the Hashemite Kingdom of Jordan, which annexed the exclusively Arab area known today as the West Bank (once called Judea and Samaria). Egypt assumed control of a strip of land along the southeastern Mediterranean coast known as the Gaza Strip. Meanwhile, the coveted city of Jerusalem was divided between the Jewish state and the Kingdom of Jordan.

Displaced Peoples

To escape the raging war of 1948, 70 percent of Palestine's Arab population fled their homes and farms. Hoping to return when things cooled down, most moved to the safety of uncontested areas in the West Bank and Gaza Strip. In addition, Arabs in the north of Palestine escaped to nearby Lebanon and Syria, while many from Jerusalem and the Galilee region found refuge in Jordan.

As things settled down, many families attempted to return to their homes, businesses, and farmlands, only to be told they were not welcome. Those who were able to make their way past Israeli soldiers found Jewish families living in their homes, using their furniture, and farming their lands.

FACT

In the aftermath of war, about 750,000 Palestinian Arabs found themselves homeless, while another 150,000 retained their property within the new Jewish state.

As most families had fled with only the clothes on their backs, they were unable to produce land deeds for Jewish officials. The only evidence most could provide was a simple skeleton key. Over the following years, the key became a common symbol for those who had lost everything to the new state. With no money to purchase property or pay for temporary housing, thousands of homeless families were exposed to the elements. This large-scale humanitarian crisis led the United Nations Relief and Works Agency (UNRWA) to move quickly; it established "temporary" refugee camps.

Viewing the camps as a demeaning, yet temporary, necessity, most Palestinian Arabs believed they would return to their homes after a few months. As the months turned into years, shacks and eventually simple cement structures replaced the original U.N.-issued tents.

ESSENTIAL

Today, refugee camps are home to more than 1 million people in the West Bank, Gaza Strip, and surrounding Arab nations, while another 2 million Palestinians live outside the camps under Israeli control.

Freedom Fighters or Terrorists?

Throughout the early 1950s, many displaced Palestinian Arabs decided they would rather die fighting than rot in filthy refugee camps. Known as the *fida'yin* ("men of sacrifice"), these men mimicked Jewish groups such as the Irgun, which had employed terror in their efforts to free Palestine from British occupation just a few years before.

The fida'yin, known to the West as "fedayeen," understood they were no match for the Israeli army. But just as the lightly armed Stern Gang had tormented the British, the fedayeen believed they could make their homeland undesirable for Jewish immigrants. Despite killing hundreds of Israeli soldiers, the fedayeen attacks actually emboldened the Jewish newcomers, inspiring them to launch counterattacks into refugee camps, killing their share of Arab fighters and civilians.

The Fix of 1956

In 1956, Egypt nationalized the Suez Canal, nullifying London's claims to the important waterway. In response, the British and French combined forces with the Israelis, who also had a bone to pick with Egypt because of fedayeen attacks staged from the Sinai. After bombing Egyptian air bases and occupying the Sinai Peninsula, the Europeans allowed Israel to manage the newly acquired Egyptian lands and destroy the fedayeen rebel camps. Within a year, pressure from the United States and other nations forced Israel to leave the Gaza Strip and Sinai Peninsula. Although the Sinai was back in Egyptian hands, Israeli operations had dealt a major blow to the fedayeen guerrillas in the region.

Hello PLO

Throughout the late 1950s and early 1960s, a period of relative peace allowed Israel to grow economically, politically, and militarily. Meanwhile, Arab nations were caught in the middle of American-Soviet rivalries. As some countries sided with the West and others looked to the U.S.S.R., the Arab world was quickly divided along Cold War lines. In addition, ideas of Arab nationalism and Islamic revolution created new movements across the Arab world.

In the midst of these changing times, Palestinians sought to regain their homeland by attacking Israel. Arab governments also desired to rid the Middle East of the Jewish state, which, in their estimation, was a Western colonial outpost. In 1964, thirteen Arab nations met in Cairo to discuss their response to the Zionist state. The Arab governments agreed that Palestinian fedayeen should be mobilized to deal with Israel. In addition, the governments trained and supplied Palestinian guerrillas in their quest for liberation.

ESSENTIAL

Yasser Arafat's movement, known as al-Fatah, translates to "conquest," but the name is also derived from the reversed first letters of its full name, *Harakat al-Tahrir al-Filastini*, meaning "Movement for the Liberation of Palestine."

In order to determine an official governing body for the Palestinians, Jordan's King Hussein gathered 400 prominent Palestinians in Jordanian-controlled East Jerusalem. Through this inaugural Palestinian National Council meeting, the Palestinian Liberation Organization (PLO) and Palestinian Liberation Army (PLA) were confirmed as the official channels for

Palestinian nationalism. Although the PLO was meant to be an umbrella organization for all Palestinians, a separate group calling itself al-Fatah emerged as the most influential resistance movement.

Yasser Arafat

With support from Syria, an influential Palestinian engineer named Yasser Arafat organized al-Fatah's members to attack Israeli positions. Because of the group's great success and Arafat's charisma, al-Fatah's popularity grew exponentially among downtrodden refugees. Realizing Arafat's popular strength, the chairman of the PLO moved to combine forces with al-Fatah.

Six Days in '67

During the mid-1960s, intense fighting erupted between Israeli and Syrian forces, bringing instability to the Soviet-backed Syrian regime. To deal with this situation, the Russians employed another of their patron states, Egypt, to defend Syria in the event of an Israeli invasion.

By spring of 1967, the Russians were anxiously watching Israeli-American relations. Meanwhile, the United States was scrambling to dissuade Israel from making any rash moves. Uncertainty reigned, until the Soviets sent bad intelligence to the Egyptians, warning them of a massive Israeli buildup on the Syrian border. Consequently, Egyptian forces rolled through the Sinai Desert toward the Israeli border, reoccupying border positions held by the United Nations since 1949. In addition, Syrian, Jordanian, and Iraqi troops moved to Israel's borders to deflect possible strikes.

Depending on whom you talk to, Israel's next move was either part of a calculated plan of expansion or a pre-emptive strike of desperation. Either way, on June 5, 1967, the Israeli air force made the first move, destroying most of Egypt's air force before its planes could leave the ground. With no air cover, the Egyptians were soundly defeated on the ground, as Israeli troops quickly took the entire Gaza Strip and most of Egypt's Sinai Peninsula. In addition, Jordanian advances were quickly repelled, as the Israeli army took East Jerusalem and all of the West Bank. Finally, the full force of the Israeli military moved north to secure a mountainous region in southern Syria known as the Golan Heights.

The Cease-Fire

After only six days of fighting, the war was officially over. As part of the cease-fire, the United Nations drafted a set of principles meant to bring lasting peace to the region. The main points of this foundational document, known as U.N. Resolution 242, are:

- The international community will not recognize territories acquired (occupied) through conquest.
- Israel's armed forces should withdraw from occupied territories (such as the West Bank and Gaza Strip).
- All states will recognize and respect the borders of all other states (that is, Arab states will recognize Israel's right to exist).
- The refugee problem is to be resolved in a just manner (meaning the more than 400,000 newly displaced Palestinians as well as those uprooted since 1948).
- All states must cooperate with the U.N.-designated special representative and adhere to the principles found in this resolution.

While Israel, Egypt, and Jordan agreed to these principles, Syria refused to accept them. In their minds, any recognition of Israel's right to exist would legitimatize colonialism and ignore the displaced Palestinian people. Nevertheless, this document's vague declarations did little to bring lasting peace. Instead, finger-pointing and inaction left Israeli occupation forces in control of Egyptian, Syrian, and Palestinian peoples, while Palestinian fighters continued their resistance efforts in Israel.

Domination and Terror

Before 1967, Arabs living in the West Bank and Gaza Strip recognized themselves as Palestinian Arabs. But, because they were living under other Arab governments, many were not moved by Palestinian nationalism. However, after the '67 War, Palestinian Arabs found their homeland occupied by a non-Arab government whose laws and language were unfamiliar. Because of this, Palestinians looked to their unique heritage while resisting the expanding Zionist state.

In the midst of this nationalist upsurge, several groups organized Palestinians to fight for their independence. Believing the international community was unaware of their suffering, the PLO, along with other guerrilla groups, brought its cause to the world stage. By hijacking airplanes, taking hostages, and choosing high-visibility targets—such as Israeli athletes at the 1972 Munich Olympics—Palestinian leaders believed they could make their plight known.

Although the PLO succeeded in securing the world's attention, images of "crazed Muslim hijackers" overshadowed any recognition of Israeli injustice. In fact, for many Europeans and Americans, this period of international terror created a lasting image of Palestinians as bloodthirsty fanatics. In many people's estimation, Israel's occupation was justified as a necessary "security" measure.

War of Atonement

After unsuccessful attempts to take back the Sinai in the early 1970s, the Egyptians were anxious to use newly acquired Soviet weaponry and training. On October 6, 1973, Egypt and Syria launched a surprise two-front offensive against Israel, with Egypt hoping to regain the Sinai and Syria desiring to reclaim the Golan Heights. Because the attack was launched on the Jewish Day of Atonement (*Yom Kippur* in Hebrew), many Israeli soldiers were unprepared for battle, giving Egyptian and Syrian forces a great advantage.

Despite Israeli resistance in the Sinai and Golan, Egyptian and Syrian armies conducted successful operations, pushing the Israeli Defense Forces (IDF) out of the occupied lands and threatening the State of Israel proper (sometimes distinguished as "Green Line Israel"). After a week of fighting, it appeared Israel might be overrun, but the United States came to the rescue, resupplying the embattled nation with superior weaponry. From near defeat, Israel managed to push the Syrians back through the Golan, advancing to within twenty-five miles of Damascus. In addition, the IDF moved Egyptian troops back through the Sinai, over the Suez Canal, to within sixty miles of Cairo.

With the Soviet Union and United States occupying opposing sides, the real threat of nuclear war led the two superpowers to draft a cease-fire just eighteen days into the battle. As part of the agreement, the United Nations drafted Resolution 338, which called for the complete implementation of U.N. Resolution 242. Despite the influential role of the United States in the region, the peace process once again stalled, as Israel continued its occupation of the Sinai, Golan, and Palestinian territories, and the PLO remained violently opposed to the Zionist state.

Peace Camps and Refugee Camps

In 1977, Israel elected Menachem Begin as its prime minister. With a hawkish view toward all Arabs, Begin's tough stance did little to bring peace in the region. Since their initial occupation of the West Bank and Gaza Strip in 1967, some Israeli extremists had begun constructing heavily fortified Jewish settlements in the occupied Arab areas. Although most Israelis were happy with the pre-1967 borders, Begin set out to claim the Arab West Bank, Gaza Strip, and Sinai Peninsula by populating them with Jewish citizens.

As these areas were outside Israel's internationally recognized borders (Green Line Israel), it was illegal to build Israeli settlements on them. Concerning these Israeli-controlled Arab areas, Prime Minister Begin declared, "What do you mean 'Occupied Territories'? If you mean Judea and Samaria, they are 'Liberated Territories.'" With statements like these, Palestinians had little reason to believe they would ever find freedom.

Camp David

Despite Begin's harsh attitude toward the Palestinians, Egypt's President Anwar Sadat shocked the world by visiting the Jewish state. While addressing the Israeli parliament, Sadat insisted that Israel relinquish the occupied territories in exchange for peace. Impressed by Sadat's risky first move toward peace, U.S. President Jimmy Carter invited the Egyptian and Israeli leaders to his Camp David retreat in September 1979. After days of deliberation, a historic agreement was made between the two nations. Israel returned the occupied Sinai Peninsula and dismantled all its settlements there, and Egypt recognized Israel's right to exist. Although this peace agreement was a monumental achievement, it failed to deal with the Palestinian territories, causing many Arabs to see Sadat as a sellout.

Lethal Lebanon

At about the same time, the PLO found a home in Lebanon, where it became entangled in the Lebanese civil war. As a result, Israel supplied the Lebanese Phalange Party's militia with weapons to fight their Lebanese Muslim rivals, who had welcomed the PLO. At the request of the Phalange and their leader Bashir Gemayel, Israel invaded Lebanon in 1982, hoping to rid the region of PLO forces once and for all.

Under the leadership of General Ariel Sharon, Israeli forces moved through Lebanon, encircling the capital city, Beirut. Understanding that the IDF wanted to remove the PLO, Lebanese Muslim leaders asked Arafat to leave the city. Gathering about 15,000 PLO and Syrian fighters, Arafat evacuated Lebanon, moving his operations to the North African nation of Tunisia. In retaliation for the Christian Phalange Party's role in expelling the PLO, Gemayel, their leader, was assassinated. Holding the Palestinians responsible, enraged Phalange militiamen sought swift retribution.

In circumstances that remain unclear, it seems Ariel Sharon ordered Israeli troops to encircle two Palestinian refugee camps while the Lebanese Phalange took their revenge. As it turns out, the Sabra and Shatila refugee camps were not full of PLO fighters. Instead, about 800 women, children, and elderly people were ruthlessly massacred. The extent of Israeli involvement in these killings remains unclear, but in 1983 upon investigation of the situation, Ariel Sharon was forced to step down from his position as Israel's Defense Minister.

FACT

The 2001 movie *Spy Game*, starring Brad Pitt and Robert Redford, shows the ugly realities of everyday life during Lebanon's civil war. With Christian and Muslim militias fighting for control of Beirut, Syrian troops occupying parts of the country, and Israeli soldiers battling Hizbullah ("Party of God") forces in southern Lebanon, Palestinian refugees and Lebanese citizens were caught in the bloody middle.

After the expulsion of PLO troops, U.S., French, and Italian peacekeepers attempted to bring stability to the splintered nation. On October 23, 1983, a massive truck bomb rocked the U.S. marine barracks, killing 241 American armed forces' members and injuring sixty others. Two minutes later, another bomb exploded at a French army barracks, killing fifty-eight French paratroopers and wounding fifteen more. As a result of these bombings, the peacekeepers left Lebanon, and the war raged on. By 1985, the Israeli army pulled most of its forces out of Lebanon, leaving a small force in the south to fight the Syrian/Iranian-supported *Hizbullah* guerrillas.

With Israel and the PLO out of Lebanon, Syrian troops remained, while domestic militias decimated the nation. Lebanon was once a unique concoction of French and Middle Eastern cultures, with beautiful ski resorts, lavish nightclubs, and the like that created a legendary playground for the world's rich and famous. After fifteen years of war, little beauty or glamour remained, and the Lebanese people were left with more than 300,000 casualties and a country in ruins.

Desperation and Uprising

In 1982, the Golan Heights were annexed into the State of Israel, and the Arab inhabitants of these lands were encouraged to accept Israeli citizenship. The West Bank and Gaza Strip remained occupied territories, and the Arab inhabitants of these lands remained nationless. By occupying the West Bank and Gaza, Israel created a "manageable buffer zone" to the Arab states. By not annexing these areas, Israel would not be required to give citizenship to hundreds of thousands of Arabs. Thus, occupation avoided the creation of an Arab majority within the Jewish state while offering temporary and synthetic territorial security. Meanwhile, day-to-day life for Palestinians went from bad to worse.

ESSENTIAL

The term "Arab Israeli" refers to indigenous Palestinians who have been given Israeli citizenship. Today, there are more than 1 million Arab Israelis, with about 75 percent calling themselves Muslims and most of the remaining 25 percent considering themselves Christians.

By 1987, Palestinians in the West Bank and Gaza had been without many basic human rights for more than twenty years, while many refugees had lived in Arab ghettos for nearly forty years. Since 1948, Israel had grown to become one of the wealthiest nations in the Middle East, yet the occupied territories remained isolated and impoverished. Cut off economically from the rest of the world, Palestinians were forced to become day laborers in Israel.

For most Palestinian workers, the daily trip from their poverty-stricken lands to Israel's luxury created mounting resentment. If only they could be freed from Israel's clutches, they too might improve their lands and enjoy prosperity. The Israeli government determined the fate of the Palestinians, until one day they revolted.

During a period known as the *intifada* ("the shaking off"), the occupied peoples vented their frustration in a massive and spontaneous popular uprising. With scores of youth taking to the streets, workers going on strike, and various other forms of civil disobedience, the Palestinians were ready for change. Aware of Israel's vastly superior weaponry, stones were used to deliver their message of exasperation. In addition, the Palestinian flag (illegal under the Israeli occupation) was flown proudly as a symbol of their desired independence. With the PLO on the sidelines in North Africa, the Palestinian people were ready to liberate themselves.

ALERT

The Islamic group Hamas was formed by the Muslim cleric Shaykh Ahmad Yasin in 1987, at the start of the intifada. Although Hamas is a Palestinian movement, its members desire an Islamic state in the occupied territories and all of historic Palestine. While other Palestinian groups, such as Islamic Jihad, also have religious goals, most Palestinian liberation movements are strictly secular.

Instead of recognizing the intifada as a serious warning sign, the Israeli government continued the occupation and suppressed the uprising, although it took some time. With Palestinians desperately wanting freedom, the IDF sought to break their will by making mass arrests, beating protestors, demolishing homes, and torturing prisoners. Despite Israel's use of psychological warfare, the Palestinians shook off the occupation for another six years.

Suicides, Strikes, and Settlements

The passion of the intifada fighters awakened many Israelis to the injustices caused by their government. In addition, forty years of life under Israeli rule brought many Palestinians to realize the Jewish state was not going to go away. With each side wanting a normal life, compromises were made in which Israeli "doves," or peacemakers, pushed for a withdrawal from the West Bank and Gaza, while Palestinian doves called for the recognition of Israel according to its pre-1967 borders.

After several years of unproductive peace talks in Madrid and Washington, D.C., secret back-channel negotiations in Oslo, Norway, produced a major breakthrough in 1993. In order to formally recognize this achievement, U.S. President Bill Clinton invited Israeli Prime Minister Yitzhak Rabin and PLO Chairman Yasser Arafat to Washington for a treaty-signing ceremony.

According to the principles of the Oslo Accords, Israel and the PLO were to mutually recognize one another. Israel was to withdraw from the occupied territories, and the PLO was to take specific steps toward ensuring Israel's security. In the face of this monumental victory for moderates on both sides, Israeli and Palestinian hawks violently opposed the arrangement. For Israel's minority of extremists, any loss of territory was unacceptable. At the same time, some fanatical Palestinian groups viewed the recognition of Israel as cowardly submission to Zionism.

Struggle and Peace

In the city of Hebron, on February 25, 1994, an Israeli settler responded to Rabin's concessions by killing twenty-nine Palestinians as they prayed at the Mosque of Abraham inside the Tomb of the Patriarchs complex. The Islamic group Hamas answered the Hebron massacre with several bombings, yet both Arafat and Rabin continued their march toward peace. As part of the Oslo Accords, Arafat was allowed to return from exile in Tunisia to establish a provisional Palestinian government known as the Palestinian Authority (PA). With the West Bank town of Jericho and most of the Gaza Strip under PA administration, it appeared the Palestinian people were on the road to liberation.

In 1994, Yitzhak Rabin continued his dovish efforts, signing a peace treaty with the Kingdom of Jordan. In addition, a second agreement was made between the PA and Israel, known as Oslo II or the Taba Accords. As part of this "interim agreement," Israeli forces would pull out of certain West Bank towns and villages in several phases. Then, at the final status talks (scheduled for May 1996), tough issues such as the fate of Jewish settlements, the nature of a Palestinian state, and control of Jerusalem would be decided.

By 1995, Egypt, the PLO, and Jordan were in the peace camp, leaving Syria (and its client state, Lebanon) as Israel's only adversarial neighbor.

In hopes of completing the peace train, Rabin approached Syrian President Hafez al-Assad with a deal in which the Golan Heights would be returned to Syria in exchange for peaceful relations. Before the train could leave the station, it was derailed: On November 4, 1995, an Israeli extremist assassinated his own prime minister.

QUESTION

Isn't the Israeli-Palestinian conflict about religion?
Although religion is a factor, it is not the main issue for most Israelis and Palestinians. Most Israelis see the Jewish state as a secular haven in which Jewish people should be able to celebrate their culture and heritage in safety and security. At the same time, the vast majority of Muslim and Christian Palestinians desire basic freedoms and human rights, unavailable to them under Israeli occupation. In the end, the conflict can be summarized as a struggle for Israeli security and Palestinian liberation.

Polarization and Pain

After Rabin's assassination, two large Palestinian suicide bombings rocked the nation, creating a drastic shift in Israeli public opinion. From the euphoria of Rabin's peace victories, the region spiraled into a pit of desperation and fear. More concerned with security than peace, the Israeli people elected the hawkish Benjamin Netanyahu as their leader. Reluctantly, the new prime minister continued with the principles of the Oslo Accords, allowing increased Palestinian autonomy in the West Bank and Gaza. At the same time, Netanyahu showed his true colors by lifting the four-year ban on settlement construction and refusing to meet with Yasser Arafat for scheduled final status talks.

Over the next two years, clashes between Palestinians and the IDF, followed by a series of bombings in Jerusalem and Tel Aviv, left the peace process at a standstill. In 1998, U.S. President Bill Clinton convinced Netanyahu to restart the peace process by signing the U.S.-sponsored Wye River Memorandum, which guaranteed Israeli withdrawal from another 40 percent of the West Bank. Like a political car bomb, implementation of the agreement divided the Israeli government. Within a year the Wye deal was suspended. That same year, a dissatisfied Israeli public replaced Netanyahu with a new leader—Ehud Barak.

Signs of Hope

As prime minister, Barak revived the Wye agreement, called for the long-awaited final status negotiations, and put a freeze on all settlement construction in occupied lands. Despite periods of disagreement and several stalemates, Barak agreed to make concessions, which allowed final status negotiations to move forward. In July 2000, Israeli and Palestinian leaders met at Camp David, hoping to produce an historic agreement, just as Israeli and Egyptian leaders had done in 1979. As it turned out, the summit was fruitless, as neither side would compromise on having Jerusalem as its capital.

By September 2000, after months of gridlock, Barak was showing signs of conciliation regarding the fate of Jerusalem. With tensions running high among frightened Israelis and frustrated Palestinians, this type of meaningful concession could have ensured lasting peace. Instead, Barak's goodwill was undermined by the right-wing Israeli hawk, Ariel Sharon.

Creating More Tension

In an attempt to show the Palestinians who was boss, Sharon and a small group of his cronies paraded across the Temple Mount, known to Muslims as *Haram al-Sharif* ("Noble Sanctuary"). Not only was Sharon's act against his own Jewish religious regulation, it was also a slap in the face to the Palestinian people, and for that matter the entire Muslim world. As a result of Sharon's calculated actions, Palestinians erupted in protest and the second intifada (known as the al-Aqsa Intifada) was born.

Although infuriated Palestinians had utilized the strategy of minimal force in the first intifada (by throwing rocks instead of firing guns), the second uprising was characterized by Palestinians who were so far beyond exasperation that they were ready to kill themselves. After more than thirty years of daily road closures, never-ending curfews, and time-consuming checkpoints, Palestinians longed for an unimpeded life.

Decades of home demolitions, early morning arrests, torture sessions, random interrogations, and "accidental" deaths had left people more than angry. Poverty, humiliation, and pain, plus years of shattered dreams, produced mind-numbing hopelessness and unimaginable rage. For many, suicide was seen as freedom, and the death of even one Israeli was viewed as a victory.

ALERT

Although nearly all Palestinians want the occupation to end, most are not willing to blow themselves up for this liberation. Similarly, most Israelis want to live in a secure nation but are not willing to wipe out the Palestinians in the process. Despite the horrible actions of Palestinian and Israeli extremists, most are willing to live in peace if it is just.

Over the following year, men and women of varying ages killed themselves and others in the name of liberation, turning many Israeli peaceniks into protective hawks. Despite U.S. efforts to foster peace, suicide bombers and Israeli reprisals eventually killed more than 700 Israelis and 1,900 Palestinians. The evaporation of the peace process, and the chaos that ensued, moved Barak to resign from his position as prime minister. Ironically, in February 2001, Ariel Sharon—the man whose actions sparked the al-Aqsa uprising—was elected prime minister on a platform of strict security and decisive retaliation.

In the wake of September 11, Sharon's hard-line attitude gained support from many Americans, who saw Palestinian attacks as part of al-Qaeda's global terror network. In the following two years, the cycle of violence worsened, as Israel's harsh reprisals only intensified Palestinian resentment and rage.

Probable Peace

In the face of ongoing violence, the hawkish leader Ariel Sharon showed uncharacteristic moderation by acknowledging the West Bank and Gaza as occupied territories and spoke of a future Palestinian state until he suffered a massive stroke on January 4, 2006. He was replaced by Ehud Olmert. Little changed under his leadership, and he was replaced in 2009 by Benjamin Netanyahu. Netanyahu and U.S. President Barack Obama engaged in talks to resolve the Israeli-Palestinian issue as late as May 2011, but the establishment of borders delineating two independent states remained an impediment to reaching a mutually satisfactory agreement.

For Palestinians living under the thumb of Israel, words are cheap, and only tangible freedom will give them relief. At the same time, fearful Israeli citizens desire a secure nation without the threat of terrorism, and only the cessation of Palestinian attacks will suffice.

After years of empty promises and failed peace plans, most Israelis and Palestinians have grown extremely cynical. Is there any hope for peace in this land? Only time will tell, but one thing is certain. The status quo will only produce more death, more pain, and more injustice.

CHAPTER 13

Egypt—Heart of the Arab World

While Israel/Palestine has been the center of regional conflict for more than half a century, Egypt has been the hub of Arab nationalism. As the most populous Arabic-speaking nation, Egypt has led the way, becoming the first independent Arab nation and the first Middle Eastern state to make peace with Israel. But with a swelling population of more than 75 million, increasing poverty, and widespread distrust of the government, militant Islamic groups have found fertile ground.

Remnants of Imperialism

After World War I, the Egyptian people were ready to shake off forty years of British control. In the spirit of Europe's nationalist movements, the Wafd Party was established to coordinate popular impetus for change. Wafd (meaning "delegation") was named after the Egyptian delegation that pled for independence from Britain at the postwar Paris Peace Conference. Run by educated professionals and wealthy elites, the Wafd Party harnessed the power of the people, channeling it into an effective nationalist movement.

FACT

While English speakers call it Egypt, the country is called *Misr* (meaning "country") by Arabic-speaking peoples. Although there are various explanations of the origins of this name, it is likely that Arab invaders were influenced by one of this region's ancient names—Mizraim.

To appease Egyptian nationalist desires, the British ended Egypt's protectorate status in 1922. Although Egypt was officially independent, the British continued to control the profitable Suez Canal and the nation through their puppet, King Fuad. By 1924, members of the Wafd Party formed most of the Egyptian government, though Fuad remained the ruling monarch and British forces remained on the ground.

Frustrated by Turkey's abolishment of the pan-Islamic office of caliph, as well as by the secular nature of Middle Eastern nationalist movements and perceived corruption in Egypt's government, Hassan al-Banna formed a youth movement known as the Muslim Brotherhood (*Al-Ikhwan*, "the Brotherhood") in 1928. Originally focused on promoting moral and social reforms, the organization became more political throughout the 1930s, eventually promoting militant action against the Egyptian government.

The Muslim Brotherhood

In what some call an Islamic revival and others see as the rebirth of Islamic militancy, the Muslim Brotherhood rallied dissatisfied Egyptians behind the utopian vision of an Islamic state. Teaching his followers, "Islam is creed and state, book and sword," Banna gathered more than 500,000 who were ready to fight for their faith.

After King Fuad's death in 1936, his son Farouk became monarch. Soon the new king's playboy lifestyle enraged conservative Egyptians and members of the Muslim Brotherhood, who responded with intentional efforts to destabilize the kingdom. Because of their militant actions, the Egyptian government banned the Muslim Brotherhood, forcing them to go underground.

United They Stand

Meanwhile, as World War II erupted in Europe, the Allies attempted to gain support from the newly established Arab nations by promoting the idea of a unified and prosperous Arab world. Although Egypt and other Arab states remained neutral during the war, the Allies managed to plant the seeds of pan-Arabism. On March 22, 1945, these seeds bore fruit, as Egypt, Iraq, Lebanon, North Yemen, Saudi Arabia, Transjordan, and Arab representatives from Palestine formed the League of Arab States (or the Arab League).

ALERT

Today, the Muslim Brotherhood movement (*al-Ikwan al-Muslimin* in Arabic) has members in more than seventy countries around the globe and holds eighty-eight seats in the Egyptian parliament after making major gains in the 2005 legislation election. The organization desires to see individual Muslims develop their faith, practice, and community, but it also states one of its primary goals as "mastering the world with Islam."

With Cairo established as the Arab League's headquarters, the Arab member states turned their attention to the region of Palestine. Because Jewish immigrants to Palestine were preparing to establish a Zionist state, Arab nations looked for ways to prevent the birth of what they viewed as a European colony. In response, King Farouk committed Egyptian troops and weaponry to a massive Arab coalition against the emerging Jewish nation. Viewing the Zionist state as an insult to the Arab people and Islam, irregulars from the Muslim Brotherhood joined the war as well.

The Arab resistance of 1948 was soundly defeated, and Israel was able to maintain the Jewish state. Nevertheless, the Arab world continued to reject the new nation as a Crusader-type colony. While most Arabs resented Western governments for meddling in their domestic affairs, they vehemently opposed the Jewish state as an unmistakable arm of Western imperialism.

Nationalism and Revolution

Blaming King Farouk for their poor training and shoddy equipment, Egyptian soldiers turned their anger toward the government. One of these dissatisfied soldiers, Gamal Abdel Nasser, organized a revolutionary movement within the Egyptian Army. Known as the Free Officers' Movement, their ultimate goal was the removal of Farouk and his government. For the Free Officers, total independence from European powers was the only way Egypt could revive its former glory.

Assassination

With the Free Officers growing in strength, the illegal Muslim Brotherhood also expanded as an underground religious and political movement. Since Egypt's defeat in the '48 War with Israel, members of the Muslim Brotherhood had turned their power against the Egyptian government, organizing demonstrations, riots, and acts of terror. In response to the group's violent acts, King Farouk is said to have ordered the death of its leader, Hassan al-Banna.

Whether or not the king ordered it, Banna was assassinated on February 12, 1949, giving him the title *al-Shaheed*, meaning "the martyr." Despite the death of their supreme leader, the Muslim Brotherhood continued their efforts to overthrow Farouk and establish an Islamic state in Egypt. At the same time, the Free Officers sought to inspire their own brand of revolution, based on secular nationalism.

The Officers' Uprising

On July 22, 1952, Gamal Abdel Nasser and several other high-ranking Free Officers gathered for a late-night meeting at El-Fishawi's, Cairo's oldest and most enchanting coffeehouse. With the sweet smell of smoldering apple tobacco emanating from Middle Eastern water pipes (*nargilas* or *shishas*) and the rich flavor of thick Arabic coffee titillating each man's palate, Nasser and his companions prepared for one of Egypt's most significant days. Believing King Farouk was ready to move against them, the Free Officers' leadership decided a pre-emptive strike was their only option.

FACT

> Traditional coffee and tea houses are an integral part of Middle Eastern society. From Istanbul to Casablanca, water pipes bubble and delicious black teas and coffees simmer, as men enjoy watching soccer contests, playing board games, and talking politics. Of Egypt's numerous coffee shops, El-Fishawi's is the oldest, with a continuous flow of smoke and coffee since 1773.

The following morning the Free Officers staged a coup d'état. After three days, King Farouk was deposed and on his way to a life of exile in Italy. The Free Officers then formed the Revolutionary Command Council (RCC) as the governing body for the new republic. With a desire to see their impoverished nation revitalized and freed from all British influence, the RCC implemented strict reforms based on secular and nationalistic ideals. Among the many changes was the requirement that all political parties dissolve, including the once-powerful Wafd Party.

Nasser's Pan-Arabism

By 1954, Gamal Abdel Nasser was the leader of an independent Arab Republic of Egypt. Over the following years, Nasser rallied Egyptians under the banner of Arab nationalism. In keeping with his original goals, Nasser wanted to remove Britain's influence over his nation, while providing prosperity to his impoverished citizens. As a result, the Egyptian president looked to the British-controlled Suez Canal, which ran directly through his country.

Although Europeans had paid for the canal's construction and King Farouk had agreed to British administration of this lucrative waterway, Nasser and many other Egyptians saw the British as exploiters. In addition, the Egyptian president recognized the canal as an important source of revenue, which could fund his planned massive Aswan High Dam project.

As a logical extension of his nationalistic goals, Nasser declared the Suez Canal Zone part of Egypt and ordered all non-Egyptians out of the area. Britain and France responded by joining forces with Israel and attacking Egypt. This conflict, known as the '56 War (or Sinai Campaign), drove Arabs further away from the West (and toward the Soviets); it also popularized Nasser as the Arab world's hero against Crusader-type, Zionist aggression.

Though most Arabs respected Nasser for his defiance and nationalism, conservative members of the Muslim Brotherhood were infuriated by the secular nature of the new republic. They thought the revolution should have been followed by an Islamic state, governed by Islamic law. Instead, Nasser and the RCC established a secular government—and were dealing with the atheist Soviets. Because of this, members of the Muslim Brotherhood attempted to kill Nasser. In response, Nasser's regime put down the rebellion. The five perpetrators were executed, and more than 4,000 Muslim Brotherhood members were arrested, causing thousands of others to flee to other Arab states.

United Arab States

With the Arab League headquartered on Egyptian soil, Nasser used the organization as a staging ground for his pan-Arab agendas. In 1958, Nasser realized part of his dream, as Syria agreed to come under his leadership in a pan-Arab state known as the United Arab Republic (UAR). Nasser then looked to Yemen as a possible partner state. Before he could go any further, a coup in Syria caused the breakup of the UAR in 1961.

The following year, civil war erupted in the Arabian kingdom of North Yemen. In the spirit of Nasser's independent Arab republic, a group of Yemeni separatists attempted to wrest power from the royal family of a Muslim cleric named Imam Muhammad al-Badr. In what was originally a civil war, Egypt and the Soviet Union soon came to the aid of their like-minded republican fighters, while the kingdoms of Saudi Arabia, Iran, and Jordan supported the royal family of Imam al-Badr.

Despite the UAR's failure, Nasser continued to use the term "United Arab Republic" for the remainder of his presidency. While Egypt and Syria ceased to be a unified state, the idea of pan-Arab strength continued to unify Arabic-speaking nations. Throughout the 1950s and 1960s, nearly every Arab nation joined the Arab League. Though the assembly was plagued with division, member states proudly declared their unity. With Nasser guiding a body of independent Arab nations, a sense of dignity was restored in the region, which had withered during centuries of non-Arab imperialism and Western colonization.

In addition to being an Arab state, Egypt recognized itself as an African nation. In 1963, the concept of pan-Africanism inspired Egypt and thirty-one other states to form the Organization for African Unity (OAU). Similar to the Arab League, the OAU sought to unify the continent under a banner of African pride. Emerging from years of Western colonization, the OAU hoped to bring stability to nations attempting to agree upon borders and form their own governments. However, the OAU disbanded in 2002, to be replaced by the African Union (AU), which consists of fifty-three African states.

ALERT

As part of the Arab world and of Africa, the countries of Egypt, Libya, Tunisia, Algeria, Morocco, and Mauritania enjoy a unique mix of Afro-Arabic culture and history. This distinct character empowered Nasser and other North African leaders to rally their citizens behind the concepts of Arab and African nationalistic pride.

War and Withering

By 1967, Egypt was receiving substantial military aid from the U.S.S.R., but the war in Yemen had drained the nation, costing many Egyptian lives and resources. In addition, Egyptian support of the anti-royalists in Yemen moved Saudi Arabia to cut off all financial aid to Nasser's regime. After the Soviets sent Egypt bad intelligence regarding Israeli troop movements in 1967, the Egyptian government ordered all U.N. peacekeepers to evacuate its border with Israel, closed the Red Sea to all Israeli ships, moved several divisions toward the Israeli border, and engaged in the "Six-Day War." Israel defeated the Egyptian forces and took all of Egypt's Sinai Peninsula.

Because of the massive losses sustained in the war with Israel, Nasser was forced to pull his troops from Yemen as well. After this great humiliation, the

Egyptian leader announced his resignation. But, Egypt's people encouraged him to remain as their president. He agreed. However, he never held the same regional influence that he had enjoyed through the late 1950s and early 1960s. Under the stresses of his failing nation, Nasser suffered a fatal heart attack on September 28, 1970, ending more than twenty years of inspiration and action.

Sadat's Peace

Known as a key leader in the 1956 Revolution and as Egypt's vice-president, Anwar al-Sadat assumed the presidency following Nasser's death. Influenced greatly by the social reforms and anti-colonialist nature of Turkey's founder, Mustafa Kemal Atatürk, Sadat sought to lead Egypt into an age of strict nationalism and prosperity.

Hoping to usher in a new era of independence and economic might, Sadat dedicated Nasser's brainchild, the Aswan High Dam, in 1970. After ten years of construction, this miracle of engineering produced a structure two miles long and more than 360 feet tall. Today, the dam retains part of the Nile in Lake Nasser, a 500-mile-long lake that stretches from southern Egypt to northern Sudan. The project increased the amount of arable land in Egypt by 30 percent and doubled its production of electricity.

The Quest for Honor

Despite the improvements offered by the Aswan project, most Egyptians continued to deal with increasing poverty and sickness and the strains of rapid urbanization. While Egypt continued to boast the Arab world's most powerful military, it was also licking its wounds from the 1967 war, as well as the humiliation caused by its withdrawal from the civil war in Yemen. In an effort to restore Egyptian pride and sovereignty, Sadat decided to reclaim the Sinai Peninsula by force.

The 1973 conflict, known to Egyptians as the 6th of October War and to the Israelis as the Yom Kippur War, was a joint effort between Syria and Egypt aimed at reclaiming lands occupied by Israel in 1967. Viewed by most Egyptians as a major victory, the '73 War united Egyptians in a revived spirit of nationalism. Although they failed to reclaim their lands, Egypt and Syria awakened Israelis to the real threat of Arab invasion. As a result, the Israeli government began to soften its grip on the Sinai.

By 1977, that sparkle was gone, and most Egyptians were again frustrated by their country's apparent weakness, Israel's defiance, and the continued deterioration of their urban living conditions. Viewing peace with Israel and the West as a necessary move toward prosperity, Sadat went against popular opinion and the political mainstream and announced his willingness to visit Israel for peace. After receiving a formal invitation, Sadat became the first leader of an Arab nation to visit there.

Peacemaker and Pariah

For many Egyptians and people throughout the Muslim World, Sadat's trip was not a positive step toward peace; they viewed it as an irresponsible action that gave credibility to the illegitimate Jewish state. Despite great opposition in the Middle East and elsewhere, U.S. President Jimmy Carter saw Sadat's action as a brave step toward peace. Inspired by Sadat's gesture, President Carter organized the Camp David peace summit of 1978. From the Camp David talks, Israel agreed to return the Sinai Peninsula to Egypt, and Sadat and Israeli Prime Minister Menachem Begin signed a historic peace treaty.

Although Sadat and Begin shared the 1978 Nobel Peace Prize for their efforts, most people in the Arab and Muslim worlds viewed Sadat as a traitor. Signing the treaty returned the Sinai to Egypt and assured the nation of substantial aid from the United States. But, in the minds of most Middle Eastern people, it ignored the plight of nearly 3 million Palestinians. Not only that, it ensured that the Arab world's most powerful nation would not be involved in resisting the Zionists.

In response to Sadat's deal, the Arab League suspended Egypt from membership and moved the organization's headquarters from Cairo to Tunis, Tunisia. In the face of this shame, Egyptians violently protested their leader's actions, with some even calling for his death.

Assassination

Despite Sadat's efforts to pacify disgruntled citizens, many remained opposed to their government's domestic efforts and its attitude toward the Palestinian crisis. Capitalizing on popular frustration, extremist groups rallied the masses in large-scale protests. Sadat answered this unrest with overwhelming force, which was met with condemnation from the international community. Incensed by their government's perceived acts of injustice and lack of piety, Islamic extremists decided to forcefully remove Sadat.

On October 6, 1981, assassins opened fire on the Egyptian president at a ceremony commemorating the 1973 war with Israel. Ironically, Sadat spent his last moments battling for life because of his struggle for peace, while this peacemaker's mortal defeat arrived during a celebration of his most successful war. With Sadat's passing, Vice President Hosni Mubarak became president of an unstable nation threatened by militants calling for Islamic revolution and moderates demanding equity and reform.

Radicals Reborn

Throughout the 1980s and 1990s, a new round of assassinations, car bombings, and other attacks threatened the secular nature of the state. As the masterminds of Sadat's assassination, the Egyptian Islamic Jihad group worked alongside another cadre of militants called *Jamaat al-Islamiyya* (meaning "the Islamic Group"). With separate leadership and distinct modes of operation, both movements desired to overthrow Egypt's secular government and replace it with a "pure" Islamic regime. While these Egyptian extremists were made up almost entirely of Sunnis, they were inspired by Iran's Shi'ite revolutionaries, who had ousted the shah and his secular government in 1979 and established an Islamic state.

Both the Egyptian Islamic Jihad group and Jamaat al-Islamiyya were the result of a rift between the members of the Muslim Brotherhood who wanted to continue their armed resistance and the brotherhood's leadership, which agreed to work peacefully within the Egyptian political system. Under the leadership of a medical doctor named Ayman al-Zawahiri, the Egyptian Islamic Jihad group waged war on the state by targeting high-level Egyptian officials and other political interests. Guided by a blind cleric named Sheikh Omar Abdel Rahman, Jamaat al-Islamiyya staged attacks on anyone and everyone, including tourists, hoping to destabilize the economy and, in turn, the government of Egypt.

Since 1993, the Egyptian Islamic Jihad group has not carried out attacks on Egyptian soil. Instead, it has joined forces with al-Qaeda and other groups to wage a global war against nations they view as a threat to Islam. While the Egyptian Islamic Jihad group has turned its attention away from Egypt,

Jamaat al-Islamiyya has continued its struggle in North Africa, as well as other parts of the world. In 1993, members of the organization bombed New York's World Trade Center, while in 1997 they carried out several attacks in Egypt, including the massacre of fifty-eight tourists near the city of Luxor.

FACT

Egyptian Islamic Jihad leader Ayman al-Zawahiri partnered with Osama bin Laden throughout the 1990s and served as al-Qaeda's number-two man, while Jamaat al-Islamiyya leader Sheikh Omar Abdel Rahman is serving a life sentence in the United States for his involvement in the 1993 attack on New York's World Trade Center. Even though U.S. Navy Seals killed bin Laden on May 2, 2011, in a surprise raid on his compound in Abbottabad, Pakistan, after a nearly ten-year search, al-Zawahiri remained in the number two position until a permanent leader was named. Bin Laden was buried at sea within twenty-four hours of his death by U.S. Navy personnel.

As planned, these attacks dissuaded travelers from visiting Egypt, bringing the nation's vital tourist industry to a standstill. (Tourism accounts for approximately 11 percent of Egypt's gross domestic product and employs about 12.6 percent of the country's work force.) While extremists wanted to undermine the secular government by crippling its economy, their plan backfired. With hundreds of thousands out of work, Egyptians didn't turn their anger toward the government; instead, they blamed the militants. Due to this outcry, Jamaat al-Islamiyya signed a cease-fire with the Egyptian government in 1999. Since this agreement, they have not carried out major attacks within Egypt, though Jamaat al-Islamiyya remained a threat to President Mubarak, who resigned in 2011, and others around the world.

President Mubarak

Under the circumstances of Hosni Mubarak's rise to the presidency, his number-one goal was to see Islamic militancy removed from Egypt. Mubarak was shot in the hand during the October 6 assassination, making him a victim of Sadat's killers as well. Although he vowed to continue

Sadat's policies toward the West and Israel, Mubarak knew he would have to make drastic changes if he was going to survive.

After an initial crackdown on members of Egypt's Islamic Jihad—the organization responsible for the assassination of Sadat—Mubarak looked for ways to stop Islamic extremism at the root. By instituting economic reforms, the new president hoped to remedy the hopelessness that turned many of Egypt's unemployed and impoverished toward the promises of radical Islamic groups. In addition, he attempted to remove certain policies that excluded religiously based political groups from the Egyptian government. By allowing the Muslim Brotherhood to hold seats in the parliament, Mubarak hoped to give controlled representation to frustrated Muslims who had been rallying outside the political arena.

Finally, Mubarak made it his mission to improve relations with the rest of the Arab world, which had virtually excommunicated the nation because of Sadat's treaty with Israel. Throughout the 1980s, various Arab states renewed diplomatic ties with Egypt. Finally, in 1989, Mubarak's state was readmitted into the Arab League. With Egypt again part of the fold, the League of Arab States moved its headquarters from Tunis back to its birthplace, Cairo.

Conflict Inside and Out

The following year, Egypt and eleven other Arab states voiced their condemnation of Iraq's invasion of Kuwait. Over the next year, President Mubarak responded by sending more than 38,000 Egyptian troops to support U.S.-led Operations Desert Shield and Desert Storm. Fighting alongside American, British, Saudi Arabian, Syrian, and other forces, Egyptian troops aided in pushing Iraq from Kuwait.

Despite his efforts to improve Egypt's standard of living, rejuvenate ties with the Arab world, and liberate the fellow Arab Muslim nation of Kuwait, Mubarak was repeatedly targeted by radical Islamists who viewed his secular laws, ties to the West, and friendship with Israel as abominations. Of the many plots to assassinate the president, in 1995 Egyptian gunmen almost succeeded in shooting Mubarak as he visited Ethiopia's capital city for a meeting of the OAU.

In response to repeated threats and attacks, the Egyptian government again cracked down on Islamic organizations believed to be involved in militant actions. Walking a fine line, the Egyptian president tried to stabilize his country by offering more freedoms to opposition groups while still holding extremist organizations accountable for their deeds. This led some critics to feel Mubarak was too soft on terrorism and others to believe he was a ruthless anti-Islamic dictator.

ESSENTIAL

Each year, about one-third of all U.S. foreign aid is sent to Egypt and Israel, with about $1.5 billion going to Egypt and $3.1 billion to Israel. The amounts going to Egypt have been declining steadily since 2002. By comparison, just over $1 billion is distributed among all the nations of sub-Saharan Africa.

Another sore spot for many Egyptians is their government's friendly relationship with Israel. In their estimation, partnership with Israel sends a message to the Palestinian people and the rest of the Arab world that Egypt condones the holding of more than 3 million Arabs under occupation. On the other hand, most Egyptians are also frustrated by their nation's poverty and huge unemployment rate, which would only worsen if the United States were to suspend the foreign aid it gives Egypt each year in return for Egypt's peaceful relations with Israel.

Colossal Constructs

By nationalizing the Suez Canal and implementing the gargantuan Aswan High Dam project, Nasser attempted to bring self-sufficiency and prosperity to his people. With the completion of the high dam, Sadat realized Nasser's dream, but even this feat was not enough to move Egypt out of its financial funk. By improving relations with the West and making peace with Israel, Sadat hoped to move Egypt into the elite circle of developed nations. But, even after the billions of dollars in aid the country has received, its average citizen remains below the poverty level.

After more than twenty years at the helm, Mubarak benefited from his predecessors' accomplishments, but he also had to deal with their failures. Revenues from the Suez Canal, improved irrigation and energy production from the Aswan High Dam, and substantial foreign aid have helped Egypt's economy, but the resulting political problems, ecological devastation, and domestic unrest have arguably done more harm than good to the nation as a whole. In the face of uncertain times, the Egyptian government looks continually for new ways to deal with its extreme poverty, exponential growth of unemployment, exploding population, and expanding extremist groups.

In the tradition of Nasser's and Sadat's megaprojects, Mubarak began his own monumental plan, the Toshka Project. His undertaking was meant to alleviate Egypt's population crunch, unemployment rate, and water problems by creating a new Nile River valley. In 1997, a huge pumping station was built, which is now moving water northwest from Lake Nasser to the Toshka depression, where it has formed massive desert lakes. From these lakes, a network of canals has been built, moving the "New Nile" farther to the north and west.

At its projected completion date in 2017, a second Nile River will flow through Egypt's western desert all the way to the Mediterranean Sea. By doubling Egypt's arable and inhabitable land, proponents believe millions will move from the crowded and desperate conditions of Cairo to the open spaces and opportunity of new western cities. In addition, advocates argue that improved living conditions will eliminate one of the factors that drive many moderate Muslims to extremism. Whether or not the Toshka Project will solve Egypt's social problems, it will be a historic day if the waters of the Nile find another path to the Mediterranean.

Until the project is completed in 2017, Egyptian leadership will need to keep their nation from slipping deeper into poverty and extremism. They will have to do it without Mubarak, though. He resigned as president in February 2011 in the face of Egyptian protests.

There are no simple answers or quick fixes for this nation. The Toshka Project is a bold new plan that will take decades to complete, but it could be the type of monumental undertaking that will bring substantial changes to Egypt's economy and quality of life. If the heart of the Arab world is made healthy, it will naturally pump its life to the rest of the body.

CHAPTER 14

Saudi Arabia—
Crossroads of Islam

Since Islam's birth, the cities of Mecca and Medina have attracted prayers and pilgrims from around the globe. Saudi Arabia's oil reserves have also drawn businessmen from all corners of the earth. Since the early 1900s, pious puritans and secular separatists throughout the Muslim world have scrutinized Saudi Arabia's affluent royals. Today, this critique has turned to explosive violence. From terror to trade, this chapter unveils the immeasurable importance of this international intersection of faith and finance.

Hashemite Protectors and the House of Saùd

Since the mid-600s, individuals claiming descent from Muhammad's Hashemite tribe have ruled the Hijaz region of western Arabia as the custodians of the holy mosques in Mecca and Medina. After nearly 400 years of Ottoman administration, the people of the Hijaz appeared to be on their way to independence as the Hashemites joined with British forces during World War I. After defeating the Ottomans, the British rewarded their Arabian allies by recognizing the independent Hashemite Kingdom of the Hijaz.

Meanwhile, on the eastern side of the Arabian Peninsula, Abdul Aziz ibn Abdar-Rahman (better known as *Ibn Saùd*—meaning "son of Saùd") ruled the kingdom of Najd, a realm created by his forefathers in the early 1800s. From their capital city, Riyadh, the Saùdi family gained control of most of Arabia through the 1920s, leaving the Hashemite Kingdom of the Hijaz as the only thing standing between them and regional domination.

In 1926, the Saùdis conquered the Hijaz, ending more than 1,300 years of Hashemite rule. Although their administration of Islam's holy cities was terminated, two Hashemite princes were each named king in the newly established nations of Iraq and Transjordan (later Jordan). Ruling nearly all of the Arabian Peninsula, Ibn Saùd became King of Najd (East Arabia) and the Hijaz (West Arabia). In 1932, the Saùdi king renamed his territory the Kingdom of Saudi Arabia, establishing his family and their unique interpretation of Islam in the heart of the Muslim world.

What's a Wahhabi?

If you've ever heard the term "Wahhabi," you might be scratching your head. Is it another religion, maybe an ethnic group, or even a cult? "Wahhabi" refers to a Muslim from the Sunni branch of Islam who has chosen to follow the conservative teachings and interpretations of an eighteenth-century theologian and teacher named Muhammad ibn Abd al-Wahhab.

The Beginnings

As a Sunni Muslim raised in Arabia, al-Wahhab began his puritanical quest in Mesopotamia, where he confronted the region's mystical Sufi

Muslims. After returning to Arabia, he turned his attention toward popular beliefs and practices in his homeland, which he saw as "un-Islamic."

Inspired by al-Wahhab's reforms, the Saùdi family aligned itself with his movement and re-established "pure" Islam in Arabia. With a policy of expansionism, the Saùdis spread al-Wahhab's theology throughout the region. Today, Islam is the state religion in Saudi Arabia, and Wahhabism is the kingdom's official denomination. Although other schools of thought are tolerated, conversion from Wahhabism to another stream of Islam is viewed as a crime against the state.

Sometimes viewed as an Islamic equivalent to Martin Luther's Protestant Reformation, al-Wahhab's reforms were also a reaction to perceived corruption in the religious establishment. Just as Luther hoped to rid Catholicism of things he deemed unbiblical, al-Wahhab sought to purify Islam of beliefs and practices he viewed as un-Qur'anic. In his sermons, al-Wahhab forbade such things as gravestones (because they could lead to idolatry), minarets (as they were not believed to be used at the time of Muhammad), and smoking (due to the intoxicating effects of tobacco). In addition to his passionate sermons, al-Wahhab wrote the *Book of Unity*, a text his followers continue to use in their quest for the unaltered Islam of Muhammad's day.

ESSENTIAL

"Wahhabism" is not synonymous with "terrorism." Although Wahhabis tend to be conservative in their religious views, most are not looking for holy war. While some believe Islamic law should be implemented throughout the world, even these apparent fanatics usually seek their dream through nonviolent proselytizing. Nevertheless, the passion and activism created by a few Wahhabi clerics has moved some followers to take up arms against any who might stand in the way of their plans.

Unitarian Uniformity

Calling themselves the *Muwahhidun*, or "unitarians," Wahhabis desire to see unity in issues of faith and conformity in areas of practice. In their view, outward appearances and expressions are directly connected to one's inward state. In other words, clothing styles, mannerisms, and specific actions prove whether or not one is a "true" Muslim.

One striking example of Wahhabism's outward influence on Saudi society is the widespread uniformity of men and women's apparel. In other parts of the Middle East, you will find a mix of traditional and modern clothing styles. You will also discover great variety among those who sport time-honored robes, headdresses, and veils. But in Wahhabist Saudi Arabia, nearly everyone dresses the same.

For women, a long black head covering (concealing all but the eyes) flows over a loose-fitting black outer garment that covers the entire body. This ensemble is usually accompanied by black gloves and sunglasses, covering any remaining skin. For men, a red-and-white checkered headdress (sometimes exchanged for an all-white head covering) is neatly creased at the front and held in place by two black camel-hair rings.

With his face exposed, the average Saudi man keeps the hair on his head short but sports some type of facial hair, ranging from a long beard to a neatly trimmed mustache. From the neck down, what appears to be a tailored white cotton shirt flows down to the ankles and is accented by leather sandals or shoes.

FACT

While outsiders may feel this uniformity is oppressive or strange, most Saudis don't consider their country's monolithic fashions unusual. Most are not consciously trying to dress the same. In fact, most don't ask why they wear what they do; it is simply the way to dress as a Saudi citizen. These Saudi uniforms are born out of a much bigger cultural construct, which views conformity as righteousness and contrast as rebellion.

In order to maintain religious order, Saudi society is monitored by a type of morality police known as the *muttawa*. If a man is not prostrated during one of the five daily prayer times, or a woman is not properly covered, the morality police are there to enforce shari'a through methods ranging from reminders to arrests. In addition to their policing efforts, the muttawa are involved in missionary activities inside Saudi Arabia and around the world.

In their understanding, the words of the Qur'an are not suggestions or subjects of debate but the only acceptable way to live.

Youth in Saudi Arabia

As you read earlier, most Saudis are at least nominally Wahhabis, but not all are actively pursuing this "pure" Islam and its stringent rules. For idealistic Saudi youth and those able to evaluate religion on an academic level, Wahhabism is extremely attractive. In some minds, literal interpretation and active implementation of God's laws is the only acceptable way to exist as a Muslim. For these individuals, anything less than total devotion and submission to the dictates of Islamic texts would be hypocrisy.

ESSENTIAL

With an estimated 20 million Muslims adhering to Wahhabi ideologies, this movement accounts for less than 2 percent of the world's 1.6 billion Muslims.

Most Wahhabis believe they are following not a certain brand of Islam but the only brand of Islam. In addition, many Wahhabis see Islam not as one of many equally valid religions but as God's only true path. As a result, serious Wahhabis make a concerted effort to spread their message through personal purity and missionary endeavors, known as *dawah*. In their estimation, all humans are Muslims at birth, but some are pulled away from Islam as they are raised in non-Muslim societies. As evidence of this, when a non-Muslim accepts Islam, this person is not called a convert, but a "revert."

God's Black Gold

Although the Saùdis managed to establish themselves as the leaders of modern Arabia's first independent kingdom, most of the region's inhabited areas remained loyal to local tribal chiefs, just as they had been in Muhammad's day and before. In addition, the relatively poor nation was void of any real infrastructure or modern conveniences, much the same as it had been for thousands of years. Other than propagating Wahhabi ideologies, the Saùdi regime didn't really change the nature of this ancient land—until the mid-twentieth century.

Only six years after establishing the Kingdom of Saudi Arabia, the royal family received what many viewed as a gift from God. In 1938, oil was discovered along Arabia's eastern coast, beginning a new age of petroleum power and prosperity. With the discovery of massive oil reserves, four U.S. companies came together to form the Arabian-American Oil Company (Aramco) in Saudi Arabia. As revenues flowed to Aramco, the Saùdis and their American friends realized huge profits. From this influx of Western funds and friends, the royal family began a program of modernization in which paved roadways, bridges, and sanitation systems were introduced. Also, the Saùdi royal government decided to cultivate its new Western business relationships into new political alliances.

The first test of its partnership came at the outset of World War II. While the Allies were trying to muster support in the Middle East, Egypt and other Arab nations chose to remain neutral. In a bold move, the Saudis joined with the United States and Great Britain, declaring war on Germany and Japan and allowing the United States to build an air base on their soil. In addition, Saudi Arabia was among the fifty-one nations that came together to establish the United Nations on October 24, 1945.

FACT

Throughout the early 1950s, King Ibn Saùd personally received more than $2 million per week from oil revenues.

Worldwide Wahhabism

In 1953, the Saùdi throne was passed to Ibn Saùd's son Saùd. As the protectors of Islam's holiest cities and one-fourth of the world's petroleum, the Saùdi family was in a unique situation. They could use their astronomical wealth to continue modernization projects, which in turn solidified their popularity in the kingdom, but they were also in a position to extend their influence beyond Arabia. Viewing their fortune as a direct result of their adherence to God's genuine laws, the Saùdis looked to continue their obedience by using billions of dollars to establish "true" Islam throughout the Middle East and the world.

Within two years of becoming king, Saùd agreed to send millions of dollars to Nasser's flowering Egyptian nation. In turn, the leaders signed a mutual defense pact. The Saudis also promised large loans to Syria and other Arab states. Because of their agreement with Cairo, the Saudis severed all ties with Britain and France after they joined Israel in the 1956 attack on Egypt. With Britain and France cut off from Saudi oil, the United States remained the major purchaser of Saudi Arabian petroleum.

For the past thirty years, Saudi Arabia has given 4 percent of its gross national product to development projects in over seventy predominantly Muslim nations.

Fractured Fraternities

In the early 1960s, when civil war erupted in Arabia's southwestern kingdom of Yemen, the Saudi and Egyptian governments found themselves at odds. Whereas the Saùdi royals sympathized with the family of Islamic clerics who had ruled the area for almost half a century, the Egyptian republic supported the revolutionary Yemeni nationalists. Because of this conflict, the Saudi-Egyptian agreement was scrapped, and King Saùd cut off all financial aid to Nasser's nation. In response, the Egyptian air force bombed several Saudi towns, causing the Saudis to mobilize for possible war with this North African neighbor. In the end, a regional war was averted, but Yemen's civil struggles continued into the 1970s.

In 1964, Saùd's brother, Prince Faisal, assumed the title of king. Under Faisal's authority, Saudi Arabia continued to lead the world in oil production and Wahhabist propagation. In 1967, as Egypt, Jordan, and Syria entered the infamous Six-Day War with Israel, Saudi Arabia sent 20,000 troops to Jordan as reinforcements. Because the United States backed the Israelis, King Faisal stopped all oil exports to America. In addition, Saudi clerics called for a pan-Islamic jihad against the "Zionist aggressors."

After the disgrace of '67, Saudi Arabia gave only limited support to the Syrian- and Egyptian-led Yom Kippur/6th of October War in 1973, though they did deny oil to all countries that supported Israel. Nevertheless, King Faisal was more concerned with his own kingdom than the plight of the Palestinians or the political problems of other Arab nations.

ESSENTIAL

In 1960, the Organization of Petroleum Exporting Countries (OPEC) was formed by the world's largest oil-producing nations. Today, Saudi Arabia is one of the organization's most influential member states.

During the late 1960s and early 1970s, Arabia's oil-rich coastal states—Bahrain, Qatar, the UAR, Oman, and Yemen—received complete independence from Great Britain. With their new autonomy, these nations gained full control of their natural resources. Inspired by these states, King Faisal fully secured his oil fields by taking control of Aramco (later to be known as Saudi Aramco). Just months later, King Faisal was assassinated, leading some conspiracy theorists to believe his killer was sponsored by the United States as a response to the Saùdi monarch's takeover of Aramco.

Bin Laden's Fortune

After Faisal's death, Prince Khalid inherited the Saùdi throne. With untold fortunes at his fingertips and most of Aramco's shares in the Saùdi family's hands, King Khalid began a five-year development plan. The equivalent of $150 billion (eventually $300 billion) was allocated to improving infrastructure, building petroleum and natural gas plants, and producing steel and cement for these massive projects.

In the late 1960s, an immigrant from Yemen named Muhammad impressed the royal family with his exceptional building skills and honorable business practices. As a result, King Faisal issued a decree naming this man's family-run construction company as the kingdom's official builders. Because of this promise, the vast majority of King Khalid's monumental modernization plans were carried out by Muhammad bin Laden and his large family.

As an immigrant to Saudi Arabia, Muhammad bin Laden worked as a laborer from the 1930s on, making just enough money to feed his growing family. After landing this royal remodeling job in the 1970s, the bin Ladens were transformed into one of the most powerful families in the kingdom. As founder of the nation's largest construction company, worth more than $5 billion, Muhammad used his financial blessings to support a large family that included many wives and about fifty children. From one of his Syrian wives, in 1957 Muhammad bin Laden received his seventeenth son, whom he named Osama.

The Making of a Mastermind

As part of the bin Laden family business, Osama worked on many large projects, including the renovation of Islam's most sacred mosques in Mecca and Medina. While working on these holy places, Osama drew closer to his Islamic upbringing. In addition, Osama was influenced by the flow of Muslim pilgrims who visited his country each year from around the world. Inspired by the perspectives of those who were putting their lives on the line for Islam, Osama developed new relationships and ideologies that would shape the rest of his life.

ALERT

Bin Laden wasn't always a "bad guy"! The United States gave about $3 billion to Afghani fighters during their decade-long war with the Soviet occupiers. Osama contributed to the same effort with financial and logistical support.

Osama's religious views moved to a new phase as he encountered the teachings of a professor named Sheikh Àbdullah Azzam. After absorbing Azzam's perspectives on the interconnectedness of politics and religion, bin Laden was inspired to take militant political action for the sake of Islam. Through his journey of faith, Osama came to a place where he felt compelled to fight those he deemed "enemies of Islam."

In 1982, Osama put his convictions to the test and traveled to the mountainous battlefields of Afghanistan, where he believed God would ensure victory over the powerful Soviet invaders. While bin Laden was actively involved in fighting the Russian infidels and financing the Afghan freedom fighters, his organizational efforts were by far the most memorable and effective contributions to the war. With many Arabs coming to the aid of their Central Asian coreligionists, Osama established a guesthouse where newcomers could stay until they were connected to a training facility or placed with a group of mujahedin ("holy warriors" in Arabic). This guesthouse came to be known as "The Base," *al-Qaeda* in Arabic, a name that would later be attached to Osama's global organizational efforts.

With Osama at war in Afghanistan, the bin Ladens' construction company continued to thrive. In 1982, King Khalid died. The new king, Fahd, continued the traditional Saùdi line of modernizing public works while attempting to preserve the conservative Islamic character of the Wahhabi kingdom. Nevertheless, radical elements questioned the king's piety and his family's friendship with the West. In order to offset these dissenting voices, in 1986, Fahd added the Islamic title "Custodian of the Two Holy Mosques" to his noble name.

FACT

Saudis in space? Yes! On June 24, 1985, Sultan ibn Salam ibn Abdul Aziz al Saùd traveled aboard NASA's shuttle *Discovery*, making him the first Saudi Arabian citizen in space.

Return to Saudi Arabia

When the Soviet Union finally withdrew from Afghanistan in 1989, Osama bin Laden returned to Saudi Arabia as a war hero. He and many other Arab mujahedin had succeeded in repelling an invading superpower from a needy Muslim nation. Inspired by their victory, Osama organized veterans of the Soviet-Afghan War to continue their struggle against non-Muslim "oppressors" in Bosnia, Chechnya, Somalia, and the Philippines.

Fresh from the euphoria of jihad, Osama was angered by what he saw as a lack of religious enthusiasm coming from the Saùdi leadership. As Iraq invaded Kuwait in 1990, bin Laden saw an opportunity to engage the back-sliding leadership of Iraq with his holy warriors. Believing his men could protect Arabia from Saddam's schemes, bin Laden presented his plans to King Fahd. Instead of accepting Osama's offer, the king embraced President George H. W. Bush's plan, allowing the United States to protect the Islamic Holy Land.

Enraged by the presence of largely non-Muslim American troops on the sacred soil of Saudi Arabia, bin Laden publicly voiced his criticism of the royal family and their relations with the West. Because of his statements, Osama's Saudi citizenship was revoked, and he was forced to leave the king-dom. By 1992, the homeless millionaire found refuge in the East African nation of Sudan. Here he continued to speak out against the Saùdi family and the 5,000-plus American military personnel remaining in the kingdom. In addition, bin Laden used his new position in Africa to partner with Egypt's Islamic Jihad group and other Islamist radicals in the area.

The Homeless Man's Horror

Within months of arriving in Sudan, Osama organized attacks on U.S. soldiers stationed in the Arabian nation of Yemen and the East African country of Somalia. By 1994, both the Saudi and American governments were pressuring Sudan to kick bin Laden out of the country. The following year Osama answered these calls by organizing the bombing of a U.S. training facility in the Saudi capital of Riyadh. Following this deadly attack, Sudan asked bin Laden to leave in 1996. Once again homeless, he returned to the country of Afghanistan, which had been embroiled in civil war since he and the Soviets left in 1989.

Protected by the familiar mountains of Central Asia, Osama made his first public declaration of war against the United States, calling all "true" Muslims to kill American "occupation" forces in Arabia. This bold statement was followed in June 1996 by a devastating truck bomb, in which nineteen American airmen were killed in eastern Saudi Arabia. Impressed by bin Lad-en's passion for jihad, Mullah Omar, spiritual leader of Afghanistan's ruling Taliban movement, voiced his support for the war against Western soldiers in Arabia. In addition, Osama's pan-Islamic propaganda encouraged Muslim extremists from around the world to join the fight from his base in the "pure" Islamic State of Afghanistan.

In 1998, Osama made several appearances in the media, broadening his previous declaration of war to include all Americans (including civilians, women, and children). Six months later, simultaneous bombs rocked U.S. embassies in Kenya and Tanzania, leaving 226 dead and many more wounded. The United States responded to these attacks by launching missiles at locations in Sudan and Afghanistan that were believed to be part of bin Laden's global terror network, al-Qaeda.

After targeting Osama bin Laden and his worldwide web of militants, the United States experienced the worst domestic attack in its history on September 11, 2001, when nineteen of Osama's associates flew highjacked commercial airliners into buildings in New York City and Washington, D.C., to kill themselves and thousands of others.

Worldwide War

The aftermath of these catastrophic events revealed 2,998 dead and many injured men, women, and children. In order to punish Osama and his Taliban hosts, the United States led an international coalition into Afghanistan as Operation Enduring Freedom. In this action, coalition forces joined with Afghan separatists to remove the Islamist Taliban regime and their militant al-Qaeda guests. In the ensuing years, bin Laden and many of his closest associates have been killed or captured, the ultraconservative Taliban government has been toppled, and a new representative government has been formed in Afghanistan.

ESSENTIAL

With fifteen of the September 11 hijackers believed to be Saudi citizens, and with other Saudis actively supporting bin Laden's efforts, the royal family has been forced to clear its name, defend its sovereignty, and uphold its religious views. In order to deal with its unsavory reputation as a "breeding ground for terrorists," the Saùdi regime has implemented a global public-relations campaign.

As a pivotal point in American history, September 11 has also changed the way things are done across the globe. From Buenos Aires to Beijing, the world's governments are working to stop Islamic militants before they act.

In addition, the threat of domestic terror has compelled the Saudi administration to spend billions of dollars on training and equipment for its antiterrorist units. As the protector of Islam's most revered cities, the Saùdi family is responsible not only for the safety of sojourners and Saudi citizens but also for the very reputation of Islam. With such great responsibilities, this wealthy Arab nation is criticized from all sides for its actions. Nevertheless, the royal family tries to retain honor, tradition, and stability in the Islamic Holy Land.

All Roads Lead to Mecca

In all of Islamic history, no location has equaled Mecca's prestige. From Muhammad's first supernatural encounter to the Qur'anic sermons given in its ancient streets, this city is inseparably part of Islam. Today, Muslims' prayers from across the globe are physically directed toward Mecca, its Grand Mosque, and the Ka'ba. Looking to the future, most Muslims believe Mecca will play a major role in an Armageddon-type battle and the final Day of Judgment. For conservatives and liberals, Arabs and Malaysians, rich and poor, the city of Mecca holds an eternal place in the heart of every follower of Islam.

While some Saudis use the Qur'an and other Islamic texts to legitimize their militancy and are willing to kill for their faith, the majority abstain from such actions. Though conservative Wahhabi practices and interpretations are popular in Saudi Arabia, there are also other shades of Islam within the kingdom. Worldwide, Islam is understood and observed in as many ways as any other major religion. Despite differences of opinion regarding faith and practice, nearly all Muslims look forward to a common experience—the pilgrimage to Mecca, known in Arabic as the Hajj.

In accordance with the specific directives of Muhammad, Sunnis and Shi'ites, "Twelvers" and Ismailis, literalist Wahhabis and mystical Sufis, conservative clerics and liberal librarians, moderate mailmen and militant mujahedin all travel to Arabia each year to complete the Hajj. While in the Saùdi kingdom, Muslims from around the globe visit the cities of Mecca and Medina to take part in prescribed rituals that date back to at least the seventh century. From the symbolic stoning of Satan, to the seven counterclockwise trips made round the Ka'ba, multitudes of men all dressed in white separate themselves from hordes of women all dressed in black as they re-enact rituals conducted by Muhammad and countless faithful after him.

Each year, about 2 million Muslims hailing from more than seventy countries enter the Saùdi kingdom during the month of pilgrimage to take part in the Hajj. This annual pilgrimage injects the Arab Wahhabi nation with a mosaic of ethnic and theological diversity. Not only that, but this yearly event brings a steady flow of money to the Islamic Holy Land and its Wahhabi custodians. Though every "true" Muslim is called to visit Mecca at least once in his lifetime, some are excused from this duty for physical or financial reasons. Even those who cannot make the sacred trek find their faith intimately connected to this Saudi city.

Facing Modern Changes

Because of growing domestic and international threats, the royal family has dramatically improved its aging military and security forces. Although Saudi Arabia has been purchasing weaponry and aircraft from the United States since the mid-1960s, by the late 1970s they had come to believe that it was necessary to upgrade their defenses considerably.

FACT

Saudi Arabia is the United States' number-one arms client. Since 1990, the Saudis have purchased over $100 billion worth of weaponry from the United States. In 2010 alone, the Saudis and the United States announced the largest U.S. arms deal in history, through which the Saudis purchased eighty-four Boeing F-15 fighter jets and more than 100 attack helicopters.

With about 20 million nationals and approximately 5.5 million non-Saudis living in the kingdom, the Saudi royals have compensated for their small population with big guns. From 1987 to 1997, the Saudis spent $262 billion to overhaul their army, air force, navy, national guard, and various police forces. Securing some of the world's most sophisticated weaponry, training, surveillance equipment, and defense systems, Saudi Arabia is now one of the best-defended nations in the region.

With billions continuing to flow toward modern security, infrastructure, and social services, much of Saudi Arabia's exterior has been transformed. However, on the inside, Saudi society has maintained many medieval practices and traditions. In the area of human rights, the international community has chastised the kingdom repeatedly. From the limitations put on women in the public sphere to the restrictions imposed upon its non-Muslim guests, the conservative laws of this Wahhabi state are far from modern.

Because of these strict regulations, some Saudis long for their society to evolve. One example of this can be seen in the vision of Riyadh's Al Faisaliah Center. The owners of this thirty-story complex opened their shopping mall/hotel/office/convention center with the idea that they would help their city progress beyond restrictive social norms. They had controversial plans to remain open during prayer times and provide an exciting and free environment, but the morality regulators stifled these "rebellious" ideas.

Swarming the mall's "mischievous" halls, the *muttawa* found many ways to suppress this moral mutiny. Ordering women to cover their heads and barring single men from entering the center on weekends, zealous religious enforcers ensured the purity of those inside. Forcing Muslim men to evacuate shops and head to mosques during prayer times, while informing non-Muslims they would need to stop shopping until the prayers were finished, the *muttawa* secured the sacred prayers of the city's citizens.

ESSENTIAL

In the Middle East and the rest of the Muslim world, Saudi Arabia's conservative Islamic laws are not the norm. As one of a few nations to implement Islamic law, the Wahhabi kingdom's ways are viewed by many Muslims as old-fashioned and extremist.

Though this story reveals the extremes of Saudi society, even mainstream Saudis are subject to what many Westerners would call restrictive religious laws. For many Saudis these rules are considered positive in that they uphold traditional Islamic values. To others, however, these constructs are frustrating remnants of a long-lost age, especially for Saudis who get a glimpse of the world outside their country.

The Saudis do not hesitate to send their young people to foreign countries to complete their educations and learn about other cultures. Under the aegis of the King Abdullah Foreign Scholarship Program established in 2005, highly qualified Saudi students attend universities in twenty-one countries to pursue a variety of academic disciplines at the undergraduate and graduate levels. They absorb more than education in the process. They also learn about—and take back to Saudi Arabia with them—Western mores and customs that are at odds with their local religious and cultural practices. The program has been so successful that the number of Saudi students studying at foreign universities continues to grow. In 2010, the program received a five-year extension.

In the 1960s Wahhabi clerics spoke against the evils of radio and television, but nearly fifty years later these apparent vices are employed to deliver Islamic teachings. Though these technologies were eventually embraced, it remains to be seen whether the pressures of postmodernism, women's liberation, and Western pop culture will change basic Wahhabi traditions.

CHAPTER 15

Iraq—British Colony to Ba'thist Beginnings

Since at least 3500 B.C., Mesopotamia has been a center of cultural and religious diversity. For hundreds of years the Ottoman Empire administered this region through three ethnically and religiously distinctive provinces. After World War I, the British combined these provinces into a single nation—Iraq. Apart from brutal dictatorships, Iraq has been the site of ongoing division and unrest. After reading this chapter, you will have a much clearer picture of the complicated nation Saddam Hussein came to rule.

Ousting Ottomans and Housing Hashemites

At the beginning of the twentieth century, the Ottoman Empire had been in control of most of the Arab world for about 400 years. In order to govern its vast Middle Eastern and European territories, Istanbul created administrative areas known as *vilayets*. The region of Mesopotamia consisted of the following territories:

- The northern vilayet of Mosul, inhabited by a majority of Kurdish and non-Arab peoples
- The central vilayet of Baghdad, predominantly populated by Sunni Arabs
- The southern vilayet of Basra, almost entirely made up of Shi'ite Arabs

Although the Arabic word *al-Iraq*—meaning "the riverside slope"—was used as a general term for these river-rich lands, it was never used for a specific Ottoman administrative area or nation-state.

After defeating the Ottomans in World War I, British and French mandate areas replaced centuries-old vilayet boundaries throughout the Middle East. In the region of al-Iraq, the ethnically and religiously distinct vilayets of Mosul, Baghdad, and Basra were merged into a single British-controlled area. While leaders in London debated the nature of their nation-building efforts, some Iraqis began to question the intentions of their powerful European guests.

ESSENTIAL

Born in the Hijaz region of western Arabia on May 20, 1883, Emir Faysal was the son of Sharif Husayn, protector of the sacred cities of Mecca and Medina. After receiving his education in Istanbul, Faysal returned to his family in Ottoman-controlled Arabia. During World War I, the Hashemites aligned themselves with the British (and T. E. Lawrence) as Faysal led the Arab revolt against Ottoman imperialism.

In March 1920, Prince Faysal of the Hashemite-ruled Hijaz (leader of the World War I Arab Revolt) established an Arab government in Damascus. Here, a council of Arab leaders named him king of Syria, while his older brother, Àbdullah, was declared king of Iraq. Inspired by the idea of an independent kingdom, Iraqi nationalists united in revolt but were quickly put down by British troops. Though Iraqi nationalists were defeated, their uprising convinced British leaders to end their direct administration of Iraq.

Only four months later, France expelled Faysal from Damascus, citing his kingly claims as a challenge to their internationally recognized mandate of Syria. With Faysal and the Arab nationalists kicked out of French-controlled Syria, the British decided they could more effectively manage the region by offering Faysal the Iraqi throne. The Hashemite prince accepted this invitation, and on August 23, 1921, he was crowned king.

As part of Faysal's arrangement, the British mandate was to be replaced by a treaty of alliance, in which Great Britain would retain certain privileges within Iraq but would no longer directly control the domestic affairs of the kingdom. The new king formed Iraq's first national government and drafted its first constitution, while Iraqi nationalists moved to form political parties. Unnerved by Iraq's independent actions, London drafted a second Anglo-Iraqi treaty in 1930, which revived many of the controls found under the post–World War I British mandate. Realizing they were not fully independent, Iraqi nationalists united to expel the lingering British colonialists.

Independence with Strings

Known to many Iraqis as the "perplexing predicament," the second Anglo-Iraqi treaty created a situation in which two governments guided the kingdom, one national and one foreign. Although London verbalized its desire to see Iraqi "self-rule," nationals recognized the impossibility of this end, given Britain's continued control of domestic affairs. Voicing their frustration with London's controls, Iraqis took to the streets in protest.

After more than a decade of broken promises and nationalist resistance, the British ostensibly ended their administration of Iraq in 1930. By drafting a new treaty of independence, Great Britain relinquished control of Iraq, with the understanding that the two countries would maintain a close alliance. Britain would remain involved in Iraqi foreign affairs, and British troops would stay at several key airbases within Iraq. After accepting the articles of this new treaty, the independent kingdom of Iraq was admitted to the League of Nations on October 3, 1932.

With their British coreligionists removed from domestic affairs, many Assyrian Christians in northern Iraq feared they would be mistreated by the kingdom's Arab Muslim government. Remembering the genocide carried out by the Ottomans just decades before, Assyrian leaders appealed to the League of Nations, asking for an autonomous region near the city of Mosul (once called Nineveh—capital of the ancient Assyrian Empire). On August 7, 1933, hardliners in the Iraqi administration answered this "rebellious" minority with force, resulting in the death of several hundred Assyrian men, women, and children and the displacement of many others.

ALERT

From 1921 to 2003, political power in Iraq remained in the hands of individuals who were both Arab and Sunni. In a region like Saudi Arabia, where the population is almost entirely Arab and Sunni, this type of leadership would be expected. In Iraq, however, where only 20 percent of the population is both Arab and Sunni, this balance of power is unusual, to say the least.

Just months after the Assyrian uprising/massacre, King Faysal died of a heart attack in Switzerland, making his son Ghazi king of Iraq. With Ghazi at the helm, the Iraqi cabinet developed a massive irrigation project in the south, a lucrative oil pipeline in the north, and a stretch of railway that connected Iraq's railroads to Europe. Despite these concrete improvements, the political situation in the Hashemite kingdom spiraled out of control, leading to a military coup in 1936. Though King Ghazi remained as the figurehead monarch, Iraq came under the direct rule of the army and its pan-Arab agendas.

Kingless Kingdom

Over the next few years, tribal disputes, political power plays, and violent protests plagued the nation as opposition groups gained new strength and military officials used their might to stay in power. In the midst of these turbulent times, King Ghazi was killed in a car crash, leaving his three-year-old son, Faysal II, as king of Iraq. In 1939, with a toddler on the throne, a regent was appointed to oversee the king's duties. In the meantime, internal struggles continued among Iraq's military leaders, who were running the nation.

ESSENTIAL

As the majority in northeastern Iraq, Kurds account for nearly 20 percent of the country's total population. While most Kurds are Sunni Muslims, less than 40 percent of Iraqis consider themselves Sunni.

Europe's Involvement

At the outset of World War II, some Arab leaders felt that an alliance with Germany and the Axis Powers would be better for the Arab world than its existing agreement with Britain and France, which continued to occupy the Arab lands of Syria and Palestine. This view spread to the popular level in the summer of 1940, as France fell to the Nazis and the future of Great Britain appeared uncertain. While some Iraqi leaders remained loyal to London, the majority decided to move away from the Anglo alliance.

To restore "stability," British troops invaded Iraq in 1941. Within thirty days, the anti-Anglo regime was defeated, and civilian politicians who were more sympathetic to British desires established a new government. By January 1942, the pro-British Iraqi administration affirmed its support for the Allies, declaring war on Germany and the other Axis Powers. Though London's intervention kept Iraq from joining the losing side during World War II, it did little to remedy Mesopotamia's fractured religious, ethnic, and political terrain.

A Nation Divided

In 1946, as Iraq joined the United Nations and helped to establish the Arab League, a Kurdish tribal leader named Mustafa Barzani formed the Kurdish Democratic Party (KDP). Hoping to secure autonomy in northern Iraq's predominantly Kurdish region, thousands of *peshmerga* (translated "those who face death") followed Barzaniin opposition to Baghdad's administration of their homeland. Though Barzani was forced to leave Iraq, the Kurdish peshmerga continued to resist Arab domination into the twenty-first century.

By 1946, ethnic fires were under control in the north, but internal political passions in Baghdad were ablaze. After forming yet another government, civilian politicians were once again usurped by a military commander. Within a year, this leader was pressured to resign, and the administration was again turned over to a civilian. Though Prime Minister Salih Jabr was not a military man, he was the first Shi'ite to rule the nation. With the country destabilized by violent clashes between young liberals and older members of the establishment, Jabr was forced to resign less than a year after taking office. With Jabr's resignation, a general once again gained control of the Iraqi government.

Instability and Revolutions

In 1953, King Faysal II turned eighteen, technically making him the ruler of Iraq. In reality, the former regent, military leaders, and powerful politicians continued to throw their weight around, making it difficult for the young leader to exercise his royal authority. With great political instability in his kingdom, King Faysal II entered Iraq into a controversial security agreement with Turkey, Iran, Pakistan, and Great Britain. Known as the Baghdad Pact, this arrangement was unacceptable to nationalists who opposed partnership with the colonialist powers. Inspired by Egyptian President Gamal Abdel Nasser's Pan-Arabism, Iraqi youth began to envision an Iraq free from the Hashemite monarch and his Western friends.

In February 1958, Syria came under the authority of Egypt in the United Arab Republic (UAR). Only two weeks later, the Hashemite kings of Jordan and Iraq combined their territories to form the Arab Union of Jordan and Iraq. As a direct response to the UAR and its revolutionary ideologies, the pro-Western Hashemites hoped the Arab Union would appease those desiring pan-Arab unity while neutralizing calls for revolution. Reacting to this Hashemite union, voices from Nasser's UAR urged Iraqis to rise up against their "corrupt" king.

Inspired by Egypt's 1952 Revolution (led by Nasser and the Egyptian Free Officers' Movement), Iraqi soldiers calling themselves the Free Officers captured Baghdad. Led by Brigadier General Abd al-Karim Qasim and Colonel Abd al-Salam Arif, the Iraqi Free Officers established their regime by killing King Faysal II, the crown prince, and other members of the royal family, as well as the Arab Union's prime minister. The following day, on July 15, 1958, Iraq was declared a republic, ending more than thirty years of Hashemite rule and less than six months of federation with the Hashemite Kingdom of Jordan.

FACT

The Iraqi flag's three stars represent Iraq, Egypt, and Syria. Following the 1958 Revolution, some Iraqi leaders hoped to join Egypt and Syria in the United Arab Republic. Before this pan-Arab plan could materialize, a coup in Syria caused the UAR to dissolve, but for many Arab nationalists this dream will never die.

Soon after Iraqi revolutionaries wrested power from King Faysal and family, the new republic's leadership was divided. While Colonel Arif and other pan-Arabists wanted to join Nasser's UAR, newly elected Prime Minister Qasim and his nationalist backers planned to focus on developing an independent Iraqi nation. Eventually, the government fragmented even farther as disputes arose between Qasim and his former nationalist supporters.

Starting the Ba'th

By the early 1960s, ideological and ethnic differences once again divided Iraq, as socialist revolutionaries set their eyes on Baghdad and Kurdish peshmerga fighters struggled for independence in the north. On February 8, 1963, the Iraqi branch of the Arab Socialist Renaissance Party (*hizb al ba'th* in Arabic) joined forces with dissatisfied members of the Iraqi Army to topple Qasim's regime. Following the coup, popular pan-Arabist Arif was asked to be president, while Renaissance (Ba'th) Party leader Ahmad Hassan al-Bakr was given Iraq's premiership.

Seizing Power

After less than a year, al-Bakr's Ba'thist administration was overthrown, and President Arif took full control of the nation. Just two years later, President Arif was killed in a helicopter crash and was replaced by his brother,

Abd al-Rahman Arif. In the absence of popular support, Arif relied on the military to maintain his position, but the reorganized Ba'th Party had other plans for Iraq.

By convincing several powerful military officials to move against Arif, Ahmad Hassan al-Bakr, his cousin (Saddam Hussein al-Tikriti), and the Arab Socialist Ba'th Party seized control of Iraq on July 17, 1968. The Ba'thists established the Revolutionary Command Council (RCC) as the new governing body, with al-Bakr as the republic's leader. Though the Ba'th Party planned to implement sweeping reforms, Iraq's ethnic diversity once again shook the nation's foundations.

Continued Kurdish Clashes

Backed by Iranian arms, Kurdish separatists effectively challenged the Iraqi army, forcing negotiations. After the Ba'thists agreed to recognize a semiautonomous Kurdish region in the north, a peace treaty was signed between Iraq's ruling Arab Ba'th Party and the Kurdish Democratic Party. However, because Baghdad did not include the oil-rich province of Kirkuk in the proposed Kurdish-controlled area, the treaty was scrapped, and civil war returned in 1974.

For al-Bakr and the RCC, the Kurds and other opposition groups were an annoyance that could not be tolerated. Al-Bakr's younger cousin, Saddam Hussein, used his knack for brutality to gain respect within the Ba'th Party.

Through a matrix of ardent nationalism and calculated political maneuvering, Hussein created a network of loyal followers within his cousin's regime that would eventually become Iraq's dreaded secret service. Saddam Hussein's sadistic reputation preceded him, but for many this man remained a mystery.

CHAPTER 16

Iraq—The Rise and Fall of Saddam Hussein

After years of instability and division, Iraq was eventually subdued by the totalitarian rule of Saddam Hussein and the Ba'th Party. In this chapter, you will uncover the details of this oppressive period while examining the intricacies of a diverse nation teetering on the edge of an unknown and uncomfortable future.

The Boy from Tikrit

On April 28, 1937, the Tikriti clan of north central Iraq gained a new member. Hussein and Subha al-Majid became the proud parents of a son, whom they named Saddam. Raised in a largely Arab and Sunni Muslim region just north of Baghdad, Saddam lost his father at an early age. When his mother remarried, Saddam was forced to live with a violent man who taught him to lie, cheat, and steal. At age ten, Saddam left his stepfather's house to live with his mother's brother in Baghdad. While under his uncle's care, the boy from Tikrit was introduced to anti-British and anti-Imperialist ideologies. From his uncle's teachings, this abused farm boy was transformed into a fiery young nationalist.

As the first expression of his passionate political views, the tenacious teen took part in an unsuccessful attempt to assassinate King Faysal II in 1956. The next year, Saddam discovered the Arab Socialist Renaissance (Ba'th) Party, promoting the same pan-Arabist and anti-colonialist ideologies he already believed in. Following the 1958 revolution, Saddam helped his older cousin (and Ba'th Party leader) Ahmad Hassan al-Bakr with an assassination attempt on the new republic's leader, General Qasim. Failing to kill Qasim, Saddam was shot in the leg and forced to flee Iraq.

After a short stay in Syria, Hussein moved to Cairo, where he remained for four years, until his Ba'thist friends successfully murdered General Qasim in 1963. With an apparent Ba'thist revolution on the horizon, Saddam returned to Baghdad. Less than a year after Saddam's return, Iraq's new leader, Colonel Abd al-Salam Arif, pushed the Ba'thists out of power. In 1964, while trying to oust Arif, Hussein and al-Bakr were thrown in prison. Two years later, Saddam escaped from his cell, where he had been plotting yet another takeover.

Tikriti Takeover

As secretary general of Iraq's Ba'th Party, Saddam was instrumental in organizing the 1968 bloodless coup that brought the Arab Socialist Renaissance (Ba'th) Party and the Tikriti clan to power. With his second cousin at the helm of Iraq's ruling Revolutionary Command Council (RCC), Hussein was named deputy chairman of the RCC and vice president of the republic.

Familiar with Iraq's turbulent history, the boys from Tikrit immediately purged the nation of ethnic, religious, and political opposition.

Through the late 1960s and early 1970s, ethnic Kurds and Turkomans, Assyrian Christians and Arab Shi'ites, conservative Sunnis and communist students were deported, arrested, tortured, and executed for their "disloyalty." Though these gruesome acts may appear to be the work of madmen, they were actually pre-emptive strikes organized by sane but paranoid politicians. These inhumane practices were a response to issues that had violently divided their nation since its foundation. For this regime, fear was the glue that would keep Iraq in one piece.

FACT

After being kicked out of Iran in 1964, Ruhollah Khomeini (spiritual leader of Iran's 1979 Islamic Revolution) settled in the Shi'ite holy city of An Najaf, Iraq. In 1978, Saddam Hussein banished Khomeini from Iraq. The following year, Khomeini's followers overthrew the shah, making the Ayatollah Khomeini supreme leader of the Shi'ite-led Islamic Republic of Iran.

Through the late 1970s, al-Bakr remained Iraq's leader in name, but in practice Hussein was running the show. On July 16, 1979, al-Bakr finally acknowledged his impotence by retiring and transferring his titles to Saddam Hussein al-Tikriti. As president of the republic, chairman of the RCC, and secretary general of Iraq's Ba'th Party, Saddam wasted no time exercising his powers and solidifying his totalitarian rule.

"Treason" and Executions

Five days after his inauguration, Hussein held an important meeting of the nation's top leaders. When all were assembled, Saddam read from a list of names, which included a high-ranking RCC official, the head of Iraq's labor unions, a leading Shi'ite member of the RCC, and twenty others. These individuals were accused of conspiring with the Syrian government in a plan that would have killed Saddam and brought Iraq into an Arab federation led by Syria's Ba'thist president Hafez al-Assad. For their "treason," each was executed, with Hussein personally killing many of the conspirators. Over the next week, as many as 450 others were put to death for their alleged involvement in the plot against Saddam.

Like many Arab states aiming to break away from capitalist colonial powers, the Ba'th Party looked to the U.S.S.R. as their superpower of choice. Though Saddam and his cronies were fierce nationalists, working with the Soviets was acceptable, given Russian rivalries with the West. In addition to their communist connection, Ba'th Party officials were enjoying new wealth due to the nationalization of Iraq's oil fields. By the late 1970s, Saddam's Iraq was one of the region's most powerful nations. Though his iron-fisted domestic policies brought a type of stability to the republic, Saddam's next threat would come from the outside.

At War with Iran

Although Saddam's secular regime harassed Shi'ite leaders throughout the 1970s (for example, by deporting the exiled Iranian cleric Ayatollah Khomeini in 1978), the 1980s began a new era of calculated anti-Shi'ite efforts. After banning the Shi'ite-led Da'wa Party and executing leading Shi'ite clerics during the spring and summer of 1980, on September 21, Iraqi forces invaded the Ayatollah Khomeini's newly established Islamic Republic of Iran. Though this was primarily a territorial dispute, the ethnic and religious aspects of this war cannot be ignored.

ESSENTIAL

While Saddam's Arab regime represented about 80 percent of Iraqis who were ethnically Arab, its largely Sunni Muslim makeup ignored the three out of four Iraqi Arabs who were Shi'ite Muslims.

Seeds of War

Since at least the early 1600s the border between "Persian" Iran and "Arab" Iraq has shifted according to the politics of the time, especially along the southern Shatt al-Arab (a waterway to the Persian Gulf, formed by the joining of the Euphrates and Tigris Rivers). In 1975, Iraq and Iran agreed to divide control of the river, but after the shah was overthrown in 1979, tensions between Saddam's secular state and Iran's revolutionary religious government revived long-standing disagreements.

Hoping to spread his revolution into the largely Shi'ite nation of Iraq, Iran's Ayatollah Khomeini denounced the Iraqi leadership as "backsliding" secularists. To undermine the Soviets and the Ayatollah, the United States courted Hussein, assuring him they would support Iraq in any military action taken against Iran. With the threat of Shi'ite revolution looming over his head, Saddam looked to the long-disputed Shatt al-Arab as a pretext for his pre-emptive strike. Knowing that Washington would back him, Saddam also planned to capture the oil-rich Iranian province of Khuzestan, which was inhabited almost entirely by Arabs.

Over the next few months, border disputes led to small-scale fighting, prompting Baghdad to withdraw from the 1975 Shatt al-Arab agreement. Four days later, on September 21, 1980, Iraqi troops crossed into Iranian territory, and Iraqi planes bombed Iranian airbases. After two months of successful operations in Iran, the Iraq army met stiff resistance, leading to a one-year stalemate. By the spring of 1982, a rejuvenated Iranian army pushed Iraqi forces out of their lands. After another year of intense fighting, Iran mounted its first offensive into Iraqi territory. Over the next few years, fighting spread into the Persian Gulf, with islands, oil platforms, tankers, and other ships being attacked. As a result, the Iran-Iraq War is also known as the first Gulf war.

FACT

In 1981, Israeli jets flew into the heart of Iraq, destroying the soon-to-be-activated Osirak nuclear reactor near Baghdad.

International Conspirators

From 1983 to 1986, as fighting continued in the Persian Gulf, Iranian troops retained control of the Shatt al-Arab and part of southern Iraq's Basra province. In the north, Iranian forces joined Kurdish separatists, taking several Iraqi border towns and operating well into Iraq's Kurdish region.

As uncovered in the so-called Iran-Contra Affair, the United States had sold more than $14 million worth of weaponry to Iran in exchange for American hostages. While Washington was technically neutral, after this double-dealing was uncovered, the Reagan administration decided to salvage its image in the Arab world by openly supporting Iraq.

By 1987, France and the Soviet Union were sending weapons to Iraq (including chemical and biological agents), while Washington was also supplying Baghdad with limited weaponry, logistical assistance, and intelligence. In addition, the U.S. Navy sent a huge armada to the Persian Gulf to "protect" the flow of oil in the region. In the process, U.S. forces carried out operations against Iranian ships, oil platforms, and tankers. On several occasions Americans mistakenly targeted civilians, as seen in the downing of an Iranian commercial airliner that resulted in nearly 300 civilian deaths.

After eight years of unthinkable carnage, the Ayatollah agreed to accept a cease-fire agreement on August 20, 1988. The Iran-Iraq War had taken more than a million lives and left another 1.7 million people wounded. Despite these harsh lessons, the boundaries between Iraq and Iran returned to their prewar positions, and the leaders who orchestrated this bloody grudge match remained in power.

At War with the World

Just five days after signing the cease-fire with Iran, Saddam Hussein began a strategic campaign against the Kurds. As retribution for the Kurdish partnership with Iran, the Iraqi town of Halabja was gassed, killing 5,000 Kurdish men, women, and children and injuring another 10,000. Over the next year, more than 180,000 Iraqi Kurds "disappeared," and about 4,000 non-Arab villages were demolished. With the distraction of war gone, Saddam was determined to put out all opposition fires, no matter what the human cost.

During the eight-year struggle with Iran, Iraqi oil exports had come to a near standstill and millions had been spent on weaponry. Saddam therefore attempted to rebuild his nation's decimated economy. Between 1988 and 1990, the ruling Ba'th Party tried to revive its petroleum industry and began to accumulate large amounts of conventional and nonconventional arms. Though Washington supported Iraq during its long war with Iran,

Saddam's stockpiling of weaponry, as well as his extreme anti-Israeli statements, prompted the United States to rethink its alliance with Baghdad.

QUESTION

Why are so many Iraqis unhappy with the United States?
For many Iraqis, the United States is an arrogant superpower that uses smaller and weaker nations for its own purposes. In the words of Saddam Hussein, "You Americans, you treat the Third World in the way an Iraqi peasant treats his new bride. Three days of honeymoon, and then it's off to the fields."

With Iraq struggling to revive its economy, Saddam looked to its successful southern neighbor—Kuwait. Though this tiny Persian Gulf state had partnered with Saddam during the Iran-Iraq War, the Iraqi leader jealously set his eyes on its petroleum. As a pretext for invasion, Hussein accused Kuwait of intentionally hurting Iraq's economy by flooding the world markets with Kuwaiti oil. Looking to Iraq's long-standing claims to southern Mesopotamia (that is, Kuwait), Saddam invaded on August 2, 1990, declaring Kuwait Iraq's nineteenth province.

Another War in the Gulf

The United Nations immediately condemned the Iraqi occupation of Kuwait, implemented an international trade embargo on Iraq, and set January 15, 1991, as a deadline for Iraqi forces to withdraw from Kuwaiti lands. With Iraqi troops in Kuwait believed to be moving toward Saudi Arabian oil fields, King Fahd accepted an American offer to protect his kingdom. Known as Operation Desert Shield, this effort to guard Saudi Arabia soon turned into a massive deployment of American troops throughout the Persian Gulf region. In response to Iraq's invasion of Kuwait, more than thirty nations, both Arab and Western, joined the U.S. buildup in the Gulf.

On January 17, 1991, with the U.N. deadline passed, Operation Desert Shield erupted into Operation Desert Storm. What began as an overwhelming air campaign expanded into a well-orchestrated ground assault, aimed at removing Saddam's soldiers from Kuwait. With armed forces from Egypt,

Syria, Saudi Arabia, and other Arab nations and troops from Afghanistan, Pakistan, Turkey, and other non-Arab Muslim nations fighting alongside soldiers from North and South America, Europe, and Asia, most of the world was united against Baghdad's Ba'thist regime.

While coalition forces were successful in their air and ground campaigns, Iraq was able to send several Scud missiles into Kuwait, Saudi Arabia, and Israel, killing many civilians and soldiers. In addition, retreating Iraqi troops set fire to about 700 Kuwaiti oil wells, which burned for months until special crews were able to contain them.

Only six weeks after the start of Desert Storm, Kuwait was cleared of Iraqi combatants. Tens of thousands of Iraqi soldiers were dead, and most of Iraq's heavy weaponry and defense systems were destroyed. Clearly defeated in Kuwait, Saddam was forced to sign a cease-fire agreement. With hostilities officially over, U.N. peacekeepers were stationed along the Kuwait/Iraq border, and most coalition forces returned to their home countries.

Suppression, Sanctions, and Suffering

During Desert Storm, coalition forces dropped leaflets and sent radio broadcasts encouraging Iraqi opposition groups to rise up against Saddam's oppressive Ba'thist regime. Believing they would have an international force behind them, Kurds in the north and Shi'ites in the south revolted. But because the war ended so quickly and coalition forces didn't continue their efforts inside Iraq, lightly armed opposition groups were left to fight the Iraqi army alone. Although Saddam's forces were substantially reduced, the remaining Iraqi military easily suppressed the Kurdish and Shi'ite revolts.

In northern Iraq, Saddam's soldiers killed thousands of Kurdish Iraqi citizens, while hundreds of thousands more escaped into Iran and Turkey. In response to these atrocities, American, British, and French troops entered the region, establishing a safe zone for the remaining 600,000 Iraqi Kurds who were threatened by Saddam's armies. In addition, a no-fly zone was enforced over the northern third of Iraq as a way of ensuring that Kurds would not be attacked from the air. In southern Iraq's Shi'ite area, Iraqi forces put down anti-Ba'thist demonstrations, killing thousands and forcing many others to flee to Iran, Jordan, and Syria. As with the north, a southern no-fly zone was set up to protect the Shi'ites from Saddam.

After the war, the United Nations continued to enforce its trade embargo, promising that sanctions would be lifted if Iraq destroyed all its chemical/biological weapons, ended its nuclear program, and allowed U.N. inspectors to confirm the completion of these measures. Because Saddam refused to comply with these stipulations, the sanctions continued for more than a decade.

Punishment

In 1992, Saddam began a drainage program of southern Iraq's marshland. By destroying this important ecosystem, Baghdad hoped to punish the Shi'ite "Marsh Arabs," whose livelihood was intricately connected to the wetlands. In addition, removing the water from this soggy region enabled Iraqi soldiers to move more freely in search of Shi'ite rebels.

ALERT

As a result of Saddam's systematic abuses of southern Iraq's "Marsh Arabs," many were killed, imprisoned, or forced to flee their ancient homeland, reducing the population of Iraqi Marsh Arabs from about 250,000 in 1991 to fewer than 40,000 in 2003.

In 1994, after two years of continuously draining southern Iraq's ancient wetlands, Saddam Hussein sent troops into the dry marshes to root out "terrorists" and any other Shi'ites who dared to oppose him. In the same year, Baghdad renewed its efforts against Kurdish Iraqis by establishing an economic embargo against the already impoverished northern region.

From Wealth to Want

Throughout the 1980s, Iraqis had grown accustomed to air conditioning, clean running water, and other modern conveniences. As the capital of an oil-rich nation, Baghdad was a bustling metropolis, complete with modern highways, tall buildings, and new cars. By the mid-1990s, after five years of U.N. sanctions, Iraq's economy was in shambles. Luxuries such as reliable electricity and sanitation services were almost nonexistent. Skilled professionals were quitting their jobs for more lucrative forms of employment, such as selling cigarettes on the street. With Iraqi currency worth little more than the paper it was printed on, food and basic medicines in short supply, and Saddam's regime firmly in place, the international community began to question the effectiveness of the embargo.

After recognizing widespread malnutrition throughout Iraq, the U.N.-sponsored Oil-for-Food Program was implemented in 1996, allowing Iraq to sell limited amounts of oil to offset the cost of its growing humanitarian needs. In May 2002, the United Nations again tried to lessen the burden on Iraqi civilians by changing the embargo to focus on military goods. Though more than $28 billion in humanitarian supplies and equipment were sent to Iraq between 1997 and 2003, the people of Iraq continued to suffer in many ways.

Ending Saddam's Regime

When U.S. President Bill Clinton ordered strategic strikes throughout Iraq in the 1998 Operation Desert Fox, American and British planes limited their attacks to hostile targets within Iraq's northern and southern no-fly zones. After the tragedy of September 11, Washington once again turned up the heat on Saddam, with President George W. Bush naming Iraq, Iran, and North Korea as the Axis of Evil. After President Bush and other U.S. officials convinced the United Nations to pass a new resolution concerned with Iraq's reported weapons of mass destruction (WMD), Baghdad's Ba'thists were once again in America's crosshairs.

Failing to obtain U.N. support for a pre-emptive strike on Iraq, the United States, Great Britain, and several other countries decided to deal with Saddam themselves. On March 19, 2003, the first of many powerful bombs rocked the Iraqi capital as Operation Iraqi Freedom got under way. Following another night of intense bombing, American and British troops camped in Kuwait moved into southern Iraq, bound for Baghdad. Over the next three weeks, some of the most powerful non-nuclear bombs known to man were guided to specific targets in a "shock and awe" air campaign. At the same time, ground troops battled their way toward Baghdad from the south, while others secured positions in western and northern Iraq.

FACT

In order to help coalition troops recognize important Ba'th Party officials, the U.S. Department of Defense issued the "Iraqi Most Wanted" set of playing cards. This dual-use deck pictured the fifty-five most important Ba'thist leaders, including Saddam Hussein as the ace of spades, his son Uday Hussein as the ace of hearts, and his other son Qusay Hussein as the ace of clubs.

Looting and Liberty

By April 14, coalition forces had gained control of Baghdad and Saddam's hometown of Tikrit, sending the toppled regime into hiding. Because most experts expected a long and bloody fight in the streets of Baghdad, no one was prepared when the government gave up the city after a matter of days. The resulting security vacuum gave the city's impoverished people the opportunity to take back what Saddam had stolen from them. Though looting was initially limited to Ba'th Party offices, it soon spread to warehouses, banks, and even museums.

After coalition forces made the transition from the role of warrior to policeman, relative order was eventually restored, but not before millions of dollars in cash, property, and artifacts were taken. Less than two weeks after Saddam's government collapsed, widespread rioting erupted as outspoken ethnic and religious leaders rallied their people, calling on foreign troops to leave their liberated lands as soon as possible. This development shocked many, but given Iraq's previous experiences with British occupation, their discomfort may be understandable. At the same time, with Saddam on the run, possible WMDs floating around, and the country devastated, coalition forces believed their continued presence was a necessity.

As American and British troops hunted for Hussein and company, many high-ranking Ba'thist officials were captured or killed, including Saddam's sons Uday and Qusay, who were slain in the northern city of Mosul (ancient Nineveh). Despite these successes, coalition forces experienced repeated attacks from suicide bombers, rocket-propelled grenades (RPGs), and snipers. Though some of these attacks were the work of Saddam loyalists, many were made by individuals of varied political, ethnic, and religious backgrounds who wanted to repel another round of foreign occupation.

Quagmire of the Conquerors

On May 1, 2003, President George W. Bush announced the end of major battle operations in Iraq. But for coalition forces, the battlefield was still hot. Though no WMDs were found, Saddam's regime was toppled. Even though the Iraqi army was no longer functioning, the "fida'yin Saddam" and other guerrillas continued sporadic attacks. With heavily armed young adults forced to police the streets of a foreign land, mortal mistakes were made. At times, troops took the lives of innocent Iraqis suspected of hostile intent, while at other times soldiers and marines lost their own lives by giving attackers the benefit of the doubt.

With Iraqi civilians dying at the hands of confused coalition forces, and citizens concerned that their liberators were now occupiers, protests increased in frequency and intensity. Soon after the fall of the Ba'thists, tribal and religious leaders gathered with American representatives to discuss Iraq's post-Saddam government, but the average Iraqi did not see the fruits of these talks until the summer of 2003.

On July 13 that year, a twenty-five-member interim administration known as the Governing Council met for its first official meeting. Because U.S. officials chose this temporary governing body, it was quickly criticized, but for the first time in Iraqi history the nation's administration was representative of the ethnically and religiously diverse populace. The twenty-two male and three female cabinet members constituted the following:

- 13 Shi'ite Muslims
- 5 ethnic Kurds
- 5 Sunni Muslims
- 1 ethnic Turkoman
- 1 Assyrian Christian

Though July saw the formation of Iraq's first indigenous representative government, August 2003 was the bloodiest month since Saddam Hussein was ejected from power. On August 7, a car bomb exploded at the Jordanian Embassy in Baghdad, killing ten. The following week, oil, water, and electrical lines were sabotaged, and on August 19, a large truck bomb ripped through U.N. headquarters in Baghdad, killing the chief U.N. envoy to Iraq and seventeen others, while injuring 100 more. To round out the month of terror, a massive car bomb rocked Friday prayers at the Imam Àli Mosque in An Najaf (home of the tomb of Àli, spiritual founder of Shi'ite Islam). In this attack, the Ayatollah Muhammad Baqir al-Hakim (spiritual leader of Iraq's Supreme Council of Islamic Revolution) was killed along with 124 other worshipers, while another 142 were wounded.

Iraq's Future?

Were these attacks the organized efforts of a lingering underground government or the work of frustrated Iraqis who wanted to avoid foreign occupation? There were colorful arguments on both sides, but it seemed to be a combination of the two. Though no WMDs were ever found, Iraqis began experiencing freedoms they hadn't seen for decades.

With little or no restrictions on morality, pornographic videos and sex theaters grew more commonplace. In response, religious leaders used their new liberty to criticize these evils and the Western "occupation" forces believed to be importing them. Many Iraqis also used their increased wages to buy satellite dishes, which were forbidden under Saddam's strict media controls. In addition, Iraqis became free to tear down the numerous pictures of Saddam Hussein that had peppered the nation for decades. They did so gladly.

As for Saddam, on December 13, 2003, American soldiers captured him hiding under a trap door at a farm in Tikrit and turned him over to Iraqi authorities. An Iraqi Special Tribunal found him guilty of crimes against humanity and sentenced him to death. He was hanged on December 30, 2006. Saddam Hussein's execution and the removal of his regime gave the average Iraqi freedom to buy, sell, watch satellite dishes and videos, and do many new things. More importantly, it helped dissolve the glue of fear from this troubled and diverse nation. But problems remained.

In the years since Hussein's removal, Iraqis have struggled to create a form of national government that will bring together the country's diverse political, ethnic, and religious groups and genders—and that will function in a secure environment. Their efforts have not always gone smoothly.

FACT

Iraq has been a forerunner in the Middle East in providing opportunities for women to participate in government. In 2005, the Iraqi constitution set aside one-quarter of legislative seats for females. Of 325 lawmakers elected in March, 82 were women, according to the Inter-Parliamentary Union. They began to gain power in 1959 with the passage of a progressive civil liberties law and the appointment of the first female minister in the Arab world.

Foreign troops have begun their withdrawal from the country and Iraqis have participated in elections to choose a Prime Minister and other officials. The officials, in turn, have created a National Council for Strategic Policies, filled cabinet posts, and increased oil production. However, thorny issues remain to be resolved.

For example, does the National Council for Strategic Policies have any real power? How much of a role does each separate political or religious group play in the government? If conservative religious factions gain significant political power, will the influence and participation of women in government be diminished? There are no immediate answers to such questions, and they will not be easy to resolve. The one certainty is this: The future of Iraq now lies in the hearts and hands of the Iraqi people, who are striving mightily to create a country that will be a model for unity and prosperity in the Middle East.

CHAPTER 17

Iran—The Shi'ite State

The Iranian plateau has produced some of the world's most colorful cultures and powerful politicians. Following World War II, America and Iran developed a strong friendship that lasted until the Islamic Revolution of 1979. Today, the United States and Iran have been at odds for more than thirty years. Why? Find out as you uncover the complexities of this corner of the globe, known to many as a hotbed of Islamic extremism.

Dynasties and Divisions

Since at least 800 B.C., Aryan peoples from the Fars/Pars tribe have lived in the region now called Iran. Long known as Persia, this land was ruled by a succession of Aryan, Greek, Arab, Mongol, and Turkic families. After the Turkic Safavid dynasty was toppled in the mid-eighteenth century, several short-lived monarchies controlled parts of Persia. Meanwhile, the powerful Russian and Ottoman empires planned to divide the region and annex its territories. In 1795, the Turkic Qajar tribe, from the southern Caspian Sea region, saved Persia from foreign annexation. Moving Persia's capital to the city of Tehran, the Qajars established a dynasty that lasted 130 years.

Through the 1800s, British-Russian rivalries inspired each empire to vie for supremacy in the region. As Russia conquered Persian provinces in Central Asia and London expanded its influence from British-controlled India into the Persian territory of Afghanistan, each empire secured economic concessions from Tehran. In a 1901 agreement, Great Britain was granted a sixty-year dispensation to exploit Persia's oil reserves, while the Qajars also promised most of Persia's customs proceeds to St. Petersburg in return for several large Russian loans.

Persia's Parliament and Predicament

In 1906, London was given concessions over Persia's tobacco industry. Believing the Qajars were jeopardizing Persia's independence, nationalists organized a constitutional revolution. As part of the new constitution, an elected consultative assembly (known as the Majlis) was given considerable authority over the kingdom's affairs. Though Persia's parliament desired to end foreign control over the country's markets, in 1907 Russia and Britain divided the kingdom into spheres of economic influence. Hoping to improve Persia's situation, the Majlis invited the successful American banker Morgan Shuster to put things in order.

As treasurer-general, Shuster was given complete control of Persia's finances. Fearing Shuster's input would produce an economically empowered Persia, Russia forced the national assembly to fire the American expert.

As World War I erupted, Persia remained neutral. Because of its strategic importance and coveted petroleum reserves, Allied and Axis armies battled for position within this nonaligned nation. After the war, Persian delegations were excluded from the Paris Peace Conference. Instead of allowing Tehran to build an independent nation-state, British officials drafted the Anglo-Iranian Treaty, basically making the Qajar kingdom a protectorate.

ALERT

Though Iran was long called Persia, just over half of the nation's people are ethnically Persian. The Turkic Azeri people make up about a quarter of Iran's population, while Kurds, Turkmen, Arabs, and other ethnic groups form the other roughly 25 percent of the populace.

Embittered by Britain's persistent imperial presence, the Majlis and other nationalists looked to expel the weak Qajar monarchy. To avoid violence, London pulled back from the direct controls afforded by the Anglo-Iranian Treaty. In 1921, military leader Reza Khan conquered the Persian capital, establishing a new government with himself as war minister and, eventually, prime minister. In 1925, more than a century of Turkic Qajar rule ended as Shah Ahmad Mizra was deposed, and Reza Khan became Persia's new shah.

Aryans All over Again

Since the Mongols conquered Persia in the thirteenth century, non-Aryan dynasties had dominated the region, but with the rise of Reza Khan, an Aryan was back on top. Associating himself with the ancient Achaemenian kings, the new shah adopted the name Pahlavi. Like other leaders of his time, Reza Shah worked to promote a clear national identity. As a way of celebrating the region's rich pre-Islamic and non-Arab heritage, Pahlavi changed Persia's name to Iran, in reference to its ancient Aryan peoples.

Emulating Mustafa Kemal Atatürk, the charismatic founder of Turkey, Reza Shah Pahlavi began a controversial program of modernization. Just as the Republic of Turkey was established as a secular state, the new shah divorced the long-married mosque and state in his own nation. Since the Safavids declared Shi'a Islam the state religion in 1501 (transforming the largely Sunni region), Shi'ite clerics (leaders of the Shi'a brand of Islam) had remained intimately involved in the kingdom's administrative affairs. Under the Pahlavi monarchy, preachers were expected to stay out of politics, and individual religious convictions were a private matter.

Reza Shah adopted the name Pahlavi (the name of an ancient form of the Persian language) in order to stress his nation's pre-Islamic Aryan history. He hoped to establish a nationalistic, secular, and modern state. The Pahlavi dynasty was Persia's first Aryan regime in more than 1,000 years.

Modern, Independent, then Occupied

Like Atatürk, Pahlavi looked to Western civilization in his quest for modernization. Through the late 1920s and early 1930s, new French-inspired law codes were introduced, breaking the tradition of governance guided by shari'a (Islamic law). In the mid-1930s, Iranian women were forbidden to wear veils in public, and all citizens were encouraged to wear Western-style clothing. Inspired by Europe's wealthy industrialized nations, Reza Shah built new factories, roads, and railways (including the Trans-Iranian Railroad) and developed a modern European-style education system.

Though Pahlavi tried to emulate the West in his modernization efforts, his nationalist agendas brought Iran closer to true independence. Soon after becoming shah, Reza negotiated the withdrawal of Russian and British troops that had been stationed in Iran since the beginning of World War I. In addition, Pahlavi abolished the special economic rights that had allowed foreigners to exploit Iran for more than 100 years. As part of his anti-colonialist efforts, Reza Shah established friendly relations with Nazi Germany, which he saw as a shining example of modernity and nationalism. With the outbreak of World War II, Reza Shah sided with Hitler and the Axis Powers, provoking Britain and Russia to invade Iran in 1941.

With Iran occupied by Allied troops, Reza was forced to turn the kingdom over to his son Mohammad Reza Pahlavi, who joined the country to the Allied cause in 1943. That same year, Iran hosted the Tehran Conference, in which U.S. President Franklin D. Roosevelt, Soviet Premier Joseph Stalin, and British Prime Minister Winston Churchill discussed their wartime partnership and postwar plans. There, the Allies assured Iran of postwar independence and financial aid.

America and the Shah

After defeating Nazi Germany in 1945, the British found their nation economically and militarily depleted, opening the way for the United States to assume much of Great Britain's importance on the world stage. Immediately after the war, the United States used its influence to pressure the Soviets out of northwestern Iran. With Hitler no longer a common enemy, the American/Soviet/British "Grand Alliance" quickly deteriorated, as the Soviet Union squared off against the United States and Great Britain.

The United States in Iran

The rivalry that developed between the United States and the Soviet Union caused each side to jockey for position in smaller countries. For Iran, alliance with the United States was a way of checking Soviet expansionism, while for the United States, Iran was a strategic base of operations in Moscow's backyard. In addition, partnership with Tehran would open the way for American companies to develop the full potential of Iran's vast oil fields.

For decades, most Iranians viewed the Anglo-Iranian Oil Company (AIOC)—born out of a 1901 deal between the Qajars and a British businessman—as a remnant of British imperialism. In 1951, the Majlis nationalized Iran's oil industry, removing what they saw as the last vestiges of foreign control. In response to the newly established National Iranian Oil Company (NIOC), London severed diplomatic ties with Tehran. Within a year, Iran's oil industry was at a standstill, as nationals lacked the technical skills needed to operate wells and refineries. By the mid-1950s, petroleum production was turned over to several European and American companies, with the understanding that half of their revenues would be given to Iran.

Cold War Connections

As Washington and Moscow battled for international influence, the United States secured its position in Iran by covertly assisting the shah (who up to this point had been subservient to the prime minister). Through an apparent partnership between British and U.S. intelligence agencies, an angry mob was paid to topple Iran's anti-Pahlavi Prime Minister Muhammad Musaddiq. With Musaddiq's removal in 1953, the U.S.-backed Shah

Mohammad Reza Pahlavi established absolute control. For decades to come, Iranians questioned his foreign connections.

Between 1953 and 1967, Iran received about $600 million in economic and military aid from the United States.

Through the latter half of the 1950s, the Middle East became a political battleground for American and Soviet ideologies. After the Egyptians aligned themselves with the communists, Washington passed a 1957 resolution known as the Eisenhower Doctrine. Under this resolution, the United States promised to aid any Middle Eastern regime that might be threatened by communism. For Iran, this offer was extremely attractive, as its economy and military would be improved by American support, and its borders would be protected. Through the late 1950s and early 1960s, Tehran and Washington continued to develop strong ties, as demonstrated by the 1959 American-Iranian Defense Agreement and the U.S. aid received by the shah.

Seeds of Revolt

With oil revenues flowing and the United States sending substantial support, Iran's economy was on the rebound. Though this upturn generated new wealth, most Iranians saw the rich getting richer and the poor getting poorer. Recognizing the growing resentment among Iran's impoverished masses, U.S. President John F. Kennedy feared the pro-American shah would be overthrown.

Hoping to stabilize the Pahlavi regime, Washington encouraged the shah to deal with his nation's social problems. The resulting 1963 White Revolution forced Iranian owners of large estates to sell portions of their land to the government. These were then divided into small farms and distributed to the less fortunate. In addition, the shah introduced Western-inspired reforms that affected Iran's education system and promoted women's rights.

Though about 4 million families were given property, Iran's *mullahs* (religious leaders) denounced the shah's actions. Because many of the dissolved estates were religious endowments and most of the policy changes challenged long-standing traditions, conservative clerics criticized the monarch. The White Revolution managed to deal with a portion of Iran's problems, but with many viewing the shah as an anti-Islamic, Western-sponsored dictator, Mohammad Reza Pahlavi's troubles were far from over.

FACT

In 1964, the shah deported a sixty-two-year-old ayatollah (highest rank for a Shi'ite cleric) by the name of Sayyid Ruhollah al-Musavi al-Khomeini. Though Khomeini was deported because of anti-Pahlavi rhetoric, in exile he was able to inspire an Iranian revolution.

By the late 1960s, Iran's oil revenues were in excess of $20 billion a year. With new wealth at his fingertips, the shah began a rapid and costly program of modernization aimed at catching Iran up to the West. Though his measures resulted in economic growth, improved living conditions, and new technologies, they had serious repercussions. Culture shock, large-scale urbanization, and inflation were just a few of the things that led Iranians to resent the Pahlavi rule. In addition, the authoritarian manner with which he implemented his changes infuriated many.

Aware of his subjects' growing dissatisfaction, the shah used secret police (known as Savak) to find and punish opposition leaders. Through the early and mid-1970s, Savak agents caught some dissidents, but the shah's dictatorial and "anti-Islamic" actions led many to look for a savior. By the late 1970s, many had discovered the teachings of a man they believed to be a liberator. For students of the Ayatollah Ruhollah Khomeini, salvation would be found in a pure Islamic state, led by Shi'ite jurists, guided by God.

Khomeini's Student Revolution

Since his deportation in 1964, the Ayatollah Khomeini had sought refuge in neighboring Iraq. While living in the Shi'ite holy city of An Najaf (burial site of the revered caliph Àli), Khomeini developed a doctrine known as the Rule of the Jurist. At its heart was the belief that secular governments should be replaced by theocracies, in which God's laws would be administered by divinely appointed *mujtahids* (experts in Islamic theology and law). As an *ayatollah* (translated "miraculous sign of God"), Khomeini had attained the most honorable title within the mujtahids, one that motivated millions to accept his every word.

Growth of a Movement

After Hussein exiled Khomeini in 1978, the Shi'ite holy man found refuge in France. In Iran, growing opposition to the shah brought the kingdom to the verge of civil war. Taking advantage of widespread dissatisfaction with the Pahlavi royals and their Western allies, Khomeini used a network of about 12,000 loyal students to propagate his revolutionary ideas. By recording the Ayatollah's sermons onto master audiotapes in France, smuggling them into Iran, then duplicating them, Khomeini's followers organized a strong national movement. Though not all Iranians embraced Khomeini's conservative religious views, many saw him as one who could liberate Iran from the Pahlavis.

By January 1979, opposition to the shah had risen to frenzied levels. With riots and demonstrations popping up across the nation, millions rallied behind the battle cry "Death to the shah," forcing the Pahlavi monarch to flee for his life. Two weeks later, the Ayatollah Khomeini triumphantly returned to a nation embroiled in revolutionary fervor.

Khomeini's students quickly made their presence known by executing members of the shah's notorious Savak secret police and hundreds of others who resisted the Islamic Revolution. With the shah gone and with most of Iran's Shi'ite mullahs and laymen behind him, Khomeini's theoretical Rule of the Jurist was becoming a reality.

A "Holy" State and Stately Hostages

On April 1, 1979, a constitution based on Islamic principles was adopted, and Iran was named a theocratic Islamic republic. After forming the Council of Guardians (a group responsible for preserving the republic's Islamic nature), Khomeini gave himself the lifetime position of *faqih*, or expert jurist.

As supreme spiritual leader of the modern Middle East's first Islamic republic, the Ayatollah strategically shaped his new state according to strict religious regulations. The republic's new laws included mandatory dress codes, a prohibition of all alcoholic beverages, capital punishment for prostitution and adultery, and other mandates aimed at upholding morality. In addition, the conservative regime attempted to purify Iran's foreign policy by ending partnerships with Western and non-Muslim governments.

FACT

In 1980, the phrase *Allahu Akbar* ("God is Great") was added to Iran's flag to recognize the Islamic republic and its supreme leader, the Ayatollah Ruhollah Khomeini.

Though Iran's Islamic Revolution caused great concern in Washington, diplomatic and economic relations continued until November 1979. When the ousted Shah Mohammad Reza Pahlavi was allowed into the United States, some Iranians feared Washington was planning to reinstate him as Iran's leader. In what they viewed as a pre-emptive strike, a group of Khomeini's students stormed the U.S. Embassy in Tehran. Taking seventy hostages, the group demanded the deposed shah be returned to Iran for trial. Despite continued negotiations, condemnation from the United Nations, threats of military intervention, a failed U.S. attempt to extract the hostages, and the ex-shah's death in July of 1980, Khomeini's militant students held their captives for more than a year.

In the midst of this international crisis, Khomeini endorsed the students' militant actions and accused America of being the "Great Satan." For most Westerners, this episode was instrumental in shaping a view of Iran as a fanatical terrorist state. Unaware of Washington's dealings with the deposed Pahlavi family and previous CIA-sponsored actions inside Iran, most Americans concluded that the Ayatollah was leading a nation of Muslim madmen bent on destroying freedom and democracy. To this day, many Westerners see Iran through the prism of fear, anger, and confusion that was formed during this unfortunate affair.

Ayatollahs and Politics

About one month after the American hostages were taken in Tehran, the Soviets invaded Afghanistan. With Cold War rivalries complicating matters, the Islamic Republic of Iran found itself precariously situated between the superpowers. Was Moscow hoping to use Afghanistan as an eastern staging area for an all-out invasion of Iran? If so, would the Americans overlook the hostage crisis to aid Tehran against the Soviets? Believing Soviet leaders were planning to seize Iran's oil reserves, Washington issued the 1980 Carter Doctrine, warning that any outside attempt to control the Persian Gulf would be viewed as an assault on U.S. interests and met with military force. Whether or not the U.S.S.R. was planning to occupy Iran, Soviet troops remained in Afghanistan for nearly a decade of costly conflict.

Though threats from Washington and Moscow were of great concern, Iran's attention was quickly diverted to Baghdad. With Shi'ite Muslims accounting for more than half of the Iraqi population, Iran's Shi'ite-led Islamic revolution was an exciting and inspirational event. In addition, Khomeini's intentional efforts to spread the revolution into Iraq made Saddam Hussein's secular regime extremely nervous. With Iran's conservative religious government calling the Iraqi regime "infidels" and the Iraqi administration supporting Iran's Kurdish and Arab separatists, regional tensions escalated.

ESSENTIAL

Iran's official language, known as modern Persian or Farsi, is also widely spoken in Afghanistan (where it is called Dari) and Tajikistan (where it is simply referred to as Tajik).

Nasty Neighbors

By the summer of 1980, a type of political/religious population exchange was under way, as the Iraqi government deported thousands of Shi'ites (many of them Iranian nationals) to Iran and Iranian counterrevolutionaries traveled to Iraq to fight against their nation's new Islamic regime. For several months, sporadic skirmishes broke out in border areas until Iraq launched a full invasion on September 21.

The conflict grew quickly into a regional and international clash. In the eyes of many around the globe, this was a war between secularism and religious revivalism. Though some attempted to paint the conflict as Arab versus Persian or Sunni versus Shi'ite, most looked beyond ethnic or denominational distinctions. Many Arabs and Sunnis supported the Ayatollah as a symbol of pure Islamic resurgence, while others stood behind Saddam Hussein as the defender of secular nationalism.

Given the Islamic Republic of Iran's apparent volatility, most Western governments sided with Iraq's Ba'th Party as the more stable regime. With American hostages being held in Iran, Washington covertly supplied aid to the Iraqis. By the summer of 1981, the Reagan administration had also complied with a number of Iran's requests (including a large sum of cash and weapons), and the hostages were released. Though this arms-for-hostages arrangement gave Iran a boost, increased American aid to Iraq created a bloody balance of power.

Trouble in Paradise

With Iran at war with Saddam and friends, the Islamic republic's administration was threatened from the inside. Though the Faqih (or "Leader of the Islamic Revolution") enjoyed supreme authority over the state, in December 1979, a new constitution created the office of president to oversee certain administrative affairs. In January 1980, Abolhassan Bani-Sadr (a Western-educated liberal) was elected president, while conservative clerics won the majority in Iran's parliament.

Opposed to Bani-Sadr's "un-Islamic" policies, the clergy-run parliament appointed a like-minded prime minister. Within a year, Bani-Sadr was pushed from power and Prime Minister Rajai took over the presidency. Two months later, Rajai was assassinated. By October 1981 the Ayatollah Ali Khamenei had been elected as Iran's third president, and the war went on. Iran had to find a way to pay for it.

To offset Iraq's massive petroleum exports, the Islamic republic attempted to expand its oil production and exporting efforts in the Persian (Arab) Gulf. The Iraqi military almost eliminated entirely the Iranians' ability to ship oil when it carried out more than 9,000 bombing runs on Iran's Khark Island terminal during the war. Ultimately, both the Iraqi and Iranian oil industries were brought to a grinding halt. With the flow of Middle Eastern oil threatened, international involvement increased throughout the 1980s. After eight years of hardship and the war with Iraq, Iran's economy was in ruins, hundreds of thousands were dead, and close to a million others were wounded.

Eager to stop the madness, Iran's citizens convinced their leaders to make peace with the Iraqi "infidels."

Switching Supreme Leaders

On June 4, 1989, less than a year after ending the war with Iraq, Iran's eighty-seven-year-old supreme leader passed away. With Khomeini's death, President Ayatollah Ali Khamenei was appointed supreme leader of the revolution. Ali Akbar Hashemi Rafsanjani was elected as the republic's fourth president. A moderate cleric keen to implement modernization, Rafsanjani was forced to balance personal views with those of his conservative colleagues. While walking a fine line between compromise and conviction, the new Iranian president expanded his powers, eliminated the office of prime minister, and improved relations with several Western governments.

ESSENTIAL

Iran's attempts to acquire enriched uranium for its atomic energy program have raised international suspicions that the Islamic republic may be seeking to develop nuclear weapons as well. In 2003, the International Atomic Energy Agency (IAEA) challenged the Iranian leadership to make their nuclear aspirations clear or face serious repercussions. Despite such challenges, Iran announced in 2009 that it was building a second uranium enrichment plant, and continued to maintain that its program was for strictly peaceful purposes. The charges and counter-charges regarding peaceful use versus nuclear weapons continue, as does Iran's nuclear building program.

Though relations with the United States improved slightly during the early years of Rafsanjani's presidency, by the mid-1990s allegations of an Iranian nuclear arms development program changed everything. In 1995, U.S. President Bill Clinton cut all ties with Iran, accusing the Islamic republic of developing weapons of mass destruction and supporting international terrorism. The following year, a U.S.-sponsored trade embargo made it illegal for any company (American or otherwise) operating in the United States to do business with Iran. Despite the embargo, Russia agreed to build a nuclear power plant in southwestern Iran.

Winds of Change

Though the people of Iran transformed their nation from a constitutional monarchy to an Islamic republic, the leadership of Iran transformed a "theocracy" into a clerical dictatorship. After the death of Ayatollah Ruhollah Khomeini in 1989, popular support for the new supreme leader, Ayatollah Ali Khamenei, and his conservative mullahs quickly dwindled. By the early 1990s, even the former supreme leader's son Ahmad Khomeini opposed Iran's leadership. In response, Khamenei's regime had Ahmad Khomeini assassinated on March 18, 1995.

A New President

In 1997, Iran elected Mohammad Khatami as the republic's fifth president. Having campaigned on a platform of tolerance and social reform, this moderate Shi'ite cleric touched on the pulse of a population ready for change. Though Khatami was the son of an ayatollah and was himself a *hojatolisalm* (distinguished Shi'ite title, just below that of ayatollah), his theological and philosophical studies produced more moderate views than those of his predecessors.

As Iran's new head of government, Khatami appointed a moderate cabinet, loosened restrictions on certain books, newspapers, films, and so on, and allowed new political parties to be licensed. In addition, President Khatami sought to improve damaged relations with the United States and other Western nations. Though conservative mullahs continued to impose repressive laws on an increasingly unhappy population, Khatami's reforms gave many Iranians hope for the future.

FACT

Today about 90 percent of Iranians are Shi'ite Muslims. Nine percent are Sunni Muslims, while Christians, Jews, Zoroastrians, and members of the Baha'i movement make up 1 percent of the population.

Through the late 1990s, Khamenei's totalitarian rule caused many to reject his authority and that of the Council of Guardians. Despite growing dissatisfaction on the streets, conservative clerics continued their oppressive acts into the twenty-first century, leading four prominent ayatollahs to deny Khamenei's position as supreme leader of the Islamic Revolution.

Ripe for Reform

In 2003, the late Ayatollah Khomeini's grandson Hussein Khomeini voiced his opposition to Khamenei and his mullahs, calling them "the world's worst dictatorship." As a symbol of his defiance, the prominent Shi'ite figure moved from Iran to Iraq, where he declared, "Iran needs democracy and separation of religion and state." In addition, Khomeini warned of an imminent popular movement in which Iran's clerical regime would be removed. Two years later, the people of Iran elected a new president, Mahmoud Ahmadinejad, who continued to carry out conservative religious policies and defy the international community by escalating the nation's nuclear building program. He was re-elected in 2009, even though the results were highly disputed domestically and internationally. Once again, Iranians took to the street in protest, to no avail. Similar protests have continued in Iran.

With members of the deposed Pahlavi family campaigning around the world for a democratic Iran, the conservative clerics might have reason to be concerned. As exiles in the National Council of Resistance of Iran (NCRI) make detailed plans to replace their nation's theocracy with a representative government, the "godly" governors are likely grumbling. The deployment of American troops to his east, in Afghanistan, and (though their numbers are dwindling) to his west, in Iraq, should leave the supreme leader slightly nervous. Accusations from the Ayatollah Khomeini's grandson might create a bit of anxiety, but it is the frustration of roughly 70 million Iranian citizens that could bring an end to Khamenei's grip on the government. There was a movement in that direction early in 2011, when protesters attempted to force government reforms, but their demonstrations fizzled out—at least temporarily. In the meantime, President Ahmadinejad and the nation's conservative Islamic regime have retained their power, and expanded their nuclear program despite protests from a large portion of the world community. The people's struggle for democracy continues as well.

Whether or not Iran's Islamic government is replaced through a popular uprising, the leadership of this nation must respect the people they are leading—including those with different ideologies and ethnicities.

CHAPTER 18

Turkey—
Modern and Democratic

For nearly 500 years, Istanbul stood as the center of Ottoman power. In the twentieth century, the empire went down in flames. From the ashes, Ankara rose as the capital of a new and vibrant Turkish republic. Only eighty years after its triumphant birth, the Republic of Turkey is a young developing nation with the potential to rise above its neighbors as the first successful Middle Eastern democracy.

Young Turk Takeover

After nearly 600 years of Ottoman rule, many of the empire's European subjects exchanged their imposed "Ottoman" identity for an ethnically based national consciousness. In 1912, these sentiments led to a war of independence in the Balkans, which produced the sovereign states of Bulgaria, Greece, Montenegro, and Serbia. In North Africa, French troops occupied the former Ottoman territories of Algeria and Tunisia, while Italian forces took what is now Libya, as well as the Dodecanese Islands in the Aegean Sea.

With the new Balkan nations formed from his northwest territories, European-controlled North Africa eroding his southwestern lands, and the Italians occupying the Aegean region on his western shores, the Ottoman sultan was threatened by Arab nationalism throughout his southeastern territories. In addition, the sultan was challenged at his doorstep, as Turkish nationalism spread through the streets of Istanbul and the villages of Anatolia.

Known to outsiders as "Young Turks," the Committee of Union and Progress (CUP) was an underground movement of fierce Turkish nationalists. Opposed to the sultan's tyrannical rule, CUP members sought to expel the despotic Ottoman family and re-establish the 1877 Constitution, while reviving the ancient glory of the Turkish people.

Nationalism

Nationalist-inspired pan-Turkism, or "pan-Turanism" (derived from "Turan," name of the Central Asian Turkish motherland), celebrated Turkish culture and ethnicity. The movement also looked to establish a Turkish homeland stretching from Eastern Europe to western China. With ethnically Turkic populations in Austrian-administered Hungary, Ottoman Anatolia, Russian-ruled Central Asia, Qajar-controlled Persia, and the newly established Republic of China, the massive pan-Turkish nation would have to be taken by force.

ESSENTIAL

Known for centuries as Asia Minor or Anatolia, the modern nation of Turkey (*Türkiye* in Turkish) was so named because of its large population of ethnic Turks.

By 1913, the CUP members' control of the parliament had placed their own leaders above the sultan. Looking to strengthen the empire's military capabilities, CUP leaders worked closely with Great Britain and Germany. But before Turkish nationalists could extend their powers into Turkic Central Asia and beyond, trouble in the Balkans set off an international conflict of global proportions.

Fatal Friendship

As World War I erupted in the summer of 1914, Istanbul's nationalist regime remained neutral. Through the first months of the war, Berlin wooed CUP leaders to its side, while London made several moves that disappointed the Turkish administration. By November, the Ottoman Empire had sided with Berlin and the Central Powers over the Allied Nations, which included Russia, a longtime Ottoman enemy, as well as Italy, France, and Great Britain, all occupiers of Ottoman territories. One hero, Mustafa Kemal, emerged after commanding the Turks' stunning victory at Gallipoli. He became the champion of Turkish nationalism and (after the fall of the Ottoman Empire) the harbinger of postwar independence.

From the Ashes of Empire

In the fall of 1918, Germany accepted defeat, bringing an end to World War I. As one of the conquered Central Powers, the Ottoman Empire was forced to cede its predominantly Arab provinces to the British and French, while accepting the presence of foreign troops in Istanbul and throughout Asia Minor. In 1920, with the empire's territory reduced to non-Arab Anatolia and a small piece of southeastern Europe, the sultan sent representatives to France to discuss a postwar resolution. Instead of offering Istanbul reasonable terms for a peaceful settlement, the Allies (minus Russia and the United States) presented their firm plans to dissolve the remaining imperial lands. Known as the Treaty of Sèvres, the treaty accepted by the Ottoman emissaries included the following points:

- Greece would gain the empire's remaining Eastern European lands, as well as most of Anatolia's Aegean coast.

- Italy was to be given southwestern Anatolia and its Mediterranean coast.
- France would connect south-central Anatolia to its existing Syrian Mandate area.
- Eastern Anatolia would be divided into independent Armenian and Kurdish states (monitored by the French).
- A swath of land connecting the important Bosporus and Dardanelles waterways (including the city of Istanbul) was to be under international control.
- A Turkish-controlled region would remain in a small portion of central Anatolia.

Picking Up the Pieces

Though the sultan embraced this treaty, Turkish nationalists refused to accept the division of their homeland. With the world's most powerful governments arrayed against them, patriotic Turkish men and women rallied behind Mustafa Kemal in a war of independence. After establishing a new parliament, known as the Turkish Grand National Assembly (GNA), Kemal and his followers set out to reclaim their territories and establish a Turkish state. By the summer of 1922, after winning several important victories in western Anatolia, Turkish forces stormed the city of Smyrna (now Izmir), pushing the Greek military into the sea.

After reclaiming the entire Aegean coast, Kemal's patriots looked north to the Dardanelles and Istanbul, where Allied troops were protecting the "international" waterway. Recognizing the rising tide of Turkish resistance, Allied forces fled their northern positions, followed soon by troops in the southern Italian zone and the French areas.

Using his World War I hero status, Mustafa Kemal concentrated the popular power of Turkish pride to outwit and outmaneuver the world's most powerful nations. Utilizing his new role as savior, Kemal encouraged the GNA to end the more than six centuries of Ottoman rule. On November 1, 1922, the sultanate was abolished.

Republic Rising

With Turkish nationalists controlling most of Anatolia, a new peace conference was held in Lausanne, Switzerland, to replace the failed Sèvres arrangement. By the summer of 1923, after eight months of deliberation, the Treaty of Lausanne was signed, ensuring Turkish sovereignty in Anatolia and a portion of southeastern Europe. In addition, Turkish and Greek officials arranged a "population exchange," in which Greek-speaking Christians in western Anatolia were uprooted from their homes and sent to Greece while Turkish-speaking Muslims were pulled from Greece and transported to Anatolia.

With the Ottoman regime removed, nationalism at frenzied levels, and Turkish sovereignty recognized by the world's most powerful nations, the empire's ashes were stirring. On October 29, 1923, new life arose as the GNA declared the long-awaited Republic of Turkey, with Mustafa Kemal as its first president. Because Istanbul had been the center of Ottoman might for nearly five centuries, the GNA chose the city of Ankara, deep within Turkish Anatolia, as the infant republic's capital.

Atatürk's Radical Reforms

As president, forty-two-year-old Mustafa Kemal assumed the arduous task of rebuilding an impoverished nation, depleted by years of war, decades of poor administration, and (in his estimation) centuries of social stagnation. At his core, Kemal believed Western civilization was superior to the Ottoman state's Islamic civilization. In his view, the Ottomans had forsaken their rich Turkish heritage for backward Arab customs and ideologies. By reviving ancient Central Asian culture and embracing European constructs, the new republic would join the great nations of the world as a proud and prosperous Turkish state.

Though Kemal was the son of Turkish-speaking parents, he was born and raised outside Anatolia, in the Ottoman-controlled city of Salonika (contemporary Thessaloniki, Greece). As a young officer in the Ottoman army, Mustafa learned to despise the empire's inefficient bureaucracy and archaic traditions. At the same time, the young Turk developed a fascination with modern Western nations and their successful secular regimes. While studying the works of Enlightenment-era philosophers and political theorists such as Jean-Jacques Rousseau and Thomas Hobbes, Kemal solidified his belief in the separation of religion and state, as well as many other psychological, sociological, and political principles.

Influenced by the controversial Turkish nationalist and sociologist Ziya Gökalp, Kemal avoided the slow and less abrasive process of making small-scale modern adjustments. Instead, the patriotic citizens of Turkey were given a type of "civilization transplant," affecting nearly every area of their lives. Of Kemal's many revolutionary reforms, the disentanglement of religious and public life was his first and most passionate order of business.

The Assembly's Disassembly

Seeking loyalty similar to Islamic Iran's to its divinely guided supreme leader, the Ottomans secured their subjects' complete devotion by combining the royal position of sultan and the divinely endowed office of caliph. Though the GNA abolished the Ottoman sultanate in 1922, the caliph was allowed to remain as a religious figurehead. Despite the caliphate's pan-Islamic significance, Turkey's secular regime viewed it as a symbol of outmoded Ottoman theocracy. On March 3, 1924, the GNA abolished the caliphate, along with several other religious/political offices.

ESSENTIAL

> The abolition of the pan-Islamic office of caliph was a massive cultural shakeup in Turkey. From the 1928 birth of Egypt's anti-secularist Muslim Brotherhood to Osama bin Laden's contempt for Turkish "apostasy," the aftershocks of this cultural temblor continue to rock the Middle East and the world.

With the most important Ottoman political and religious institutions removed, Kemal and the GNA continued their secularization campaign by abolishing state-sponsored Islamic schools and courts, dissolving the Ministry of Waqfs (religious endowments), banning religious brotherhoods, and closing sacred shrines. Though Ottoman reformers had introduced some European-style laws, the GNA entirely replaced the nation's "God-given" laws with secular European codes. In this widespread regulatory overhaul, polygamy was outlawed, Muslims were given the right to change their religion, and women were given equal rights in certain areas.

In 1925 the state moved deeper into its citizens' private lives by outlawing the fez (a bucket-shaped head covering worn by Muslim men throughout the Ottoman Empire) and forcing men to wear Western-style brimmed hats. For conservative Muslims, brimmed hats were unacceptable, as they would hamper proper prostration during prayers. In addition, Kemal encouraged Turkish women to leave their veils at home. For traditionalists, this request was as risqué as asking Western women to bare their breasts.

New Speak—Renewed Identity

Though the Turkish language has been spoken for thousands of years, it was without a written form until migrating Turks met Arabic-speaking Muslims. As a result, Turkish was rendered on paper for the first time with Arabic characters. Viewing the Arabic script as a cumbersome foreign influence, Kemal adopted the Latin alphabet used by most Western nations. Seeing the Arabic language as archaic and alien, the Turkish president ordered the Qur'an to be translated into Turkish, while the call to prayer (recited throughout the world in Arabic) was to be done only in the Turkish language.

As part of Kemal's ardent nationalist agenda, the Turkish language was to be "purified" of non-Turkish words borrowed from Arabic and Persian. Cities with non-Turkish names were given Turkish names. Thus, the Greek city of Smyrna was called Izmir, Armenian Antep became Gaziantep, and so on. History books were rewritten to present Turkic tribes as the source of world civilizations and to establish an ancient Turkish presence in Anatolia. Though his nationalist predecessors envisioned a massive pan-Turkic nation, Kemal focused on a much smaller Anatolian Turkish homeland.

FACT

Though experts say the first Turkic tribes migrated from Central Asia to Anatolia as early as 1000, many Turks believe that ancient Anatolia's Hittite peoples (2000 to 1200 B.C.) were Turkish.

With an increasingly unified national identity, Turkey continued to synchronize itself with European ideologies and institutions. Among Kemal's many changes was the calendar. The lunar Islamic calendar (based on Muhammad's escape from Mecca to Medina) was replaced by the internationally recognized solar Gregorian calendar (centered on the birth of

Jesus Christ). In a further attempt to align Turkey with Western markets, Kemal established the Saturday and Sunday "*vikend*," making the Friday prayer day a workday. As if these changes didn't make the point abundantly clear, the clause recognizing Islam as Turkey's state religion was deleted from the country's constitution in 1928.

New Names

From his personal affection for Western clothing and entertainment to his love for Turkish *raki* (a distilled liquor with strong anise flavor) and *meze* (Middle Eastern–style dips and appetizers), Mustafa Kemal was a man of modern ambitions and ethnic pride. As a testament to this unique fusion of philosophies, in 1934 a law was passed requiring all citizens to adopt Turkish surnames. Though last names were a Western phenomenon, this directive was also meant to unify the nation with a single Turkish identity.

In accordance with the surname law, Kemal took on the name Atatürk, meaning "Father of the Turks." Though the term "Father" is a fitting title for someone who secures a national homeland, no word or phrase can express the undying respect, admiration, and love most Turks feel for this man. Though Atatürk departed this world on November 11, 1938, his grand vision and attitudes are alive to this day.

Kemalist Clergy

After Atatürk's untimely death, his right-hand man, Ismet Inönü, and other like-minded leaders continued preaching the message of modernism, secularism, and nationalism. As the protectors of Kemal's adolescent secular nation, Turkey's leaders were left with many difficult decisions. Though Atatürk's sweeping changes paved the way for a future Western-style democracy, many social and economic issues stood in the way.

Despite popular support for Kemal's secular system, the threat of Islamic extremism worried the inexperienced administration. Atatürk's efforts to create a strong national identity encouraged most citizens to place tribal and ethnic allegiances on the back burner, but subversive movements continued to menace Turkish national unity (especially in the east). Believing the young state was not yet ready for full democracy, Kemal's successors implemented strict controls over their citizens.

On July 25, 1951, Turkey adopted Statute 5816, which states, "Anyone who publicly insults or curses the memory of Atatürk shall be imprisoned with a heavy sentence of between one and three years." While this may seem harsh, more severe punishments are doled out for defacing or destroying statues, busts, or representations of the late Mustafa Kemal Atatürk.

Out of the Darkness Into the Fire

For nearly a decade, xenophobic and ethnocentric leaders closed Turkey off to many outside influences, curbing Kemal's cosmopolitan vision. After World War II, a ray of light was allowed in as Turkey became a charter member of the United Nations. The following year, in 1947, Turkey accepted economic and military aid from the United States, which hoped to gain Ankara's allegiance against the communists. While administrators tried not to take sides in the Soviet-American Cold War competition, things changed as Turkish troops entered the Korean War in 1950 as part of a U.N. force. By 1951, after a year of bloody conflict against communists, Turkey made its position abundantly clear by joining the anticommunist North Atlantic Treaty Organization (NATO).

In 1950, in Turkey's first open elections, the opposition Democratic Party defeated President Inönü and the ruling People's Republican Party. Over the next decade, Prime Minister Adnan Menderes and the Democrats relaxed many of Atatürk's secularist policies while creating new laws to ensure the absolute authority of the state. Focusing on health care, education, and infrastructure, the new government moved to modernize the cities and villages of Anatolia. These massive development programs inched Turkey closer to Kemal's modernist dream. However, Ankara's habitual overspending created devastating inflation and left many laborers unpaid.

By 1960, a deteriorating economy and dissatisfaction among Turkey's emerging young intellectuals and professionals moved Prime Minister Menderes to seek the support of Turkey's more conservative rural populations. As a result, the Democratic Party moved further away from Atatürk's secularism toward a more pro-Islamic stance. Concerned by the government's blatant disregard for foundational Kemalist principles, the Turkish military stepped in to protect their savior's secular state.

Politicians, God, and Generals

On May 27, 1960, a second Turkish republic was born as General Cemal Gürsel and his National Unity Committee wrested power from the deviant Democrats. To punish those who had strayed from Kemal's pure path, the High Court of Justice was established. In the end, close to 600 Democratic leaders were found guilty, leading to the execution of Prime Minister Menderes and eleven others.

In an effort to avoid future wandering from the true Kemalist track, the new government drafted a new constitution, split the GNA into a two-chamber parliament, and created a protective Constitutional Court. Though former President İnönü was narrowly re-elected as Turkey's premier, just four years later the conservative Justice Party (basically a revamped Democratic Party) and its leader, Süleyman Demirel, were voted into power.

Over the next five years, Turkey's political situation spiraled out of control. Clashes between rightists (often Sunni Muslims) and leftists (largely from the heterodox Alevi tradition) left thousands dead, threatening the unity of Kemal's secular state. Recurring urban terror attacks, growing unrest among the impoverished, and violent Kurdish separatist groups challenged the government's authority and competency. In 1971, the military once again used its might to secure the floundering state, as martial law was imposed and Prime Minister Demirel was forced to resign.

ESSENTIAL

After the fall of the Soviet Union, Turkish nationalists revived pan-Turkic passions by establishing ties with the newly independent Central Asian republics. As the ancestral Turkic homeland, Turkey gave financial and logistical support to countries such as Kazakhstan and Turkmenistan. In addition, the central government hoped these nations would see Turkey as a secular, modern, and Muslim example.

The 1973 elections ushered the People's Republican Party and its leader, Bülent Ecevit, into power. Within a year, Turkey was at war in Cyprus over Greek plans to annex the island's largely Turkish northern region. Though Turkish victories in Cyprus revived nationalist pride, political, religious, and ideological differences ignited a new period of civil unrest within the year. This ended in 1980 with yet another military coup and period of martial law.

With General Kenan Evren in charge, civil order was restored, thousands (including GNA leaders) were arrested, a new constitution was created, and the parliament was reduced to a single chamber.

Following the 1983 elections, civilian rule was re-established as the new Motherland Party gained control of the GNA. As centrists, the Motherland Party sought to end Turkey's internal feuds (conservative versus liberal, East versus West, and religious versus secular) by focusing on compromise and reconciliation. In the words of Motherland Party leader and former Prime Minister Turgut Özal, "Turkey has no further need of reforms or continual revolution . . . Freedom of thought and speech, freedom of religion together with secularism as its guarantee, and freedom of enterprise will lead us to become a great civilized and civilizing power once again."

Internal Struggle—East or West?

From the birth of the republic, Mustafa Kemal clearly stated his desire to see Turkey Westernized and modernized to the level of European nations. Though Atatürk died before realizing his dream, others proudly carried the baton. As a founding member of the United Nations and the only predominantly Muslim nation in NATO, Turkey became an important bridge between the Muslim East and Christian West. By 1959, formal economic bridges were also extended westward as Turkey applied for full membership in the newly established European Economic Community (EEC). Without granting Turkey full membership, the 1963 Ankara Agreement and 1970 Protocol paved the way for Turkey's gradual integration into the EEC.

ALERT

Many Americans are surprised to hear that Turkey has surpassed the United States in its empowerment of women. In 1993, Tansu Çiller was elected as Turkey's first female prime minister, while the U.S. has yet to see a female vice president or president.

In 1993, EEC members formed the supranational European Union (EU). As the EEC's longest-standing associate member, Turkey applied for full membership in the new coalition. Though the EU continued to strengthen ties with Turkey, a number of social and economic concerns kept the European powerhouse from giving Ankara a definitive answer. While many Turks believed membership in the EU would cure Turkey's economic crisis, some looked east to Islam for their salvation.

Example or Disgrace?

In the 1995 elections, East/West differences came to a head as the pro-Islamist Welfare Party ousted Çiller from power. In response, two moderately conservative parties formed a coalition against the victorious Welfare Party, temporarily keeping the Islamists from controlling the government. Within a year this partnership fell apart, allowing Necmettin Erbakan and his Welfare Party to set up the Turkish republic's first pro-Islamic government.

Statements from Prime Minister Erbakan such as, "We will create an Islamic currency . . . an Islamic United Nations, an Islamic NATO, and an Islamic version of the EU" startled European leaders already hesitant about bringing Turkey into their ranks. Erbakan's promises to reclaim Jerusalem for Islam and save Turkey from the European "infidels" worried leaders around the world.

With Atatürk likely turning over in his grave, Turkey's Kemalist generals once again intervened, forcing Erbakan to step down in 1997. In the following year, Kemalists banned Erbakan's Welfare Party (the largest group in Parliament), moving the elderly Bülent Ecevit back to the post he had filled in the 1970s.

The Kurdish Question

As Kemalists worked to salvage their damaged image in the West, the opportunity arose to capture republic enemy number one, Kurdish guerrilla leader Abdullah Öcalan. Though Öcalan's arrest and punishment would likely ruffle the feathers of European human rights groups and politicians, Kemalists' hatred for this man was greater than any political or economic concerns.

Since the early 1980s, Öcalan and his Kurdistan Workers Party (PKK) militia had waged a bloody war of independence in Turkey's eastern provinces. Viewed as terrorists by most Turks and as freedom fighters by many Europeans, the Kurdish question was an extremely touchy issue for both sides. In the face of imminent European condemnation, Turkish commandos (likely with the aid of American and Israeli operatives) extracted the Kurdish leader from his refuge at the Greek embassy in Nairobi, Kenya. A truly international affair, Öcalan's arrest touched off a global firestorm of finger-pointing and scolding, but in Turkey it was celebrated as if they had won soccer's World Cup.

ALERT

Head coverings mean different things for women in different countries. If an Iranian woman wears a veil, she may or may not be a pious Muslim. As a citizen of the Islamic Republic of Iran, she is following the norm for women in her country. If a Turkish woman wears a veil, she is more than likely making a statement of her conservative Islamic views. As a citizen of the secular Republic of Turkey, her modest dress is going against the modernist grain.

After Turkey's celebrations subsided, and the "terrorist" mastermind was issued a death sentence, European pressure (and Öcalan's willingness to do anything to save his neck) moved Ankara to reduce his punishment to life in prison. With their leader's life secured, PKK rebels ended more than fifteen years of armed struggle as they laid down their weapons and agreed to work peacefully within the Turkish political system. Ironically, the year that began with harsh European criticisms of Ankara's actions ended with a conditional invitation for Turkey to eventually become a full member of the European Union.

Sacred and Secular Synthesized?

The dawn of the twenty-first century produced more of the same as the pro-Islamic Virtue Party was banned from the GNA but the Islamic-based Saadet Party was born. Hoping to improve their chances for EU membership, Turkish officials abolished the death penalty, removed laws recognizing men as "head of the household," gave women full legal equality, and lifted restrictions on Kurdish broadcasting and education.

After winning the 2002 elections, the pro-Islamic Justice and Development Party replaced the aged Bülent Ecevit and his secularist People's Republican Party. Though viewed with suspicion by many in the West, Justice and Development Party leaders unveiled a synthesis of East/West orientations, promising to promote Islamic values while adhering to the secular principles of Turkey's constitution. As prime minister, Recep Erdoğan set out to bridge the gap between modern secular urbanites and the more traditional and conservative rural populations. Though many continue to question the sincerity of the Justice and Development Party's secularist claims, it seems for now that they have reached a healthy balance between Turkey's cultural and ideological extremes.

One Nation Looking Forward

As one of the Middle East's most stable nations, Turkey sits on the edge of two continents and two civilizations. Turkey's pro-Western and secular foundations are unique for the region, but the nationwide esteem for Mustafa Kemal Atatürk is the republic's most distinctive quality. Just as religious texts are interpreted in many ways, Kemal's vision for Turkey has been construed in many ways over the past eight decades.

ALERT

Though European culture has greatly influenced Turkey, today the tides are changing. In 2003, Turkish pop star Sertab Erener surpassed artists from twenty-five other nations to win the coveted Eurovision title. Known as "Turkey's Shakira," Sertab is one of several Turkish superstars, such as male vocalist Tarkan or the edgy punk rock group Athena, who have gained huge success in Europe and around the globe.

A Nation of Potential

Since Persian and Greek armies clashed on the Aegean coast nearly 2,500 years ago, Anatolia has remained a vital link between Europe and Asia. Though Ankara is allied with the United States, Washington's regional plans are often at odds with Turkish public opinion. Turkish leaders are placed in the precarious position of maintaining their valuable relationship with the United States, while avoiding unpopular decisions that could create instability and give extremists a platform for critique.

Improving relations with Greece (Turkey's traditional enemy to the west) and renewed ties to Iran (the despised radical regime to the east) provide a glimpse of the powerful role Turkey could play in the region. Though Ankara has loosened restrictions on its ethnic and religious minority groups, many Europeans feel the republic has a long way to go before it can be a stable partner.

FACT

Turkey's inflation rate averaged 39.78 percent from 1965–1910. It reached a high of 138.71 in May 1980 and has fluctuated from 12 percent in 2008 to 4 percent in 2011.

With widespread unemployment (12.4 percent in 2011) and roller-coaster-type inflation rates leaving the Turkish economy well below European standards, many wonder if this nation will ever meet the criteria set by EU officials.

Poised for Success

In the face of Turkey's perplexing problems, one word encapsulates this proud people—potential! No matter how bad things have been, Turkey has the tools to become one of the world's most powerful nations. Turkey's highly educated, free-thinking, and cosmopolitan thirty-something crowd is eagerly waiting to make its mark as the authoritarian ways of an aged political establishment are proving inadequate. With more than half of Turkey's citizens under the median age of 28.8 as of June 2010, a massive population of intelligent, tech-savvy, and stylish youth is preparing for change.

If twentieth-century totalitarian tactics are forsaken, and a new generation is empowered with "freedom of thought, speech, religion, and enterprise," then these words of Motherland Party's Turgut Özal will be more than rhetoric. Though ethnic and religious distinctions may have threatened the Turkish identity eighty years ago, today these differences can be celebrated within one powerful and self-confident nation. When the multiethnic and multireligious people of Turkey are allowed to live freely without fear, then Atatürk's dream will finally become a reality, and Turkey will lead the region into a new era of peace and prosperity.

FACT

Turkey's drawn-out EU membership application process has been inching forward. The organization's analytical examination of the EU legislation began in October 2005. Since then, the EU has closed two chapters (provisionally) and opened negotiations on twelve chapters, one as recently as June 2010. On February 18, 2008, the Council accepted a revised Accession Partnership with Turkey. The process is long and arduous, but once completed it will benefit Turkey and the EU.

Meanwhile, Turkey continues to perform a delicate balancing act as the "go-between" bringing the West and the Middle East together, as it has done throughout the recent wars and political uprisings in Iraq, Afghanistan, Libya, and other countries while dealing with the demands of its own volatile population. It is a role that, because of its geographical location, Turkey cannot escape—but that it has played well.

CHAPTER 19

Tackling the Tough Issues

Now that you've been introduced to the Middle East's heritage, peoples, cultures, history, and politics, it is necessary to examine a few of the larger concepts that define the region and perplex the West. From the shame/honor-based worldview, which can move a father to kill his beloved daughter in the name of family honor, to the monumental issues moving Western and Islamic civilizations to the brink of catastrophe, this chapter will provide valuable insights into this unsettling new millennium.

Understanding Shame/Honor Societies

If you were raised in Europe or North America, you were more than likely taught to value truth and despise deception. As a Westerner, you probably base your decisions on your concept of right and wrong. You do, say, and act as you feel, as long as it doesn't break the law or hurt anyone. If you properly follow the rules, you are innocent; if you knowingly go against these directives, you are guilty.

Though most of the world's cultures recognize a difference between right and wrong, other factors may be of greater importance in their daily lives. For instance, in many African and South American tribal societies, fear of the spirits/gods causes individuals to base their actions on what will anger or appease these powerful beings. If sacrificing an innocent child will convince the gods not to destroy a village, then the infant is killed. By Western standards, the tribal leaders are guilty of murder, but in their culture they are revered for their heroism.

ESSENTIAL

Some cultures are focused on maintaining honor and avoiding shame. In others, fear of more powerful supernatural forces guides the society, while still others see punishing the guilty and protecting the innocent as their number-one aim. Though most cultures are based on one of these three perspectives, aspects of all three play some role in every civilization.

In the Middle East, India, and most of Asia (including China, Korea, and Japan), yet another worldview places honor above all things. While these societies may fear the wrath of a higher power and punish lawbreakers, they are most concerned with maintaining honor and avoiding shame. Consequently, telling a lie could be viewed as neither right nor wrong but as an honorable action, if it was meant to protect one's group. However, if the deception was selfishly motivated, then it would be considered a shameful act.

Coffee and Confederation

In the Middle East, personal friendships and tribal alliances are fully dependent upon issues of honor and shame. While mutual respect can forge honor-based unions that remain strong for generations, these associations can self-destruct because of a single dishonorable action. The symbolic use of coffee in traditional Bedouin diplomacy provides a clear illustration of this time-honored relational system.

As a sign of his honor and to uphold the reputation of his tribe, a Bedouin man will offer a cup of rich coffee to any passerby. This first cup, known as *salaam* (meaning "peace"), communicates the host's hospitable and nonaggressive intentions. After a period of conversation, the guest may be offered a second cup of coffee, called *sadaqa* (meaning "friendship"). Through this cup, the host recognizes the guest's honorable qualities and conveys his desire to pursue a friendship. If the guest continues to show himself respectable and sincere, then the alliance is sealed with a third cup of coffee. Known as *issayf* (translated "the sword"), this final drink shows the host's willingness to fight alongside his new friend. Unless this person dishonors the host or his tribe, the host is obligated to protect and stand by his friend, even to death.

From the tent of an Arab nomad to the villa of a Turkish nightclub owner, your mannerisms, choice of words, and countless other actions will communicate your level of respect for those around you and the degree to which you should be respected. From insisting that a guest take the best seat in your house to the chair you choose when visiting another person's home, a litany of gestures will convey your desire to honor or dishonor others.

Group Dynamics

In this society, the opinions and norms of one's group often overshadow an individual's personal desires. Whether family, tribe, ethnic group, religious community, or nation, one member's shameful act or victimization dishonors every member. As a result, the group is responsible for restoring its honor. By covering or compensating for the shameful act, honor can be restored, but if this is not an option, the group is obliged to take revenge. Though this arrangement usually ensures stability within a group, tribal/sectarian feuds are often produced by each side's duty to deal with damaged honor.

Because each side feels the need to restore its honor, third-party intervention is often the only way intergroup conflicts can be resolved. In the case of Iraq, Saddam Hussein's tyrannical regime used ruthless measures to maintain order. By suppressing conflicting ethnic, religious, and tribal groups, dictators use fear to dissuade opposing parties from fighting one another. However, if an oppressive ruler is removed or unable to exercise his power, age-old conflicts quickly re-emerge.

ALERT

There's no "me" in "we"! In shame/honor-based societies, the entire group will feel the repercussions of one member's offense. For instance, if your sister is accused of being promiscuous, and you are engaged to be married, your future in-laws would likely call off the wedding to avoid union with your family's shame.

While Middle Eastern dictators have employed terror to ensure temporary stability, other leaders have used traditional mediation techniques to reach lasting resolutions. From the wisdom of King Solomon, seen in his response to two women arguing over one baby, to Muhammad's skillful mediation between warring tribes in Arabia, impartial and intelligent leaders have resolved complex conflicts for thousands of years.

FACT

Though Jordan is in many ways a modern country, with trendy night-clubs, a regional center for human rights, and a king whose first language is English, its officials look the other way as hundreds are killed in the name of family/tribal honor each year. In contrast, many Jordanians, who look to the United States as an example of modernity and human rights, are appalled by the legality of abortion in America and the 1.2 million fetuses aborted each year.

In the traditional Palestinian peacemaking process, known as *sulha*, a mediator is chosen not only to determine guilt or innocence but also to uphold familial honor. If the accused is found innocent, the accusers are forced to pay a fee to the accused and their family as a way of restoring damaged honor. If the accused is found guilty, the perpetrator is punished, while his family is compelled to pay a fee to the victim and their family. In the end, tribal feuding is averted, as the perpetrator's family is shamed and the victim's family has its honor restored, leaving the shamed group to determine how it will restore honor within itself.

Is Islam a Violent Religion?

If you were in the United States after September 11, 2001, you more than likely heard people asking and answering the question, "Is Islam a violent religion?" Though you likely heard some people explaining the events of September 11 as a natural outgrowth of Islam's inherently militant nature, it is just as likely that you remember others presenting Islam as a religion of peace. So which is it? Can Islam be violent and peaceful at the same time?

This difficult question to answer could be asked of any of the world's major religions. Can any religious tradition be branded "violent" or "peaceful?" A quick review of history reveals periods of violence and peace in nearly every religious tradition. You might be thinking, "What about the battles Muhammad fought—didn't he teach his followers to fight for Islam?" This may be true, but in the Hebrew Scriptures, the Book of Joshua (revered by Jews and Christians alike) is full of death and destruction, with men, women, and children dying at the hands of God's holy warriors. Does this make Judaism an inherently violent religion? Were the Crusades a natural outgrowth of violence condoned by passages in the Bible? What about World War I? With a combined total of 37 million casualties, this European war claimed many more lives than any of Muhammad's desert skirmishes.

Throughout history, billions have died at the hands of Jews and Christians, but few would label Judaism or Christianity as violent religions. Some would argue that God instructed Joshua and his men to kill pagans for a specific purpose and time and that today, Judaism is focused on morality, faith, and peace. Others would say that Jesus Christ introduced nonviolence and personal sacrifice as an alternative to ancient Judaism's "an eye for an eye and a tooth for a tooth" mentality. Nevertheless, individuals from each tradition continue to participate in their nations' armed forces with what they believe to be scriptural and divine backing.

A Matter of Interpretation

In the twenty-first century, most Muslims look at violence found in the Qur'an as something that was necessary for a time. Now that Islam is no longer in danger of extinction, more peaceful methods should be the norm. Though Muhammad fought to resist the enemies of Islam in the seventh century, today the vast majority of Muslims believe their struggle is one of personal purity and devotion.

The Qur'an does call for violence in some circumstances, but it also instructs devotees to be merciful and to seek peaceful resolutions to conflict. Just as a Christian or Jewish person may be compelled to protect her nation or family, many Muslims are ready to do the same. This in no way makes Islam, Christianity, or Judaism violent religions. However, because Islamic and Hebrew scriptures reference bloodshed at various points, these traditions may not be wholly considered "peaceful" religions either.

Rather than examining a certain religion's scriptures or history, you may choose to explore the actions of its current adherents. Though the Hebrew and Islamic scriptures apparently condone violence, and though Jews, Christians, and Muslims have taken part in many violent battles together and against one another, the vast majority of today's Jewish, Christian, and Muslim worshipers are concerned with morality, spirituality, prosperity, and peace. Nevertheless, minorities from each of these traditions believe they have a divine obligation to fight those who oppose or contradict their religious beliefs.

Consider Your Sources

No matter what you see in the news or hear from "experts," not all Muslims are terrorists. Through the media, Westerners have been shown the Muslim hijacker, the Muslim car bomber, and the wild-eyed Muslim revolutionary with Kalashnikov and burning American flag in hand. These are the exception and not the rule. Muslim terrorists do exist, but they only make up about 3 percent of the global Muslim population. Unfortunately, extremists receive most of the media's coverage. Even American terrorists from Christian backgrounds who shoot abortion doctors, bomb government buildings, and massacre their classmates get a good deal of airtime. Does this mean all

Americans from Christian backgrounds are terrorists? No. These incidents are seen through the perspective of your everyday experiences dealing with peace-loving Americans.

Explosions and acts of terror in the Middle East are newsworthy, but spice-shop owners offering tea and coffee to tourists or poor farmers giving foreigners a meal and a place to sleep don't get the ratings. Without experiencing this hospitality firsthand, it is impossible to fully grasp the peaceful nature of this region. Most Muslims will give you the benefit of the doubt no matter what your nationality or religion may be.

ESSENTIAL

The victims in many acts of violence in the Middle East are not foreigners. They are more often than not residents of the countries in which the violence is perpetrated, even when the primary targets may be foreigners. That was illustrated by the wave of protests that swept across the Middle East in early 2011.

Granted, the United States has more violent crime than any Muslim country. In fact, no Middle East country appears in the list of the top ten countries in the world with the highest crime rates. Two, Syria and Yemen, are included in the list of the top ten countries with the lowest crime rates. Statistics aside, does that mean you should be afraid to step out of your front door? Of course not! Nor should you be fearful of visiting the Middle East. You probably shouldn't run through Gaza City waving an Israeli flag, but you wouldn't drive through an African American community flying a Confederate flag, either.

Islamic Revivalism and Militancy

Though most Muslims want to live righteous and peaceful lives, some are violently opposed to the West and its influences on the Muslim world. These revivalists advocate a return to more traditional Islamic values, with many attempting to resurrect seventh-century Arabian civilization. These revivalists believe life was the way God intended it to be during Muhammad's time.

Thus they seek to rebuild a type of medieval society in which women are suppressed, men are forced to grow beards, and foreign influences are forbidden.

In addition, individuals with this mindset want their secular governments to give way to theocratic systems in which Islamic law would govern all areas of life. Revivalists are most prevalent in Saudi Arabia, Sudan, Iran, Pakistan, and Algeria, but they can be found in just about any Muslim nation (and many non-Muslim lands). Though most revivalists are willing to accomplish their goals through peaceful methods, they may also take up arms in their religious quest.

A Planet Divided

For extremists, the world is divided into the "House of Islam" (Muslim-controlled areas) and the "House of War" (non-Muslim-controlled lands). In their minds, Muslims must use any means necessary to expand the House of Islam around the globe. If peaceful methods succeed in furthering the cause of Islam, then so be it, but if the spread of Islam is hampered or the Islamic way of life is threatened, "true Muslims" are obliged to fight nonbelievers and apostate Muslims.

QUESTION

Are many Muslims also part of al-Qaeda?
Of the world's estimated 1.57 billion Muslims (as of 2010), only about 5,000 are members of al-Qaeda, although the exact number is difficult to ascertain. And not all terrorists are members of al-Qaeda.

For al-Qaeda members, militancy is an honorable answer to the shame brought on their lands by Western cultural, economic, and political dominance. Though most Muslims consider the killing of innocent civilians to be evil and un-Islamic, militant revivalists believe non-Muslims and "backsliding" Muslims are part of an evil conspiracy to rule the world. In their view, a cosmic war is playing out on Earth between the forces of good and evil. In this great struggle there are no civilians; everyone is either a partner or an enemy of God. What fair-minded Muslims and non-Muslims view as cowardly acts of terror, combatants consider the only honorable response to Western oppression and corruption.

Between Frustration and Aggression

Apart from obvious cultural and religious differences, historical and political barriers have been erected between Middle Eastern and Western peoples. Though most Muslims are not militant revivalists, many are frustrated by what they see as a history of Western domination and exploitation. For millions, the line between frustration and aggression is becoming thinner, though most continue to pursue justice through peaceful methods.

The Crusades began more than 900 years ago, but the memory of this European Christian offensive remains fresh in the minds of many Muslims, Jews, and Middle Eastern Christians. As a symbol of Western aggression, the Crusades are often referenced by present-day clerics who believe American and European governments are against Islam. As the flames of frustration are fanned, many express their anger, but few are ready to kill civilians.

The history of European colonialism is yet another sore point for many. From right-wing fanatics to leftist nationalists in the Middle East, the embarrassment caused by this period has left deep ruts of resentment throughout the region. Blaming colonialists for widespread poverty and political weakness, many Muslims believe the region could thrive if Western "puppet-masters" would cut their strings.

ESSENTIAL

In the American and European guilt/innocence way of thinking, "collateral damage" (the death of civilians) is excused because the killing is unintentional. In the Middle East's honor/shame mentality, however, it is irrelevant whether or not a person intends to take a life. If someone is killed intentionally or accidentally, their family is not only grieved but also dishonored. The perpetrator is held responsible for their loss, and this death must be avenged.

Combined with constrictive controls put in place during the British and French mandates, broken promises and double-dealing during postwar peace conferences have created a shroud of shame across the Middle East that remains to this day. Though Western-inspired nationalist movements eventually produced independent states, most of these countries have been or are currently controlled by repressive regimes (often supported by Western governments).

Clashing Civilizations or Civilized Collaboration?

Since the September 11 attacks, people have discussed the possible "clash of civilizations." In this scenario, Islamic and Western civilizations would find their differences insurmountable, and because of diametrically opposed agendas, the world would erupt into a global conflict of apocalyptic proportions. Though many doomsday theorists and some religious extremists believe these differences are destined to summon Armageddon, current small-scale tensions don't necessarily spell out World War III.

Though individuals on the edges of the Western and Islamic mainstreams are likely to continue their inflammatory statements and fanatical forecasts, these two great civilizations were formed on the same planet and have the potential to coexist peacefully. There are fundamental differences between the cultural constructs, but there are also similarities that can serve as bridges of understanding.

CHAPTER 20

Anything but Status Quo

The Middle East has been a dynamic region in the early years of the twenty-first century. Several countries in the region have undergone internal political and religious struggles that have led them to the brink of collapse. Others have expanded their international roles in an effort to attain regional dominance and exercise more power in global affairs. Their internal upheavals may be nothing more than growing pains as individuals assert their rights to freedom and ultimately create a bigger role for their countries in an ever-changing global economic and political environment.

Geopolitical Constants in Flux

Political, religious, and economic unrest are as common in the Middle East as oil in Saudi Arabia and Libya. The unrest came to a head at the beginning of 2011 as uprisings that began in Tunisia, Egypt, and Yemen in January spread throughout the region.

The uprisings ranged from controlled demonstrations in city streets to civil wars. Some countries' leaders, such as President Ali Abdullah Saleh in Yemen, survived demands for their removal, although their holds on power were tenuous at best. Others, such as President Bashar al-Assad in Syria, promised long-overdue reforms to stay in power. Hosni Mubarak of Egypt and Tunisian President Zine el-Abidine Ben Ali, who had ruled the country for twenty-three years, were ousted.

FACT

Long tenures are a fact of life for rulers in the Middle East. Examples include Tunisian President Ben Ali (twenty-three years), Egyptian President Mubarak (thirty years), the father-son Syrian Presidents Assad (forty years), King Fahd of Saudi Arabia (twenty-three years), and Libyan President Gadaffi (thirty-two years).

For the most part, the uprisings were part of the never-ending cycle of unrest in the region described earlier. In some cases, they impacted the rest of the world to some extent, which highlights the fact that the Middle Eastern countries cannot—and do not—operate in a vacuum.

Oil Continues to Play a Role

Four Middle East countries rank among the top five oil exporters in the world. Nations across the globe depend on those four for significant amounts of their petroleum products. The unrest in early 2011 was particularly unsettling, since two of the four, Saudi Arabia and Iran, compete strongly for political dominance in the region and adopted competing sides in affected countries such as Bahrain and Syria.

Consequently, every bit of political unrest in the Middle East sends shudders through people around the world, especially in countries that do not produce significant amounts of their own oil. But oil is not the only geopolitical factor at play in the Middle East. Military activity contributes to the unrest.

Saudi Arabia is the world's leader in oil exports. It exports close to 9 million barrels a day, including both crude oil and petroleum products. That is more than numbers three, four, and five combined (the UAR, Iran, and Kuwait, respectively). (Russia is second on the list.) That explains why oil and the Middle East are synonymous.

Outside Military Influence

Military conflicts aimed at settling political differences in the Middle East are not uncommon. Since 2001 there has been an increasing number of nonregional military interventions in Middle East countries, ranging from the war on terrorism in Iraq and Afghanistan to NATO's 2011 intervention in the civil war in Libya. That has caused strife between governments in feuding Middle East countries, especially between Iran and Saudi Arabia.

While many Middle East governments cope with internal power struggles, Saudi Arabia and Iran vie for religious and political dominance in the entire region through different strategies and tactics. Bahrain became a battleground of sorts for those two countries in early 2011.

The U.S. Navy reactivated its Fifth Fleet in 1995 to direct operations in the Persian Gulf and Arabian and Red Seas and established its headquarters at Manama, Bahrain. Even though the navy has reduced its visibility in Bahrain in recent years, its presence remains a source of friction in the region.

The Iranian government saw the political unrest in Bahrain in 2011 as a chance to expand its influence subtly and diminish Western countries' power there. One of Iran's goals was to encourage the Bahrain government to force the U.S. Navy's Fifth Fleet, which is headquartered there, to seek another home. Saudi Arabia exacerbated the situation when it deployed 1,500 troops to Bahrain to help the government keep the peace.

Ostensibly, the Saudi troops entered Bahrain to intercede on behalf of the minority—but ruling—Sunnis in the country. Realistically, their purpose was to mitigate Iranian influence and exercise Saudi leadership. The situation epitomized the struggle for power in the Middle East as individual countries try to expand their spheres of influence. Iran is often in the middle of such battles for the wills and minds of the region's people, which is a source of continuing unrest in the Middle East.

The differences between Sunnis and Shi'ites have been well documented throughout this book. It is important to note that they played a major role in the unrest that spread through the region in 2011. Granted, one of the largest causes of the disturbances was attributed to a demand for democracy among the citizens of the various countries. But religion played a part as well. The irony is that in countries dominated by Sunnis—e.g., Egypt, Yemen, and Tunisia—Shi'ites demanded more political power. In the relatively few countries where Shi'ites hold a significant majority, such as Iran and Bahrain, Sunnis clamored for a larger say in government. Sunnis and Shi'ites alike want at least an equal say in government no matter where they live.

FACT

A salient case of religious differences between Muslims and non-Muslims occurred in 2005 when a Danish newspaper printed cartoons perceived by Muslims to be disrespectful to the prophet Muhammad. Islam prohibits any pictorial representations of the Prophet, let alone cartoons. The issue sparked protests in Middle East countries and evoked a letter of protest to the Danish Prime Minister signed by ambassadors from ten Arab countries.

The religious differences between Sunnis and Shi'ites in Middle East countries in general are a perpetual issue as the people try to establish a balance of power between them. Until they find that balance, true peace will not be a reality in the Middle East.

At War with Itself

There may be a finite number of countries in what is defined nebulously as the Middle East, but they do not always see eye-to-eye. That is due to the power struggle between and among various countries and religious sects within them. Iran and Saudi Arabia again play roles in their "war for influence." Each has its allies and enemies, both within the region and globally. Consider Iran and Syria.

Iran and Syria are often cited as supporters of global terrorism. As a result, Syria has suffered from poor relations with many non–Middle Eastern countries over the years. But its relations with more moderate regional countries have not always been cordial due partly to the repressive tactics of Syrian President al-Assad and his father, Hafez al-Assad, who ran the country with an iron fist before him.

ESSENTIAL

The sometimes brutal tactics used by the Assads in Syria and by deposed President Saddam Hussein in Iraq are related to religious factors. The Assads belong to the Allawites, who resorted to repression to maintain their grip on most of the key government and military positions in Syria. Similarly, Hussein repressed the majority Shi'ites (and Kurds) in Iraq to ensure that Sunnis maintained their power.

The same types of struggles exist between countries such as Iraq and Turkey, which have long been at odds over the Kurdish question. Even though Turkey provided some support for the Kurds in the northern part of Iraq, it also had concerns about its own security, especially as U.S. troops pulled out of Iraq in 2011.

The Turks were concerned with an incursion of Iraqi Kurds belonging to the PKK crossing their border and instigating violence. The Turks wanted strong border protection between the two countries to prevent PKK infiltration. They also wanted to limit Iran's influence in Iraq as the Turks and Iraqis forged stronger business bonds. The two countries engaged in $10 billion worth of bilateral trade in 2011, but very little of it took place in the northern part of Iraq, where it rose only 30 percent between 2006 and 2010. Such trade between Middle Eastern countries is essential as Iraq struggles to attract foreign investment to rebuild its economy and deteriorating infrastructure.

Relationships such as those between Turkey and Iraq, including their mutual goal of limiting Iranian influence, and the interplay among Syria, Saudi Arabia, and Iran are commonplace in the Middle East—which is by no means a "one size fits all" region.

Countries and Their Internal Struggles

Lebanon has been in a precarious position geographically and politically for years. It is not at peace with other Arab countries in the region or with Israel. It has long-standing border disputes with Syria and Israel, particularly over the Israeli-occupied Golan Heights.

The country suffered through a fifteen-year civil war (1975–1990) among Shi'ites, Sunnis, and Christians, which ended only when Syrian army elements intervened. And political parties fighting for power within the country drew in Israel in June 2006 when Hamas members captured Israeli soldier Gilad Shalit in a cross-border raid. Shalit remains in Hamas custody, which ensures continued friction between Lebanon and Israel.

ESSENTIAL

In 2008 Hizbullah won a series of street battles with other groups to seize control of the Lebanese government. Hizbullah's victory created an imbalance in political power. It formed a coalition government with the March 14 coalition, a Christian-Sunni alliance. Then, in January 2011, Hizbullah forced the government's collapse, once again throwing the country into political chaos.

There is also a political divide between Hizbullah and the country's temporary Prime Minister, Saad Hariri, over the role of Iran in the internal affairs of Lebanon and other Middle Eastern countries. Hariri decried Iran's interference in Lebanon and Middle Eastern countries in general in opposition to Hizbullah's support of Iranian influence.

There was a familiar refrain in Hariri's claim, as he averred that Saudi Arabia is Lebanon's most important ally. Once again events in a single country centered around the struggle for influence between Iran and Saudi Arabia, which prevents any integration in the region.

Hamas Versus Fatah

The civil war that erupted in 2006 between the two primary Palestinian political parties, Hamas and Fatah, is indicative of the ongoing struggles between factions in the region. Hamas recorded significant political gains through the electoral process in Palestine in the early years of the twenty-first century. That prompted a conflict called by various names, e.g., the "Conflict of Brothers" and "*Wakseh*," an Arabic term that denotes self-inflicted damage.

The military fighting between the two parties began in 2006. They established a Palestinian unity government in 2007, but that did not end the hostilities. That same year they fought the Battle of Gaza against each other, after which Hamas took control of the Gaza Strip and removed Fatah officials.

ESSENTIAL

Israel and key Western countries such as the U.S. and Britain support the Fatah leader, Mahmoud Abbas, in the Palestinian conflict. They refuse to recognize Hamas until it recognizes Israel, accepts agreements made by the Palestinian Authority under the previous Fatah-led administration, and denounces violence. The stalemate over these issues contributes to the political instability in the region.

Middle Eastern government officials in other countries, such as Egypt and Syria, have stakes in the outcome of the Hamas-Fatah split, and encouraged the two sides to reconcile, which they did in April 2011, when they reached an agreement to reunite their governments. Their internal struggles have impacted a host of other countries inside and outside the Middle East, as is the case throughout the region.

Turkey: Middle East or West?

Turkey is in a tough position economically and geographically when it comes to Middle East versus West. It is the only Middle Eastern country in a position to be a member of the European Union (EU). But countries in the Middle East look to Turkey for guidance as well. The balancing act is difficult for the country.

FACT

It may be several more years before Turkey is admitted as a full member of the EU. It was not recognized officially as a candidate for full membership until December 12, 1999. Six years later the negotiation process to grant it full membership began. A final decision may not come until 2015—and there is no guarantee that Turkey will be admitted.

Western countries expect Turkey to play a significant role in their interactions with the Middle East. In the 2011 unrest, Turkey consented to act as a "protecting power" for the United States during Libya's civil war. In that capacity, Turkish representatives served as consular officers on behalf of U.S. citizens in Libya and passed messages between the two countries.

Meanwhile, there was a bit of unrest in Turkey in light of declining press freedom and freedom of expression in the country. That happened as Turkish diplomats pressed for stability in Bahrain and Libya and held meetings in Cairo to forestall protests there against the army and discuss the ongoing Israeli-Palestinian conflict. All this was going on while NATO was using an air base in Izmir, Turkey, as a command center to conduct its operations in Libya. The dichotomy demonstrated Turkey's peculiar dual role in the Middle East as it seeks a "home" somewhere between it and the West.

Iran Flexes Its Muscles

Iran has been a thorn in the side of Middle Eastern and Western countries for several years, especially because of its nuclear intentions. Nuclear programs are relatively rare in the Middle East, but more countries are starting their own to balance Iran's.

The new programs starting in the Middle East may be more for individual countries' self-protection against Iran than for practical purposes. Conversely, Iran's more developed program is as much a provocation as it is a tool for providing energy to the country. It is akin to Iran's deployment of navy ships through the Suez Canal in 2011 for the first time since 1979. Such tactics are used to keep other Middle Eastern countries off balance and guessing at what Iran's next provocation might be, such as forming "unholy" alliances with nations normally outside of its sphere of influence.

ESSENTIAL

In recent years Egypt worked out a nuclear cooperation agreement with Russia; France promised to help Morocco begin a nuclear energy program; and Syria and Turkey announced the development of a joint energy company that includes nuclear power plants. Saudi Arabia, Libya, Jordan, Qatar, Kuwait, the UAE, Bahrain, and Oman are also launching nuclear programs.

Iran and Venezuela

Over the past several years, the presidents of Venezuela and Iran have pursued strong economic and political ties between their countries. Their meetings have led to numerous agreements to cooperate in projects such as oil and gas, trade, and construction.

The relationship between Iran and Venezuela is predicated on their leaders' mutual distrust of the West and their opposition to international sanctions and threat of military action against Iran over its nuclear program. The alliance is a factor in Iran's relations with Middle East countries as well, most of which do not have strong ties with Venezuela outside OPEC.

Iran, China, and North Korea

Iran has also formed ties with North Korea and China to help develop its nuclear program. China blocks sanctions imposed by Western countries on Iran, while North Korea provides technological aid and weapons assistance.

One of the Middle East's concerns is that Iran is forming alliances with countries that increase its military, nuclear, and economic power globally to the detriment of the region. Moreover, it is lending assistance to Syria to upgrade that country's nuclear program.

FACT

Iran signed a $40 billion deal with China in July 2009 that allows China to refine Iranian oil. The value of the two countries' bilateral trade that year, excluding the refining deal, was $36.5 billion, which made China Iran's largest trading partner. The figure surpassed Iran's trade with the European countries, which amounted to $35 billion, primarily in the energy sector.

Reaching Out to Syria

Syria has acknowledged that it is pursuing nuclear power programs. Israel has suggested that the Syrians are building nuclear weapons for illicit purposes, which poses a danger to its welfare. (Israel has long been secretive about its own programs. It neither confirms nor denies its nuclear arms capabilities, if any.)

Syria has refused since 2008 to let International Atomic Energy Association (IAEA) inspectors look at a site destroyed by Israeli warplanes in 2007. The inspectors investigated the site after the bombing and reported that the collection of uranium particles they found there proved the Syrians were conducting nuclear activity.

Iran and Syria are working together closely on the latter's nuclear program, which, if not used strictly for peaceful purposes, can adversely affect the balance of power in the region. The growth of nuclear programs in the Middle East is something that all the countries in the region must monitor closely.

Struggle for Democracy

The first few months of 2011 were a time of unrest in the Middle East. Citizens' protests demanding improved social programs and more democracy began in Tunisia and Egypt and spread quickly throughout the region. As a result, President Zine el-Abidine Ben Ali of Tunisia left the country on January 14th. Fouad Mebazaa replaced him.

Ben Ali's counterpart in Egypt, President Hosni Mubarak, resigned on February 11th. The Supreme Council of Egyptian Armed Forces stepped in to lead the country, but that did not appease the people, who continued to protest the lack of progress in implementing social reforms and giving citizens more say in government. Leaders in other countries read the tea leaves carefully and took steps to avoid similar fates.

Although tea is a popular drink in the Middle East, it is only grown in two countries in the region: Turkey, in the mountains near the border of Georgia, and Iraq, where it is new. The Iraq Agricultural Department announced in July 2010 that tea has been grown successfully in the province of Al Diwaniyah. Kuwait is the second largest tea-drinking country per capita in the world. Turkey is the fourth.

Moroccan King Mohammed VI promised significant constitutional reforms. Kuwait's emir, Sheikh Nasser Sabah Al-Ahmed Al-Jaber Al-Sabah, accepted the resignation of the state's cabinet. Yemen's President Saleh resigned, but when protesters gathered in the streets in late March, the king rescinded his promise.

What the Citizens Are Seeking

In general, protesters sought two goals: leadership changes and better job opportunities. They had more specific protests within individual countries. In Algeria, they rallied against a new law that diminished the value of college diplomas by giving equal status to less-qualified degree holders in the job market. Egyptians rallied for pay raises to offset price inflation for food.

Some protesters marched to support their counterparts in other countries. Iranians demonstrated to support Egyptians, Bahranians, and Tunisians. Saudis protested to support Bahranian reformists as well.

Often, government officials met the protesters with violence. Yemeni security forces used tear gas and bullets to stop protesters. So did Syrian police. Civil war erupted in Libya where Gadaffi tried to maintain his grip on power. NATO intervened on rebels' behalf by implementing a "no fly" zone to inhibit the Libyan air force from bombing its own people and carrying out missile attacks on Gadaffi-held territory. The entire region was in disarray.

Although anti-government protests in the Middle East are not new, the wave of unrest in 2011 drew unwanted attention from around the world. The demonstrations disrupted day-to-day events in people's lives and spread beyond the region in ways that most previous protests had not.

ALERT

Over one-third of the people in Upper Egypt live below the international poverty line of $2 a day. Approximately 20 percent of all Egyptians are below that poverty line, and another 20 percent are about a dollar or so above it. In all, almost half the Egyptian population is living in extreme poverty.

Effects on Regional Peace

The uprisings in the region created instability that threatened peace even in the countries that were not affected directly by protests. They created mutual assistance efforts by government leaders designed to keep the protests from spreading and enveloping the entire region.

Leaders inside and outside the Middle East initiated negotiations to settle the protests and end the escalating violence in different countries. Saudi Arabia invited President Saleh and representatives of Yemen's opposition to Riyadh for talks. The Gulf Cooperation Council got involved as well. Their efforts were rebuffed.

FACT

The Gulf Cooperation Council (GCC) comprises several economically stable states in the Middle East: UAR, Bahrain, Saudi Arabia, Oman, Qatar, and Kuwait. They formed the organization to pursue mutual political and economic goals, including joint business ventures, scientific research, the creation of a common currency, and a unified military presence. No country in the Middle East could stay out of the disorder besetting the region.

As Long as Israel Stays Where It Is

As long as Israel stays where it is geographically, there will be unrest in the Middle East. Only two countries in the region, Egypt and Jordan, have peace treaties with Israel. Those treaties were jeopardized by the 2011 uprisings in the Middle East.

Political leaders in other nearby countries point to Israel as one of the sources of the unrest in the region. Iran threatens to eliminate Israel, Hariri in Lebanon links Iran and Israel together as the biggest instigators in the unrest, and even Sudan claims that Israel has fired rockets into it.

The long-standing situation of Israel versus the rest of the Middle East is a problem that festers as the region undergoes its growing pains. There are periods of calm on all of Israel's borders, interrupted by intermittent attacks by anti-Israeli groups from one country or another. They, in turn, engender responses from Israel, claims of human rights violations by all sides . . . and the cycle perpetuates itself.

Settlements Come, Settlements Go

One of the biggest stumbling blocks in establishing peace between Palestine and Israel and, by extension, other Middle Eastern countries, is the settlement issue. The Israeli government frequently grants citizens permission to build new homes on occupied territories in the West Bank and East Jerusalem.

ESSENTIAL

Estimates suggest that approximately 500,000 Israelis in occupied lands live in settlements that, according to international law, are illegal. Israel rejects the claim of illegality. Government leaders across the globe say that as long as the settlements exist, there is little to no chance of an equitable resolution of the two-state solution—or real peace.

Palestinians note that East Jerusalem, one of the areas in which new settlements are being built, will be the capital of their future state if a two-state solution is ever realized. They oppose Israeli control over the area in particular and settlements in general. The issue must be resolved if the deadlock between the two entities is to be broken.

How Long Can This Go On?

The question of how long the political, religious, and economic struggles in the Middle East will last has confronted the region for centuries. The answer is seemingly "forever," based on what has happened both in larger countries such as Pakistan and Afghanistan and in smaller ones such as Dubai and Bahrain.

Afghanistan has been a battleground for years. Russia, Britain, the United States and its coalition allies, the Taliban, al-Qaeda . . . the list of countries and groups that have fought across the Afghan landscape is long and varied, as have been the issues involved.

One of the most significant issues in Afghanistan is the people's quest for self-determination. That is at the heart of the twenty-first-century unrest in the Middle East: people trying to gain control of their own destinies.

ESSENTIAL

The United States launched an offensive in Afghanistan in October 2001 to find and destroy terrorists who sought a safe haven in the country after the September 11 catastrophe in New York City. It enlisted the aid of several countries in the Middle East to eradicate them from their own borders. That effort has contributed to a decade of unrest in the region as individuals, political groups, and governments take sides in the war on terrorism.

Afghanistan faces a long rebuilding process as it emerges from years of war. The international community is providing humanitarian relief and assistance, security, financial aid to fund infrastructure projects across the country, and political support for a democratic framework. Projects such as those being conducted in Afghanistan are being duplicated throughout the Middle East as the current century progresses.

Pakistan

Pakistan is on the eastern fringe of the Middle East both geographically and politically. Like Afghanistan, it is a battleground in the war against terrorism. Western countries rely on Pakistan as an ally in their effort to rid the region of terrorists, while the Pakistani government struggles to determine exactly how much help it wants to provide.

FACT

Pakistan has one of the more complex government structures in the Middle East. It is best described as a federal parliamentary system. The president, who is elected indirectly, is both the head of state and commander in chief of the Pakistani Armed Forces. The prime minister, also elected indirectly, is the head of government. There is also a cabinet of ministers comprising members from both chambers of the federal legislature to assist the prime minister.

Pakistan is more closely involved with Asian countries than with the Middle East, although it has a pronounced relationship with Turkey. The unrest in the Middle East prompted Pakistani President Asif Ali Zardari to visit Turkey in April 2011 to discuss its effects on both countries and their specific economic and cultural bilateral dealings.

It's Not Just the Large Countries

Smaller countries in the Middle East suffer from the same problems as their larger counterparts. Often they have fewer resources to help them weather their crises. Yemen is a perfect example.

Yemen is one of the poorest countries in an overall poor region. Its economy was based almost exclusively on oil exports. As the twenty-first century began, Yemen's oil production dropped as its population began growing. To compound matters, another problem endemic to the region afflicted the country: dwindling water resources.

Until recently, Yemen derived 70 percent of its revenues from petroleum resources—which also accounted for one-quarter of its gross domestic product. The lack of diversity in Yemen's economy became one of the government's root problems as the oil supplies diminished, and contributed to political unrest by 2011.

The Yemeni government, led by President Ali Abdullah Saleh since 1978, acted to improve the country's economy and provide jobs for its citizens. It implemented an economic reform program in 2006 to reduce reliance on non-oil products and attract more foreign investment. Three years later the program bore some fruit when Yemen exported liquefied natural gas in October 2009 as part of this diversification effort.

Natural gas is a mostly methane product that can be extracted from non-oil products, such as coal.

In January 2010 a group named the Friends of Yemen, comprising Americans, Yemenis, and Yemeni-Americans interested in promoting the country's welfare, formed to support economic and political reform efforts. The International Monetary Fund provided a big boost in August 2010 when it approved a three-year $370 million program to fund those efforts. However, the government's attempted reforms take time, which does not provide immediate satisfaction for residents' demands for jobs and security.

President Saleh had two major problems in 2011. First, Yemenis believed he had been in power too long and did not have a full grasp of the country's problems. Second, Western countries were questioning his efforts to drive insurgents and secessionists from Yemen, where they were trying to take advantage of the unrest to seize power. As a result, Saleh promised to give up his presidency by the end of 2011; however, he reneged.

Despite the Saleh government's ambitious endeavors, Yemen continues to face difficult long-term challenges at a time when its residents are demanding short-term results.

Bahrain

The two major concerns in Bahrain are political and economic. Politically, if Iran gains influence in Bahrain, that could create more instability in the world's oil markets, which is a source of concern for many countries outside the Middle East. Economically, the country is not in dire straits, although its focus is changing from oil to financial services and tourism.

FACT

The first oil in the Middle East was discovered in Bahrain, in 1931. There have been no additional resources discovered since then, and forecasts suggest that the oil will be depleted in ten to fifteen years, depriving the country of a significant portion of its income.

Bahrain has gradually lost its position as the region's financial center. Dubai has achieved that distinction. Nonetheless, Bahrain has experienced steady financial growth in recent years. In the first three quarters of 2010, the rate of growth was about 4.3 percent. Nevertheless, the country has not been immune to the wave of unrest that swept the region in 2011.

Dubai

Dubai epitomizes Middle Eastern countries' struggles to balance their history, religions, and culture with the rest of the world. The country hosts the world's richest horse race, the Dubai World Cup, now worth $10 million, and boasts the world's tallest building, the 2,717-foot-tall Burj Khalifa.

The growing number of people who attend the races contributes to the burgeoning status of Dubai as an international crossroads and global transport hub. The government is transforming Dubai into a first-class tourist destination and a center of international business as it diversifies from a trade-based, oil-reliant economy to one based more on real estate and financial services.

FACT

French skyscraper climber Alain Robert ascended the Burj Khalifa on March 28, 2011. The climb was rife was symbolism. The presence of the world's tallest building in one of the Middle East's smallest countries epitomizes the region's struggle to make its mark in the world community, even if it means taking chances.

Yet, there is still strict enforcement of religious law at times, which creates a paradox as Dubai struggles to bridge the gap between the old and new worlds, between modernism and religious tradition.

FACT

More than 50,000 horse race fans attend the Dubai World Cup meeting each year, which contributes heavily to the country's economy and reputation as a tourist destination.

Religion Versus Democracy

One of the central issues in the 2011 unrest in the Middle East revolves around the question of whether Muslims can exercise their democratic freedoms. There are no clear-cut answers.

ESSENTIAL

Democracy in the Middle East cannot always be defined in Western terms. Many countries in the region hold elections and their leaders may be called presidents, but the presidents are not always elected. Election results are sometimes questionable, and government leaders use intimidating tactics to monitor individual voters. Thus, Middle Eastern elections may not be a true test of democracy.

The real question is how much freedom each government, whether secular or theocratic in structure, allows its citizens. In some Middle Eastern countries, the people were not rebelling against Islam in 2011. Mostly, they were seeking more individual freedom and a larger say in government. There is little or no danger of Middle Eastern countries moving away from Islam. It is more a matter of the people in them seeking more individual freedom within the constricts of their religion.

Whether democracy and Islam can coexist is a question for scholars to debate. Time will provide at least part of the answer after the outcomes of the 2011 protests are better understood.

The Future

The Middle East is faced with a significant balancing act: how to fit in with the rest of the world economically and politically while maintaining its unique traditions and culture. The region cannot isolate itself from the countries outside its borders, nor does it want to. It is part of the global community and must act accordingly.

FACT

Islamic banks—i.e., those that conform to a system of banking consistent with the principles of Islamic law—are a tradition in the Middle East. They have made a comeback in recent years to provide banking services to people living in Muslim communities. Significantly, shari'a-compliant assets reached about $400 billion throughout the world in 2009. The potential market is $4 trillion.

Leaders of the countries within the region realize it is not the Middle East against the world, or vice versa. Like their counterparts across the globe, they must grapple with cohesion versus confusion, with the former as their goal. They have been undergoing serious growing pains in the first decade of the twenty-first century as they strive to reach that goal.

There are no easy answers to resolving the Palestinian versus Israeli situation, placating the protesters in the many "hot spots" in the region, creating jobs, decreasing reliance on non–Middle East countries for technological services, or planning for a non-oil economy. But there is hope for the region based on the progress demonstrated in individual countries that are models for the entire Middle East.

Bright Spots

Qatar is one of the bright spots in the Middle East. Its growing economy is a model for other countries in the region, and it will host the 2022 soccer World Cup, which has accelerated large-scale infrastructure projects such as a metro system and a Qatar-Bahrain causeway. The event will showcase the Middle East and what it can accomplish.

Qatar was one of the few Middle East countries to escape serious political unrest in 2011. That was due largely to its solid, expanding economy and prospects for continued growth in the future. In fact, in 2010, Qatar experienced the world's highest growth rate, ranked second only to Liechtenstein in per capita income, and has the world's lowest unemployment rate.

FACT

Oil and gas account for more than half of Qatar's GDP, 85 percent of its export revenues, and 70 percent of its government income. It has enough proved oil reserves (15 billion barrels) to last another thirty-seven years and 14 percent of the world's proved reserves of natural gas. Qatar is also attracting private and foreign investment in non-energy sectors.

The adage "Employed people are happy people" applies to Qatar. Yet, its government does not ignore the rest of the Middle East. The country supplied fighter planes to a NATO coalition that interceded in the 2011 Libyan civil war, which was not a popular tactic in some Middle East countries, such as Iran. Despite that, this emirate comprising only 850,000 people is emerging as a leader in the Middle East and a reliable partner for countries outside the region.

Technology

Technology provides hope for the future. Social networking websites such as Facebook are invaluable tools for people to spread information, contact one another about protests, and conduct debates about public policy, among other uses. (Conversely, a government can use the networks to squelch debate or disseminate public relations information—or can simply shut them down.)

ESSENTIAL

The media revolution involved in the 2011 unrest may prove to be beneficial for the people of the Middle East. The expansion of digital technology and more innovative use of the media may spur citizens' demands for democracy, and lessen governments' willingness and actions designed to inhibit their protests.

Real-time communications will enable people in Middle East countries to become more aware of what is going on in the region, and facilitate their abilities to express their political and religious views.

An Increasing Need for Infrastructure

There are other favorable signs that the Middle East is growing in prestige and importance globally. Metropolitan areas are expanding rapidly in some countries, particularly Saudi Arabia, Bahrain, and the UAR. Consequently, jobs will be created as local authorities strive to upgrade the infrastructures of these communities to keep pace with the growth.

FACT

By mid-2011, Iraqis were able to buy flat-screen TVs, computers, refrigerators, stoves, and clothing from China, Turkey, Iran, and South Korea. Oil production was increasing, the dinar was stabilizing, and the economy was growing an average of 5.2 percent annually based on figures between 2007 and 2011. The central bank had foreign reserves of about $50 billion.

There are drawbacks to the burgeoning populations and demands for improved infrastructures. Currently, most Middle Eastern countries do not have the capability to upgrade the needed facilities, especially water and wastewater, roads and rails, traffic and transportation, and underground infrastructures without outside help. Domestic businesses with the technological and logistical expertise needed to cope with tasks in these areas currently do not exist in sufficient number. Experts in specialties such as planning competence, services, machines, and construction supervision still must be hired from outside the region.

Iraq presents a classic example of a country in need of infrastructure upgrades—and of opportunity. In 2003 the country had no economy to speak of, as civil war and the incursion of international military forces created chaos across the country. By 2011, foreign armies began their withdrawal and a newly formed government took control of the country, albeit tenuously.

The Iraqi government still had a lot of work to do to restore stability, but the country experienced a major step forward in economic development—and gave cause for hope to the rest of the region.

Addressing the Problems

Middle East government officials are taking steps individually and collectively to address the problems created by growing populations, including political unrest and shortages of water. They send students to excellent schools around the globe to acquire educations that can be applied back home, engage in international joint venture business projects, and hold local, regional, and international seminars to exchange knowledge.

They work together to promote projects in organizations such as the Organization of the Islamic Conference (OIC), an organization that includes fifty-seven countries spread over four continents. It is the world's second largest intergovernmental organization, ranked below only the United Nations. Its goal is to protect the interests of the Muslim world by promoting international peace across the globe.

In short, these Middle Eastern countries are striving to earn their places among the world's elite nations. That is their future, whether it is derived from unexpected sources or local experts rebuilding technologically advanced infrastructures.

APPENDIX A

Timeline: Prehistory to the Present

PREHISTORY—Ancient Monotheists: Adam, Enoch (Idris), Job (Ayyoub), Noah (Nuh), etc.

7000 TO 3500 B.C.—Sumerians develop world's first civilization in southern Mesopotamia (contemporary Iraq)

5500 TO 3500 B.C.—Egyptians develop civilization along Nile River (northeast Africa), establishing northern and southern kingdoms

3500 B.C.—Sumerians invent wheel

3200 B.C.—Sumerians create world's first written language

3100 B.C.—Egyptian kingdoms united by Pharaoh Menes

2800 B.C.—Papyrus writing sheets invented by Egyptians

2500 B.C.—Phoenicians settle along northeastern Mediterranean coast

2500 B.C.—Sumerian *Epic of Gilgamesh* written

2200 B.C.—Hittites establish civilization in Anatolia (present-day Turkey)

2100 B.C.—Abraham (Ibrahim) born in Mesopotamian city of Ur

2050 B.C.—Isaac (Is-haq) born in Canaan (present-day Israel/Palestine)

2000 B.C.—Jacob (Yakub) born in Canaan

2000 B.C.—Babylonian civilization established in central Mesopotamia

1900 B.C.—Joseph (Yusuf) born in Canaan

1850 B.C.—Israelites enslaved in Egypt

1800 B.C.—Birth of Assyrian Empire in northern Mesopotamia

1750 B.C.—Assyrian Empire conquered by Babylonians

1700 B.C.—King Hammurabi develops detailed law code for Babylonian Empire

1530 B.C.—Babylonian Kingdom destroyed

1520 B.C.—Moses (Musa) born in Egypt

1440 B.C.—Israelites Exodus from Egypt/Conquest of Canaan

1440 TO 1400 B.C.—Moses receives Ten Commandments and pens Torah

1350 B.C.—Pharaoh Amenhotep IV rejects polytheism

1200 B.C.—Hittite Kingdom destroyed

1200 TO 800 B.C.—Assyrian Empire slowly re-established

1000 B.C.—Persian prophet Zoroaster preaches monotheism

1000 B.C.—Kingdom of Saba' (Sheba) established in southwestern Arabia

1000 TO 950 B.C.—Kingdom of Israel established, Jerusalem built, and Temple of Solomon erected

930 B.C.—Kingdom of Israel splits into Israel (North) and Judah (South)

722 B.C.—Israel destroyed by Assyrians

700 B.C.—Assyrian capital moved to Nineveh (present-day Mosul, Iraq)

612 B.C.—Assyrian Empire conquered by Medes

605 B.C.—King Nebuchadnezzar establishes Neo-Babylonian (Chaldean) Empire

600 B.C.—Medes establish empire in northern Mesopotamia and Aryana (Iran)

586 B.C.—Judah conquered by Neo-Babylonians (Chaldeans) and exiled to Babylon

550 B.C.—Median Empire conquered by Persians; Persian Empire established

539 B.C.—Babylon conquered by Persians

538 B.C.—Citizens of Judah (Jews) return from exile in Babylon

500 B.C.—Nomadic Arab "Nabataeans" settle in present-day southern Jordan

490 TO 479 B.C.—Greco-Persian Wars

331 B.C.—Alexander the Great conquers Persian Empire; Greek Empire born

264 B.C.—Punic Wars begin between Carthage and Rome

146 B.C.—Rome captures Carthage

133 B.C.—Roman Empire controls North Africa

100 B.C.—Nabataeans establish the city of Petra

27 B.C.—Roman Empire's Pax Romana begins

3 B.C.—Jesus, son of Mary (Esa ibn Marium) born in Bethlehem

A.D. 30—Jesus' crucifixion

A.D. 40 TO 95—Christian Scriptures written

A.D. 50 TO 70—Persecution of Christians in Judea and spread of Christianity

A.D. 70—Destruction of Jerusalem Temple and expulsion of most Jews of Judea

A.D. 135—Rome removes all remaining Jews from Province of Judea

A.D. 224—Sassanians revive glory of Persian Empire

A.D. 284—Roman Empire divided into East and West

A.D. 303—Great persecution of Christians by Emperor Diocletian

A.D. 312—Roman Emperor Constantine converts to Christianity

A.D. 325 TO 451—Series of Church Councils determine Christian Orthodoxy

A.D. 330—Constantinople becomes capital of "Christian" Roman Empire (Byzantine Empire)

A.D. 447—Attila the Hun takes Balkans and Asia Minor (minus Constantinople) from Byzantines

A.D. 476—Rome destroyed by Germanic warriors

A.D. 527—Justinian expands and strengthens Byzantine Empire

A.D. 570—Muhammad ibn Àbdullah born in Mecca, Arabia

A.D. 610—Muhammad receives first revelation of Qur'an

A.D. 622—Muhammad and his followers escape to Yathrib (later Medina)

A.D. 632—Muhammad's death; revelation of Qur'an ends

A.D. 632—Abu Bakr becomes leader; Medina is capital of Islam

A.D. 634—Abu Bakr dies; Ùmar leads Muslim community

A.D. 640—Muslim armies conquer Persia, Egypt, and eastern Mediterranean

A.D. 644—Ùmar assassinated; Ùthman in command

A.D. 656—Ùthman killed; Àli becomes supreme leader

A.D. 661—Àli assassinated—last of the "Rightly Guided Caliphs"

A.D. 662—Umayyad dynasty established; Muslim capital moved from Medina to Damascus

A.D. 680—Husayn killed in city of Karbala

A.D. 685—"Dome of the Rock" built in Jerusalem

A.D. 733—Umayyads expand Islamic domains stretching from Spain to India

A.D. 750—Abbasid dynasty takes control from Umayyads; capital of Islam moved to Baghdad

A.D. 900—Small Umayyad kingdom established in Spain

A.D. 969—From Cairo, Fatimids establish rival dynasty to Abbasids

1040—Seljuk Turks move into Mesopotamia and Syria

1054—Separation of the Eastern "Orthodox" and Western "Catholic" churches

1055—Fatimids occupy Abbasid Baghdad

1071—Seljuks defeat Byzantines in eastern Anatolia, capture Emperor

1097—Start of Western "Christian" Crusades in Middle East

1169—Salah al-Din (Saladin) expels Crusaders from Egypt

1187—European colonialists expelled from Jerusalem by Salah al-Din

1250—Mamluks take Fatimid Egypt, establish dynasty

1258—Mongols destroy Baghdad and Abbasid dynasty

1291—Last Crusader colonialists expelled from the Middle East

1299—Osman's Turkic tribe expands power from northwestern Anatolia

1370—Ottomans (Osmanli) establish dynasty, move into Eastern Europe

1402—Timur the Lame (Tamerlane) defeats Ottomans, captures Sultan

1448—Ottomans regroup and take Kosovo in Balkans

1453—Ottoman Sultan Mehmed conquers Constantinople; end of Byzantine Empire

1492—Spanish Inquisition displaces many Jews and Muslims

1500s—European kingdoms develop economic ties with Muslim world

1501—Safavid dynasty set up in Persia and Central Asia

1517—Mamluk dynasty toppled; Ottomans gain most of Arab world

1526—Mughal dynasty begins in present-day India, Pakistan, and eastern Afghanistan

1529—Sultan Süleyman besieges Vienna; Ottoman "Golden Age" begins

1555—Peace treaty signed between (Sunni) Ottomans and (Shi'ite) Safavids

1600s—European colonies established in Americas, Africa, and Southeast Asia

1623—Safavid Shah Abbas takes Ottoman city of Baghdad

1631—Taj Mahal built by Mughal emperor

1683—Ottomans besiege Vienna again

1700s—European navies control the world's seas

1735—Weakened Ottomans lose territory to Russia

1757—Islamic Mughal Empire conquered; India controlled by Great Britain

1795—Safavid dynasty overthrown by Turkic Qajar tribe in Persia

1800s—European powers move into Muslim North Africa, Persia, and Central Asia

1839—Ottomans Westernize and reorganize

1880—Zionism (Jewish nationalism) born out of European nationalistic fervor

1882—British occupy Egypt

1882—First migration of European Jews to Palestine

1896—Publication of Theodor Herzl's *Der Judenstaat* ("The Jewish State")

1901—British granted oil rights in Persia

1906—Constitutional Revolution in Persia

1908—Young Turk Revolution

1913—Ottomans lose most of European territories to nationalist movements

1914—World War I sparked by tensions in former Ottoman Balkan lands

1914—Ottomans join Germany and the Central Powers

1915—Huysayn McMahon correspondence

1915—Ottoman victory at Gallipoli; Mustafa Kemal becomes Turkish hero

1916—Sykes-Picot Agreement

1917—Balfour Declaration

1918—Arabia, Syria, and Mesopotamia fall from Ottoman to British control

1918—Ottomans withdraw from war. Central Powers surrender, ending World War I

1919—Paris Peace Conference determines European influence over Middle Eastern lands

1919—British and French mandate areas replace Ottoman vilayet system

1919—Egyptian nationalist Wafd Party established

1920—Faysal named king of Syria by Arab nationalists; French expel him

1920—Treaty of Sèvres; Turkish War of Independence

1921—The Jewish paramilitary organization Haganah formed

1921—Faysal named king of Iraq; Abdullah made king of Transjordan

1922—British protectorate terminated; Egypt first independent Arab state

1923—Turkish republic declared with Mustafa Kemal as president

1924—Turkey abolishes pan-Islamic caliphate

1925—Reza Khan topples Qajars and becomes shah of Persia

1926—Saùdi family takes Hijaz region from Hashemites

1928—Islam no longer recognized as state religion in Turkey's constitution

1928—Muslim Brotherhood formed in Egypt

1929—Massacre of sixty-seven Jews in Jerusalem by Arabs in response to rumors that Jews were massacring Arabs

1932—Iraq becomes independent state

1932—Saùdi family announces united kingdom of "Saùdi" Arabia

1934—Mustafa Kemal takes name Atatürk

1935—Persia formally called "Iran"

1935—Oil discovered in Arabian Peninsula

1936—Iraqi military coup makes Hashemite king figurehead

1938—Kemal Atatürk's death

1939—"White Paper" ends British support for Zionism; Palestinian state promised

1939—Beginning of World War II

1941—Iran sides with Germany; British and Russians invade Iran

1941—Iraq sides with Germany; British troops invade Iraq

1942—Pro-Allied administration formed in Iraq

1943—New shah sides with Allies

1945—Birth of Arab League; end of World War II; birth of United Nations

1946—French mandate ends; Syria and Lebanon granted independence

1946—Zionist terrorists bomb Jerusalem's King David Hotel

1948—Massacre of 245 Palestinians by Jewish radicals in the village of Dayr Yasin

1948—Jewish State of Israel declared; Arab-Israeli war begins

1949—Jordan and Egypt sign cease-fire agreement with Israel

1950—Turkish troops part of U.N. force in Korean War

1951—Turkey joins NATO

1951—Iran's oil industry nationalized

1952—Egyptian Free Officers' Revolution

1953—Apparent CIA-supported removal of Iranian prime minister

1953—Arab Republic of Egypt declared

1954—Gamal Abdel Nasser named president of Egypt

1955—Baghdad Pact signed

1956—Nasser nationalizes Suez Canal

1956—British, French, and Israeli forces attack Egypt

1957—Eisenhower Doctrine put in action

1958—Egypt and Syria form United Arab Republic (UAR)

1958—Jordan and Iraq form Arab Union

1958—Iraqi Free Officers assassinate King Faisal in Iraq, overthrow the monarchy, and declare a republic

1959—American-Iranian Defense Agreement

1960—Birth of the second Turkish republic

1960—Organization of Petroleum Exporting Countries (OPEC) formed

1961—Syria pulls out of UAR

1961—Kuwait granted independence from Great Britain

1962—Egypt and Saudi Arabia clash over civil war in Yemen

1963—Short-lived Ba'th Party coup in Iraq; pan-Arabists take over

1963—Egypt helps to form Organization for African Unity (OAU)

1963—White Revolution in Iran

1964—Ayatollah Khomeini kicked out of Iran, settles in Iraq

1964—Arab nations agree to support Palestinians through PLO

1965—Yasser Arafat's al-Fatah movement gains popular support

1967—Israel strikes Egypt; Six-Day War; Palestinian areas occupied by Israel

1967—U.N. Resolution 242 drafted

1968—Complete Ba'th Party takeover in Iraq; Revolutionary Command Council formed; power to Tikriti clan

1969—Arafat becomes leader of PLO

1970—Nasser's death; Anwar al-Sadat new Egyptian president

1970—Aswan High Dam completed

1971—Bahrain, Qatar, United Arab Emirates, and Oman receive independence

1972—Palestinian militants kill Israeli athletes at Munich Olympic Games

1973—Egypt and Syria attack Israel on October 6 (Yom Kippur)

1973—Soviet-American sponsored cease-fire and U.N. Resolution 338

1974—Turkey at war with Greece over island of Cyprus

1975—Iraq and Iran agree on disputed territories

1975—Start of civil war in Lebanon

1977—Egyptian President Sadat speaks to Israeli parliament

1978—Ayatollah Khomeini deported from Iraq

1978—Camp David Peace Accords

1979—Israeli-Egyptian Peace Treaty; Egypt kicked out of Arab League

1979—Islamic Revolution in Iran, American hostages taken

1979—Afghan-Soviet War begins

1979—Saddam Hussein named president of Iraq

1980—Start of Iran-Iraq War (Gulf War)

1980—Turkish generals take over government; martial law instituted

1981—Israel destroys Iraqi nuclear reactor outside Baghdad

1981—Sadat assassinated; Hosni Mubarak new Egyptian president

1981—Syria's Golan Heights annexed by Israel

1982—Israel invades Lebanon; 800 Palestinians massacred at Sabra and Shatila refugee camps

1983—Bombing of U.S. Marine barracks in Beirut

1984—Civil war starts between Kurdish PKK guerrillas and Turkish military

1985—First Saudi Arabian citizen in space

1985—Israeli forces pull out of Lebanon

1987—Palestinian intifada begins

1988—Iran-Iraq War ends; Iraqi Kurds gassed by Saddam Hussein's regime

1988—Egyptian author Naguib Mahfouz awarded Nobel Prize in Literature

1989—Egypt readmitted to Arab League

1989—U.S.S.R. pulls troops out of Afghanistan, ending long and bloody war

1989—Ayatollah Khomeini's death

1990—Iraq invades Kuwait/Nation declared Iraq's nineteenth province

1991—U.S.-led Operation Desert Storm (second Gulf War); Kuwait liberated; sanctions and "no-fly zones" imposed on Iraq

1993—Turkey elects first female prime minister

1993—Oslo Peace Accords; Palestinian intifada ends

1994—Israel and Jordan Peace Treaty; Oslo II (Taba Accords)

1994—Saddam Hussein orders attacks on Shi'ites in southern Iraq

1995—United States cuts all ties with Iran

1995—Jewish extremist assassinates Israeli Prime Minister Yitzhak Rabin

1996—Series of Palestinian bombings; clashes between Palestinians and Israeli Defense Forces

1996—Osama bin Laden threatens U.S. soldiers in Arabia; bombing of U.S. facility

1997—Members of Jamaat al-Islamiyya massacre 58 tourists in Luxor, Egypt

1998—U.S.-led Operation Desert Fox in Iraq

1998—Osama threatens all Americans around the world

1998—U.S. embassies in Kenya and Tanzania bombed; al-Qaeda targets struck in Sudan and Afghanistan

1998—U.S.-sponsored Wye River Peace Deal

1999—Jamaat al-Islamiyya signs cease-fire with Egyptian government

1999—Kurdish Leader Abdullah Öcalan captured; Turkey given conditional invitation for EU membership

2000—Camp David II; fate of Jerusalem sticking point

2000—Ariel Sharon sparks second Palestinian uprising (the al-Aqsa Intifada)

2001—Ariel Sharon elected Israeli prime minister

2001—September 11 attacks in United States

2001—United States strikes al-Qaeda with Operation Enduring Freedom in Afghanistan; Taliban removed from power

2003—U.S. President Bush unveils plan for Middle East free-trade zone

2003—U.S.-led Operation Iraqi Freedom removes Saddam Hussein and Ba'th Party

2003—Representative Governing Council formed in Iraq; ongoing suicide bombings and popular unrest; capture of Saddam Hussein

2004—Yasser Arafat dies on November 11, 2004

2005—Mahmoud Ahmadinejad assumes presidency of Iran

2006—Hamas wins a majority of seats in the Palestinian Legislative Council and forms a government

2006—Egyptian writer and Nobel Prize in Literature recipient Naguib Mahfouz dies

2007—Israeli Air Force planes reportedly bomb a partly constructed nuclear reactor apparently of North Korean design, although the Israelis neither confirm nor deny it

2007—Hamas and Fatah form a Palestinian unity government

2008—Hamas and Fatah sign an agreement in Saana, Yemen, on March 23 that calls for a return of the Gaza Strip to the pre-June 2007 situation

2008—Israel attacks the Gaza Strip in an offensive known as "Operation Cast Lead" in December 2008 in response to years of almost daily rocket fire from the Gaza Strip at southern Israel

2008—Iran signs $40 billion deal with China for oil refining services

2009—Benjamin Netanyahu becomes Prime Minister of Israel for the second time

2010—U.N. Security Council announces fourth round of sanctions on Iran in continued attempts to curb the country's nuclear development program

2010—President Obama announces end of combat operations in Iraq

2010—World's tallest building opens in Dubai

2010—Saudi Arabia purchases $60 billion worth of advanced aircraft from the United States

2011—Political protests spread throughout Middle East

2011—Hosni Mubarak resigns

2011—Civil war rages in Libya, which draws in NATO

2011—U.S. Navy Seals kill Osama bin Laden

2011—Hamas and Fatah sign a peace agreement that unites them

APPENDIX B

Further Reading and Resources

Books

Atatürk: The Biography of the Founder of Modern Turkey by Andrew Mango (The Overlook Press, NY: 1999)

Between Memory and Desire: The Middle East in a Troubled Age by R. Stephen Humphreys (University of California Press, CA: 2001)

Building a Successful Palestinian State by Kenneth I. Shine and Steven N. Simon (Rand Publishing, CA: 2007)

The Coming Revolution: Struggle for Freedom in the Middle East by Walid Phares (Threshold Editions, NY: 2010)

Coptic Egypt by Jill Kamil (The American University Cairo Press, Cairo, Egypt: 1996)

Crescent & Star: Turkey Between Two Worlds by Stephen Kinzer (Farrar, Straus and Giroux, NY: 2001)

From Beirut to Jerusalem by Thomas L. Friedman (Anchor Books, NY: 1990)

Hamas vs. Fatah: The Struggle for Palestine by Jonathan Schanzer (Palgrave Macmillan: 2008)

A History of the Arab Peoples by Albert Hourani (MJF Books, NY: 1991)

The Middle East: Fourteen Islamic Centuries by Glenn E. Perry (Prentice Hall, NJ: 1983)

A Modern History of the Kurds by David McDowall (I.B. Tauris, NY: 1997)

Sulha: Palestinian Traditional Peacemaking Process by Elias J. Jabbour (House of Hope Publications, Shefar'Am, Israel: 1996)

Magazines and Journals

International Journal of Middle East Studies, edited by Juan R. I. Cole (Cambridge University Press, NY: 2003)

Islam and Christian-Muslim Relations, edited by John L. Esposito & David Thomas (Carfax Publishing, PA: 2003)

Journal of Palestine Studies, edited by Hisham Sharabi (University of California Press, CA: 2003)

Middle East International Review, produced by Winning Communications (Dubai, United Arab Emirates: 2003)

Washington Report on Middle East Affairs, edited by Richard H. Curtiss (American Education Trust, Washington, D.C.: 2003)

Videos

Blood and Tears. Image/Think Films, 2006.
www.amazon.com/Blood-Tears-Abdel-aziz-Rantisi/dp/B000P29GJY

Byzantium: The Lost Empire, by John Romer. Top Documentary Films, 2000.
http://topdocumentaryfilms.com/byzantium-lost-empire/

Egypt's Golden Empire. PBS, 2002.
www.shoppbs.org/product/index.jsp?productId=1402878&keywords=egypt%27s+golden+empire

A Dangerous Man: Lawrence After Arabia. Anchor Bay Entertainment, 1998.
www.amazon.com/Dangerous-Man-Lawrence-After-Arabia/dp/B0024UNHSG/ref=sr_1_1?ie=UTF8&s=digital-video&qid=1306934387&sr=8-1

Israel's Shattered Dreams, by Victor Schonfeld. MPI Home Video, 1990.

🖰 *www.amazon.com/Israels-Shattered-Dreams-Victor-Schonfeld/dp/6301694155/ref=sr_1_3?ie=UTF8&s=video&qid=1306934540&sr=8-3*

The Middle East, 1963. National Archives and Records Administration, 2010.

🖰 *www.amazon.com/The-Middle-East-1963/dp/B0050GCFR0/ref=sr_1_1?ie=UTF8&qid=1306933263&sr=8-1*

The Seven Wonders of the Ancient World. Questar Video, 2002.

🖰 *www.questar1.com*

Six Days in June: The War That Redefined the Middle East. PBS, 2007.

🖰 *www.shoppbs.org/product/index.jsp?productId=2792235&cp=&sr=1&kw=six+days+in+june&origkw=Six+Days+in+June&parentPage=search&searchId=51914380794*

Tales from Arab Detroit, by Joan Mandell. ACCESS & Olive Branch Productions, 1995.

🖰 *www.arabfilm.com*

Travels in Europe: Turkey. Small World Productions, 1995.

🖰 *www.smarttravels.tv/*

Websites

Al Jazeera (English)

🖰 *http://english.aljazeera.net/*

Middle East News—BBC World Service

🖰 *http://news.bbc.co.uk/1/hi/world/middle_east*

Middle East Newspapers and News Sites in English

🖰 *www.world-newspapers.com/east.html*

Middle East Religious Studies

Christianity (Orthodox)—*www.rbsocc.org*

Christianity (Protestant)—*www.gospeloutreach.net*

Christianity (Roman Catholic)—*www.vatican.va*

Islam (Shi'ite)—*www.shia.org*

Modern Judaism—*www.jewfaq.org*

Middle East Research and Information Project

🖰 *www.merip.org*

Washington Report on Middle East Affairs

🖰 *www.wrmea.com*

Organizations and Associations

Americans for a Just Peace in the Middle East
P.O. Box 1086, Santa Barbara, CA 93102

🖰 *www.ajpme.org*

Campus Watch: Monitoring Middle East Studies on Campus
1500 Walnut St., Suite 1050, Philadelphia, PA 19102

🖰 *www.campus-watch.org*

The Cooperation Council for the Arab States of the Gulf

🖰 *www.gcc-sg.org/eng*

Council on American-Islamic Relations (CAIR)

🖰 *www.cair.com*

The Fares Center for Eastern Mediterranean Studies at Tufts University
Cabot Intellectual Center, 160 Packard Ave., Medford, MA 02155

🖰 *http://farescenter.tufts.edu*

Middle East Studies Association of North America
1219 N. Santa Rita Ave., The University of Arizona, Tucson, AZ 85721

🖰 *www.mesa.arizona.edu*

Organization of the Petroleum Exporting Countries

🖰 *www.opec.org*

Index

We Have
EVERYTHING
on Anything!

The Everything® list spans a wide range of subjects, with more than 500 titles covering 25 different categories:

Business	History	Reference
Careers	Home Improvement	Religion
Children's Storybooks	Everything Kids	Self-Help
Computers	Languages	Sports & Fitness
Cooking	Music	Travel
Crafts and Hobbies	New Age	Wedding
Education/Schools	Parenting	Writing
Games and Puzzles	Personal Finance	
Health		